The Lectionary 2020

First published in Great Britain in 2019

Society for Promoting Christian Knowledge
36 Causton Street
London SW1P 4ST
www.spck.org.uk

British Library Cataloguing-in-Publication Data
A catalogue record for this book is available from the British Library

ISBN 978-0-281-08099-1
ISBN 978-0-281-08100-4 spiral-bound
ISBN 978-0-281-08098-4 cased (moleskin)

1 3 5 7 9 10 8 6 4 2

Designed by Colin Hall, Refined Practice
Typeset by Fakenham Prepress Solutions, Fakenham, Norfolk NR21 8NL
Printed in Great Britain by Ashford Colour Press

Produced on paper from sustainable forests

CONTENTS

UNDERSTANDING THE LECTIONARY

Common Worship on left-hand page

August 2020 *Common Worship*

		Sunday Principal Service Weekday Eucharist		Third Service Morning Prayer	Second Service Evening Prayer
23 Sunday	**THE ELEVENTH SUNDAY AFTER TRINITY (Proper 16)**				
G	*Track 1* Exod. 1.8 – 2.10 Ps. 124 Rom. 12. 1–8 Matt. 16. 13–20	*Track 2* Isa. 51. 1–6 Ps. 138 Rom. 12. 1–8 Matt. 16. 13–20		Ps. 104. 1–25 Jonah ch. 2 *or* Ecclus. 3. 17–29 Rev. ch. 1	Ps. 95 2 Kings 6. 8–23 Acts 17. 15–end *Gospel*: John 6. 56–69 *or First EP of Bartholomew* Ps. 97 Isa. 61. 1–9 2 Cor. 6. 1–10 **R ct**
24 Monday	**BARTHOLOMEW THE APOSTLE**				
R **DEL 21**	*The reading from Acts must be used as either the first or second reading at the Eucharist.*	Isa. 43. 8–13 *or* Acts 5. 12–16 Ps. 145. 1–7 Acts 5. 12–16 *or* 1 Cor. 4. 9–15 Luke 22. 24–30		*MP*: Ps. 86; 117 Gen. 28. 10–17 John 1. 43–end	*EP*: Ps. 91; 116 Ecclus. 39. 1–10 *or* Deut. 18. 15–19 Matt. 10. 1–22

Column 1

- **Date**
- **Colour:** An upper-case letter indicates the liturgical colour of the day. A lower-case second colour indicates the colour for a Lesser Festival while the Lectionary upper-case letter indicates the continuing seasonal colour.
- **DEL:** Week number of Daily Eucharistic Lectionary.

Column 2

- Name of the Principal Holy Day, Sunday, Festival or Lesser Festival;
- a note of other Commemorations for mention in prayers;
- any general note that applies to the whole *Common Worship* provision for the day;
- one of the options where there are two options for readings at the Eucharist or Principal Service.

Readings: Readings occur in this column only in two circumstances.

1. **On Sundays after Trinity** where there are two 'tracks' for the Principal Service readings (where there is a choice of first reading and psalm, but the second reading and Gospel are the same in both tracks), Track I appears in this column.
2. **On Lesser Festivals throughout the year** where there are readings for that festival that are alternative to the semi-continuous Daily Eucharistic Lectionary, these also appear in this column.

Column 3

On Principal Feasts, Principal Holy Days, Sundays and Festivals this gives the Principal Service Lectionary, intended for use at the main service of the day (in most churches the mid-morning service), whether or not it is a Eucharist.

On other weekdays this gives the Daily Eucharistic Lectionary for those wanting a semi-continuous pattern of readings and a psalm for Holy Communion. It is most useful in a church where there is a daily celebration and a core community that worships together day by day, though its use is not restricted to that.

Column 4

On Principal Feasts, Principal Holy Days, Sundays and Festivals this gives the Third Service Lectionary. Many churches will have no need of it, for it comes into use only if the Principal and Second Service Lectionaries have been used. Its most likely use is at Morning Prayer (when this is not the Principal Service). Where psalms are recommended for use in the morning, these also appear in this column.

On other weekdays this provides the psalmody and readings for Morning Prayer. Where two or more psalms are appointed, the psalm in bold italic may be used as the only psalm. Psalms printed in round brackets ( ) may be omitted if they are used as an opening canticle at Morning Prayer. Where † is printed after the psalm number, the psalm may be shortened if desired. For those wishing to follow the Ordinary Time psalm cycle throughout the year (except for the period between 19 December and the Epiphany and from the Monday of Holy Week to the Saturday of Easter Week), this is printed as an alternative to the seasonal provision.

Column 5

On Principal Feasts, Principal Holy Days, Sundays and Festivals this gives the Second Service Lectionary, intended for use when a second set of readings is required. Its most likely use is in the evening, when the Principal Service Lectionary has been used in the morning. Sometimes it might be used at an evening Eucharist. Where the second reading is not a Gospel reading, an alternative to meet this need is provided. Where psalms are recommended for use in the evening, these also appear in this column.

On other weekdays this provides the psalmody and readings for Evening Prayer. Where two or more psalms are provided, the psalm in bold italic may be used as the only psalm. Psalms printed in round brackets ( ) may be omitted if they are used as an opening canticle at Evening Prayer. Where † is printed after the psalm number, the psalm may be shortened if desired. For those wishing to follow the Ordinary Time psalm cycle throughout the year (except for the period between 19 December and the Epiphany and from the Monday of Holy Week to the Saturday of Easter Week), this is printed as an alternative to the seasonal provision.

Book of Common Prayer and space for notes on right-hand page

Book of Common Prayer

August 2020

	Calendar and Holy Communion	Morning Prayer	Evening Prayer	NOTES
	THE ELEVENTH SUNDAY AFTER TRINITY			
G	1 Kings 3. 5–15 Ps. 28 1 Cor. 15. 1–11 Luke 18. 9–14	Ps. 104. 1–25 Jonah ch. 2 *or* Ecclus. 3. 17–29 Rev. ch. 1	Ps. 95 2 Kings 6. 8–23 Acts 17. 15–end *or First EP of Bartholomew* Ps. 97 Isa. 61. 1–9 2 Cor. 6. 1–10 **R ct**	
	BARTHOLOMEW THE APOSTLE			
R	Gen. 28. 10–17 Ps. 15 Acts 5. 12–16 Luke 22. 24–30	(Ps. 86; 117) Isa. 43. 8–13 John 1. 43–end	(Ps. 91; 116) Ecclus. 39. 1–10 *or* Deut. 18. 15–19 Matt. 10. 1–22	

Column 6

- Liturgical colour (***see column 1***).

Column 7

- The name of the Principal Holy Day, Sunday, Festival or Lesser Festival;
- any general note that applies to the whole Prayer Book provision for the day and an indication of points at which users may wish to draw on *Common Worship* material on the opposite page where the BCP has no provision;
- the Lectionary for the Eucharist on any day for which provision is made.

Column 8

This provides the readings for Morning Prayer, together with psalm provision where it varies from the BCP monthly cycle.

Column 9

This provides the readings for Evening Prayer, together with psalm provision where it varies from the BCP monthly cycle.

A letter to indicate liturgical colour in this column indicates a change of colour for Evening Prayer. The symbol in bold lower case, **ct**, indicates that the Collect at Evening Prayer should be that of the following day.

Column 10

Space for notes.

ABBREVIATIONS OF BOOKS OF THE BIBLE

Old Testament

Gen. (Genesis)
Exod. (Exodus)
Lev. (Leviticus)
Num. (Numbers)
Deut. (Deuteronomy)
Josh. (Joshua)
Judg. (Judges)
Ruth
Sam. (Samuel)
Kings
Chron. (Chronicles)
Ezra
Neh. (Nehemiah)
Esth. (Esther)
Job
Ps(s). (Psalms)
Prov. (Proverbs)
Eccles. (Ecclesiastes)
Song of Sol. (Song of Solomon)
Isa. (Isaiah)
Jer. (Jeremiah)
Lam. (Lamentations)
Ezek. (Ezekiel)
Dan. (Daniel)
Hos. (Hosea)
Joel
Amos
Obad. (Obadiah)
Jonah
Mic. (Micah)
Nahum
Hab. (Habakkuk)
Zeph. (Zephaniah)
Hag. (Haggai)
Zech. (Zechariah)
Mal. (Malachi)

Apocrypha

Esd. (Esdras)
Tobit
Judith
Wisd. (Wisdom of Solomon)
Ecclus. (Ecclesiasticus)
Baruch (Baruch)
Song of the Three (Song of the Three Children)
Susanna (The History of Susanna)
Prayer of Manasseh
Macc. (Maccabees)

New Testament

Matt. (Matthew)
Mark
Luke
John
Acts (Acts of the Apostles)
Rom. (Romans)
Cor. (Corinthians)
Gal. (Galatians)
Eph. (Ephesians)
Phil. (Philippians)
Col. (Colossians)
Thess. (Thessalonians)
Tim. (Timothy)
Titus
Philem. (Philemon)
Heb. (Hebrews)
Jas. (James)
Pet. (Peter)
John (letters of John)
Jude
Rev. (Revelation)

MAKING CHOICES IN *COMMON WORSHIP*

Common Worship makes provision for a variety of pastoral and liturgical circumstances. It needs to, for it has to serve some church communities where Morning Prayer, Holy Communion and Evening Prayer are all celebrated every day, and yet be useful also in a church with only one service a week, and that service varying in form and time from week to week.

At the beginning of the year, some decisions in principle need to be taken.

In relation to the Calendar, whether to keep The Epiphany on Monday 6 January or on Sunday 5 January.

In relation to the Lectionary, the initial choices every year to decide in relation to Sundays are:

- which of the services on a Principal Feast, Principal Holy Day, Sunday or Festival constitutes the 'Principal Service'; then use the Principal Service Lectionary (column 3) consistently for that service through the year;
- during the Sundays after Trinity, whether to use Track I of the Principal Service Lectionary (column 2), where the first reading stays over several weeks with one Old Testament book read semi-continuously, or Track 2 (column 3), where the first reading is chosen for its relationship to the Gospel reading of the day;
- which, if any, service on a Principal Feast, Principal Holy Day, Sunday or Festival constitutes the 'Second Service'; then use the Second Service Lectionary (column 5) consistently for that service through the year;
- which, if any, service on a Principal Feast, Principal Holy Day, Sunday or Festival constitutes the 'Third Service'; then use the Third Service Lectionary (column 4) consistently for that service through the year.

And in relation to weekdays:

- whether to use the Daily Eucharistic Lectionary (column 3) consistently for weekday celebrations of Holy Communion (with the exception of Principal Feasts, Principal Holy Days and Festivals) or to make some use of the Lesser Festival provision;
- whether to follow the first psalm provision in column 4 (morning) and column 5 (evening), where psalms during the seasons have a seasonal flavour but in ordinary time follow a sequential pattern; or to follow the alternative provision in the same columns, where psalms follow the sequential pattern throughout the year, except for the period between 19 December and The Epiphany and from the Monday of Holy Week to the Saturday of Easter Week; or to follow the psalm cycle in the Book of Common Prayer, where they are nearly always used 'in course';
- whether to use the Additional Weekday Lectionary (which begins on page 116) for weekday services (other than Holy Communion). It provides a one-year cycle of two readings for each day (except for Sundays, Principal Feasts, Principal Holy Days, Festivals and during Holy Week). Since each of the readings is designed to 'stand alone' (that is, it is complete in itself and will make sense to the worshipper who has not attended on the previous day and who will not be present on the next day), it is intended particularly for use in those churches and cathedrals that attract occasional rather than regular congregations.

The flexibility of *Common Worship* is intended to enable the church and the minister to find the most helpful provision for them. But once a decision is made, it is advisable to stay with that decision through the year or at the very least through a complete season.

All Bible references (except to the psalms) are to the New Revised Standard Version, Anglicized edition (1995). Those who use other Bible translations should check the verse numbers against the NRSV. References to the psalms are to the *Common Worship* Psalter.

BOOK OF COMMON PRAYER

A separate Lectionary for the Book of Common Prayer is no longer issued. Provision is made on the right-hand pages of this Lectionary for BCP worship on all Sundays in the year, for the major festivals and for Morning and Evening Prayer. The Epistles and Gospels for Holy Communion are those of 1662, with the additions and variations of 1928, now authorized under the *Common Worship* overall provision. The Old Testament readings and psalms for these services, formerly appended to the Series One Holy Communion service, may be used but are not mandatory with the 1662 order.

Readings for Morning and Evening Prayer, which are the same as those for *Common Worship*, are set out in the BCP section for Sundays and weekdays. The special psalm provision of the BCP is given; however, where the *Common Worship* psalm provision is used, verse numbering may occasionally differ slightly from that in the BCP Psalter, and appropriate adjustment will have to be made (a table of variations in verse numbering can be found at www.churchofengland.org/prayer-and-worship/worship-texts-and-resources/common-worship/daily-prayer/psalter/psalter-verse). Otherwise the Psalter is read in course daily through each month.

The Calendar observes BCP dates when these differ from those of *Common Worship*; for example, St Thomas on 21 December. Additional commemorations in the *Common Worship* Calendar are not included, but those who wish to observe them may use the *Collects and Post Communions in Traditional Language: Lesser Festivals, Common of the Saints, Special Occasions* (Church House Publishing).

The Lectionaries of 1871 and 1922, to be found in many copies of the BCP, are still authorized and may be used, but – with the exception of the psalms and readings for Holy Communion mentioned above – the Additional Alternative Lectionary (1961) is no longer authorized for public worship.

Although those who use the BCP, for private or public worship or both, are free to follow any of the authorized lectionaries, there is much to be said for common usage across the Church of England, so that the same passages are being read by all. It is of course appropriate that BCP readings should be taken from the Authorized or King James Version for harmony of style, with the daily recitation of the BCP Psalter.

The integrity of the BCP as the traditional source of worship in the Church of England is not in any way affected by the use of a common lectionary for the daily offices.

CERTAIN DAYS AND OCCASIONS COMMONLY OBSERVED

Plough Sunday may be observed on 12 January 2020.

The Week of Prayer for Christian Unity may be observed from 18 to 25 January 2020.

Education Sunday may be observed on 13 September 2020.

Rogation Sunday may be observed on 17 May 2020.

The Feast of Dedication is observed on the anniversary of the dedication or consecration of a church, or, when the actual date is unknown, on 4 October 2020. In *Common Worship*, 25 October 2020 is an alternative date.

Ember Days. *Common Worship* encourages the bishop to set the Ember Days in each diocese in the week before the ordinations, whereas in BCP the dates are fixed.

Days of Discipline and Self-Denial in *Common Worship* are the weekdays of Lent and all Fridays in the year, except all Principal Feasts and festivals outside Lent and Fridays between Easter Day and Pentecost. The eves of Principal Feasts are also appropriately kept as days of discipline and self-denial in preparation for the feast.

Days of Fasting and Abstinence according to the BCP are the forty days of Lent, the Ember Days at the four seasons, the three Rogation Days, and all Fridays in the year except Christmas Day. The BCP also orders the observance of the Evens or Vigils before The Nativity of our Lord, The Purification of the Blessed Virgin Mary, The Annunciation of the Blessed Virgin Mary, Easter Day, Ascension Day, Pentecost, and before the following saints' days: Matthias, John the Baptist, Peter, James, Bartholomew, Matthew, Simon and Jude, Andrew, Thomas, and All Saints. (If any of these days falls on Monday, the Vigil is to be kept on the previous Saturday.)

KEY TO LITURGICAL COLOURS

Common Worship suggests appropriate liturgical colours. They are not mandatory, and traditional or local use may be followed.

For a detailed discussion of when colours may be used, see *Common Worship: Services and Prayers for the Church of England* (Church House Publishing), *New Handbook of Pastoral Liturgy* (SPCK) or *A Companion to Common Worship: Volume I* (SPCK).

When a lower-case letter accompanies an upper-case letter, the lower-case letter indicates the liturgical colour appropriate to the Lesser Festival of that day, while the upper-case letter indicates the continuing seasonal colour.

W White
𝔚 Gold or white
R Red
P Purple (may vary from 'Roman purple' to violet, with blue as an alternative; a Lent array of sackcloth may be used in Lent, and rose pink on The Third Sunday of Advent and Fourth Sunday of Lent)
G Green

PRINCIPAL FEASTS, HOLY DAYS AND FESTIVALS

Principal Feasts and other Principal Holy Days (Ash Wednesday, Maundy Thursday, Good Friday) are printed in **LARGE BOLD CAPITALS** in the Lectionary.

There are no longer proper readings relating to the Holy Spirit on the six days after Pentecost. Instead they have been located on the nine days before Pentecost.

When Patronal and Dedication Festivals are kept as Principal Feasts, they may be transferred to the nearest Sunday, unless that day is already either a Principal Feast or The First Sunday of Advent, The Baptism of Christ, The First Sunday of Lent or Palm Sunday.

Festivals are printed in the Lectionary in **SMALL BOLD CAPITALS.**

For each day there is a full liturgical provision for the Holy Communion and for Morning and Evening Prayer. Most holy days that are in the category 'Festival' are provided with an optional First Evening Prayer. Its use is entirely at the discretion of the minister. Where it is used, the liturgical colour for the next day should be used at that First Evening Prayer, and this has been indicated in the provision on the following pages.

LESSER FESTIVALS AND COMMEMORATIONS

Lesser Festivals (printed in **medium-bold roman** typeface) are observed at the level appropriate to a particular church. The readings and psalms for The Common of the Saints are listed on page 10. In addition, there are special readings appropriate to the Festival listed in the first column. The daily psalms and readings at Morning and Evening Prayer are not usually superseded by those for Lesser Festivals, but the readings and psalms for Holy Communion may on occasion be used at Morning or Evening Prayer.

Commemorations are printed in the Lectionary in *italic* typeface. They do not have collect, psalm or readings, but may be observed by mention in prayers of intercession and thanksgiving. For local reasons, or where there is an established tradition in the wider Church, they may be kept as Lesser Festivals using the appropriate material from The Common of the Saints. Equally, it may be desirable to observe some Lesser Festivals as Commemorations.

If a Lesser Festival or a Commemoration falls on a Principal Feast, Principal Holy Day, Sunday or Festival, it is not normally observed that year, although it may be celebrated, where there is sufficient reason, on the nearest available day. Lesser Festivals and Commemorations which, for this reason, would not be celebrated in 2019–20 are listed on pages 9–10, so that, if desired, they may be mentioned in prayers of intercession and thanksgiving.

LESSER FESTIVALS AND COMMEMORATIONS NOT OBSERVED IN 2019–20

The Lesser Festivals and Commemorations (shown in italics) listed below fall on a Sunday or during Holy Week or Easter Week this year, and are thus not observed in this Lectionary.

COMMON WORSHIP

2019

December

1 *Charles de Foucauld, Hermit in the Sahara, 1916*
8 The Conception of the Blessed Virgin Mary
29 Thomas Becket, Archbishop of Canterbury, Martyr, 1170

2020

January

12 Aelred of Hexham, Abbot of Rievaulx, 1167
Benedict Biscop, Abbot of Wearmouth, Scholar, 689
19 Wulfstan, Bishop of Worcester, 1095
26 Timothy and Titus, Companions of Paul

February

23 Polycarp, Bishop of Smyrna, Martyr, c. 155

March

1 David, Bishop of Menevia, Patron of Wales, c. 601
8 Edward King, Bishop of Lincoln, 1910
Felix, Bishop, Apostle to the East Angles, 647
Geoffrey Studdert Kennedy, Priest, Poet, 1929

April

9 *Dietrich Bonhoeffer, Lutheran Pastor, Martyr, 1945*
10 William Law, Priest, Spiritual Writer, 1761
William of Ockham, Friar, Philosopher, Teacher, 1347
11 *George Augustus Selwyn, first Bishop of New Zealand, 1878*
16 *Isabella Gilmore, Deaconess, 1923*
19 Alphege, Archbishop of Canterbury, Martyr, 1012

May

21 *Helena, Protector of the Holy Places, 330*
24 John and Charles Wesley, Evangelists, Hymn Writers, 1791 and 1788

June

1 Justin, Martyr at Rome, c. 165
14 *Richard Baxter, Puritan Divine, 1691*
28 Irenaeus, Bishop of Lyons, Teacher, c. 200

July

19 Gregory, Bishop of Nyssa, and his sister Macrina, Deaconess, Teachers, c. 394 and 379
26 Anne and Joachim, Parents of the Blessed Virgin Mary

August

9 Mary Sumner, Founder of the Mothers' Union, 1921
30 John Bunyan, Spiritual Writer, 1688

September

6 *Allen Gardiner, Founder of the South American Mission Society, 1851*
13 John Chrysostom, Bishop of Constantinople, Teacher, 407
20 John Coleridge Patteson, first Bishop of Melanesia and his Companions, Martyrs, 1871
27 Vincent de Paul, Founder of the Congregation of the Mission (Lazarists), 1660

October

4 Francis of Assisi, Friar, Founder of the Friars Minor, 1226
11 *Ethelburga, Abbess of Barking, 675*
James the Deacon, Companion of Paulinus, 7th century
25 *Crispin and Crispinian, Martyrs at Rome, c. 287*

November

8 The Saints and Martyrs of England
22 *Cecilia, Martyr at Rome, c. 230*
29 *Day of Intercession and Thanksgiving for the Missionary Work of the Church*

December

6 Nicholas, Bishop of Myra, c. 326
13 Lucy, Martyr at Syracuse, 304
Samuel Johnson, Moralist, 1784

BOOK OF COMMON PRAYER

2019

December
8 The Conception of the Blessed Virgin Mary

2020

March
1 David, Bishop of Menevia, Patron of Wales, *c.* 601

April
19 Alphege, Archbishop of Canterbury, Martyr, 1012

May
3 The Invention of the Cross

June
1 Nicomede, Priest and Martyr at Rome (date unknown)

October
25 Crispin, Martyr at Rome, *c.* 287

November
15 Machutus, Bishop, Apostle of Brittany, *c.* 564
22 Cecilia, Martyr at Rome, *c.* 230

December
6 Nicholas, Bishop of Myra, *c.* 326
13 Lucy, Martyr at Syracuse, 304

THE COMMON OF THE SAINTS

The Blessed Virgin Mary
Genesis 3. 8–15, 20; Isaiah 7. 10–14; Micah 5. 1–4
Psalms 45. 10–17; 113; 131
Acts 1. 12–14; Romans 8. 18–30; Galatians 4. 4–7
Luke 1. 26–38; l. 39–47; John 19. 25–27

Martyrs
2 Chronicles 24. 17–21; Isaiah 43. 1–7; Jeremiah 11. 18–20; Wisdom 4. 10–15
Psalms 3; 11; 31. 1–5; 44. 18–24; 126
Romans 8. 35–end; 2 Corinthians 4. 7–15; 2 Timothy 2. 3–7 [8–13]; Hebrews 11. 32–end; 1 Peter 4. 12–end; Revelation 12. 10–12a
Matthew 10. 16–22; 10. 28–39; 16. 24–26; John 12. 24–26; 15. 18–21

Teachers of the Faith and Spiritual Writers
I Kings 3. [6–10] 11–14; Proverbs 4. 1–9; Wisdom 7. 7–10, 15–16; Ecclesiasticus 39. 1–10
Psalms 19. 7–10; 34. 11–17; 37. 31–35; 119. 89–96; 119. 97–104
I Corinthians 1. 18–25; 2. 1–10; 2. 9–end; Ephesians 3. 8–12; 2 Timothy 4. 1–8; Titus 2. 1–8
Matthew 5. 13–19; 13. 52–end; 23. 8–12; Mark 4. 1–9; John 16. 12–15

Bishops and Other Pastors
I Samuel 16. I, 6–13; Isaiah 6. 1–8; Jeremiah 1. 4–10; Ezekiel 3. 16–21; Malachi 2. 5–7
Psalms 1; 15; 16. 5–end; 96; 110
Acts 20. 28–35; I Corinthians 4. 1–5; 2 Corinthians 4. 1–10 (*or* 1–2, 5–7); 5. 14–20; 1 Peter 5. 1–4
Matthew 11. 25–end; 24. 42–46; John 10. 11–16; 15. 9–17; 21. 15–17

Members of Religious Communities
I Kings 19. 9–18; Proverbs 10. 27–end; Song of Solomon 8. 6–7; Isaiah 61.10 - 62.5; Hosea 2. 14–15, 19–20
Psalms 34. 1–8; 112. 1–9; 119. 57–64; 123; 131
Acts 4. 32–35; 2 Corinthians 10.17 - 11.2; Philippians 3. 7–14; 1 John 2. 15–17; Revelation 19. 1, 5–9
Matthew 11. 25–end; 19. 3–12; 19. 23–end; Luke 9. 57–end; 12. 32–37

Missionaries
Isaiah 52. 7–10; 61. 1–3a; Ezekiel 34. 11–16; Jonah 3. 1–5
Psalms 67; 87; 97; 100; 117
Acts 2. 14, 22–36; 13. 46–49; 16. 6–10; 26. 19–23; Romans 15. 17–21; 2 Corinthians 5.11 - 6.2
Matthew 9. 35–end; 28. 16–end; Mark 16. 15–20; Luke 5. 1–11; 10. 1–9

Any Saint
Genesis 12. 1–4; Proverbs 8. 1–11; Micah 6. 6–8; Ecclesiasticus 2. 7–13 [14–end]
Psalms 32; 33. 1–5; 119. 1–8; 139. 1–4 [5–12]; 145. 8–14
Ephesians 3. 14–19; 6. 11–18; Hebrews 13. 7–8, 15–16; James 2. 14–17; 1 John 4. 7–16; Revelation 21. [1–4] 5–7
Matthew 19. 16–21; 25. 1–13; 25. 14–30; John 15. 1–8; 17. 20–end

SPECIAL OCCASIONS

The Guidance of the Holy Spirit
Proverbs 24. 3–7; Isaiah 30. 15–21; Wisdom 9. 13–17
Psalms 25. 1–9; 104. 26–33; 143. 8–10
Acts 15. 23–29; Romans 8. 22–27;
1 Corinthians 12. 4–13
Luke 14. 27–33; John 14. 23–26; 16. 13–15

The Commemoration of the Faithful Departed
Lamentations 3. 17–26, 31–33 *or* Wisdom 3. 1–9
Psalm 23 *or* 27. 1–6, 16–end
Romans 5. 5–11 *or* I Peter 1. 3–9
John 5. 19–25 *or* 6. 37–40

Rogation Days
Deuteronomy 8. 1–10; 1 Kings 8. 35–40; Job 28. 1–11
Psalms 104. 21–30; 107. 1–9; 121
Philippians 4. 4–7; 2 Thessalonians 3. 6–13;
1 John 5. 12–15
Matthew 6. 1–15; Mark 11. 22–24; Luke 11. 5–13

Harvest Thanksgiving

Year A
Deuteronomy 8. 7–18 *or* 28. 1–14
Psalm 65
2 Corinthians 9. 6–end
Luke 12. 16–30 *or* 17. 11–19

Year B
Joel 2. 21–27
Psalm 126
1 Timothy 2. 1–7 *or* 6. 6–10
Matthew 6. 25–33

Year C
Deuteronomy 26. 1–11
Psalm 100
Philippians 4. 4–9 *or* Revelation 14. 14–18
John 6. 25–35

Mission and Evangelism
Isaiah 49. 1–6; 52. 7–10; Micah 4. 1–5
Psalms 2; 46; 67
Acts 17. 12–end; 2 Corinthians 5.14 - 6.2;
Ephesians 2. 13–end
Matthew 5. 13–16, 28. 16–end, John 17. 20–end

The Unity of the Church
Jeremiah 33. 6–9a; Ezekiel 36. 23–28;
Zephaniah 3. 16–end
Psalms 100; 122; 133
Ephesians 4. 1–6; Colossians 3. 9–17;
1 John 4. 9–15
Matthew 18. 19–22; John 11. 45–52; 17. 11b–23

The Peace of the World
Isaiah 9. 1–6; 57. 15–19; Micah 4. 1–5
Psalms 40. 14–17; 72. 1–7; 85. 8–13
Philippians 4. 6–9; 1 Timothy 2. 1–6;
James 3. 13–18
Matthew 5. 43–end; John 14. 23–29; 15. 9–17

Social Justice and Responsibility
Isaiah 32. 15–end; Amos 5. 21–24; 8. 4–7;
Acts 5. 1–11
Psalms 31. 21–24; 85. 1–7; 146. 5–10
Colossians 3. 12–15; James 2. 1–4
Matthew 5. 1–12; 25. 31–end;
Luke 16. 19–end

Ministry (including Ember Days)
Numbers 11. 16–17, 24–29; 27. 15–end;
1 Samuel 16. 1–13a; Isaiah 6. 1–8; 61. 1–3;
Jeremiah 1. 4–10
Psalms 40. 8–13; 84. 8–12; 89. 19–25;
101. 1–5, 7; 122
Acts 20. 28–35; 1 Corinthians 3. 3–11;
Ephesians 4. 4–16; Philippians 3. 7–14
Luke 4. 16–21; 12. 35–43; 22. 24–27;
John 4. 31–38; 15. 5–17

In Time of Trouble
Genesis 9. 8–17; Job 1. 13–end; Isaiah 38. 6–11
Psalms 86. 1–7; 107. 4–15; 142. 1–7
Romans 3. 21–26; 8. 18–25;
2 Corinthians 8. 1–5, 9
Mark 4. 35–end; Luke 12. 1–7; John 16. 31–end

For the Sovereign
Joshua 1. 1–9; Proverbs 8. 1–16
Psalms 20; 101; 121
Romans 13. 1–10; Revelation 21.22 - 22.4
Matthew 22. 16–22; Luke 22. 24–30

			Sunday Principal Service Weekday Eucharist	Third Service Morning Prayer	Second Service Evening Prayer

December 2019

1 Sunday	**THE FIRST SUNDAY OF ADVENT** *Common Worship* Year A begins				
P			Isa. 2. 1–5 Ps. 122 Rom. 13. 11–end Matt. 24. 36–44	Ps. 44 Mic. 4. 1–7 1 Thess. 5. 1–11	Ps. 9 (*or* 9. 1–8) Isa. 52. 1–12 Matt. 24. 15–28
2 Monday	Daily Eucharistic Lectionary Year 2 begins				
P			Isa. 4. 2–end Ps. 122 Matt. 8. 5–11	Ps. ***50***; 54 *alt.* Ps. ***1***; 2; 3 Isa. 25. 1–9 Matt. 12. 1–21	Ps. 70; ***71*** *alt.* Ps. ***4***; 7 Isa. 42. 18–end Rev. ch. 19
3 Tuesday	*Francis Xavier, Missionary, Apostle of the Indies, 1552*				
P			Isa. 11. 1–10 Ps. 72. 1–4, 18–19 Luke 10. 21–24	Ps. ***80***; 82 *alt.* Ps. ***5***; 6; (8) Isa. 26. 1–13 Matt. 12. 22–37	Ps. ***74***; 75 *alt.* Ps. ***9***; 10† Isa. 43. 1–13 Rev. ch. 20
4 Wednesday	*John of Damascus, Monk, Teacher,* c. *749; Nicholas Ferrar, Deacon, Founder of the Little Gidding Community, 1637*				
P			Isa. 25. 6–10a Ps. 23 Matt. 15. 29–37	Ps. 5; ***7*** *alt.* Ps. 119. 1–32 Isa. 28. 1–13 Matt. 12. 38–end	Ps. 76; ***77*** *alt.* Ps. ***11***; 12; 13 Isa. 43. 14–end Rev. 21. 1–8
5 Thursday					
P			Isa. 26. 1–6 Ps. 118. 18–27a Matt. 7. 21, 24–27	Ps. ***42***; 43 *alt.* Ps. 14; ***15***; 16 Isa. 28. 14–end Matt. 13. 1–23	Ps. ***40***; 46 *alt.* Ps. 18† Isa. 44. 1–8 Rev. 21. 9–21
6 Friday	**Nicholas, Bishop of Myra, *c.* 326**				
Pw	Com. Bishop *also* Isa. 61. 1–3 1 Tim. 6. 6–11 Mark 10. 13–16	*or*	Isa. 29. 17–end Ps. 27. 1–4, 16–17 Matt. 9. 27–31	Ps. ***25***; 26 *alt.* Ps. 17; ***19*** Isa. 29. 1–14 Matt. 13. 24–43	Ps. 16; ***17*** *alt.* Ps. 22 Isa. 44. 9–23 Rev. 21.22 – 22.5
7 Saturday	**Ambrose, Bishop of Milan, Teacher, 397**				
Pw	Com. Teacher *also* Isa. 41. 9b–13 Luke 22. 24–30	*or*	Isa. 30. 19–21, 23–26 Ps. 146. 4–9 Matt. 9.35 – 10.1, 6–8	Ps. ***9***; (10) *alt.* Ps. 20; 21; ***23*** Isa. 29. 15–end Matt. 13. 44–end	Ps. ***27***; 28 *alt.* Ps. ***24***; 25 Isa. 44.24 – 45.13 Rev. 22. 6–end **ct**
8 Sunday	**THE SECOND SUNDAY OF ADVENT**				
P			Isa. 11. 1–10 Ps. 72. 1–7, 18–19 (*or* 72. 1–7) Rom. 15. 4–13 Matt. 3. 1–12	Ps. 80 Amos ch. 7 Luke 1. 5–20	Ps. 11; [28] 1 Kings 18. 17–39 John 1. 19–28

	Calendar and Holy Communion	Morning Prayer	Evening Prayer	NOTES
	THE FIRST SUNDAY IN ADVENT			
P	Advent 1 Collect until Christmas Eve Mic. 4. 1–4, 6–7 Ps. 25. 1–9 Rom. 13. 8–14 Matt. 21. 1–13	Ps. 44 Isa. 2. 1–5 1 Thess. 5. 1–11	Ps. 9 (*or* 9. 1–8) Isa. 52. 1–12 Matt. 24. 15–28	
P		Isa. 25. 1–9 Matt. 12. 1–21	Isa. 42. 18–end Rev. ch. 19	
P		Isa. 26. 1–13 Matt. 12. 22–37	Isa. 43. 1–13 Rev. ch. 20	
P		Isa. 28. 1–13 Matt. 12. 38–end	Isa. 43. 14–end Rev. 21. 1–8	
P		Isa. 28. 14–end Matt. 13. 1–23	Isa. 44. 1–8 Rev. 21. 9–21	
	Nicholas, Bishop of Myra, c. 326			
Pw	Com. Bishop	Isa. 29. 1–14 Matt. 13. 24–43	Isa. 44. 9–23 Rev. 21.22 - 22.5	
P		Isa. 29. 15–end Matt. 13. 44–end	Isa. 44.24 - 45.13 Rev. 22. 6–end **ct**	
	THE SECOND SUNDAY IN ADVENT			
P	2 Kings 22. 8–10; 23. 1–3 Ps. 50. 1–6 Rom. 15. 4–13 Luke 21. 25–33	Ps. 80 Amos ch. 7 Luke 1. 5–20	Ps. 11; [28] 1 Kings 18. 17–39 Matt. 3. 1–12	

		Sunday Principal Service Weekday Eucharist	Third Service Morning Prayer	Second Service Evening Prayer
9 Monday				
P		Isa. ch. 35 Ps. 85. 7–end Luke 5. 17–26	Ps. 44 *alt.* Ps. 27; ***30*** Isa. 30. 1–18 Matt. 14. 1–12	Ps. ***144***; 146 *alt.* Ps. 26; ***28***; 29 Isa. 45. 14–end 1 Thess. ch. 1
10 Tuesday				
P		Isa. 40. 1–11 Ps. 96. 1, 10–end Matt. 18. 12–14	Ps. ***56***; 57 *alt.* Ps. 32; ***36*** Isa. 30. 19–end Matt. 14. 13–end	Ps. ***11***; 12; 13 *alt.* Ps. 33 Isa. ch. 46 1 Thess. 2. 1–12
11 Wednesday	Ember Day*			
P		Isa. 40. 25–end Ps. 103. 8–13 Matt. 11. 28–end	Ps. ***62***; 63 *alt.* Ps. 34 Isa. ch. 31 Matt. 15. 1–20	Ps. ***10***; 14 *alt.* Ps. 119. 33–56 Isa. ch. 47 1 Thess. 2. 13–end
12 Thursday				
P		Isa. 41. 13–20 Ps. 145. 1, 8–13 Matt. 11. 11–15	Ps. 53; ***54***; 60 *alt.* Ps. 37† Isa. ch. 32 Matt. 15. 21–28	Ps. 73 *alt.* Ps. 39; ***40*** Isa. 48. 1–11 1 Thess. ch. 3
13 Friday	**Lucy, Martyr at Syracuse, 304** *Samuel Johnson, Moralist, 1784* Ember Day*			
Pr	Com. Martyr *or* *also* Wisd. 3. 1–7 2 Cor. 4. 6–15	Isa. 48. 17–19 Ps. 1 Matt. 11. 16–19	Ps. 85; ***86*** *alt.* Ps. 31 Isa. 33. 1–22 Matt. 15. 29–end	Ps. 82; ***90*** *alt.* Ps. 35 Isa. 48. 12–end 1 Thess. 4. 1–12
14 Saturday	**John of the Cross, Poet, Teacher, 1591** Ember Day*			
Pw	Com. Teacher *or* *esp.* 1 Cor. 2. 1–10 *also* John 14. 18–23	Ecclus. 48. 1–4, 9–11 *or* 2 Kings 2. 9–12 Ps. 80. 1–4, 18–19 Matt. 17. 10–13	Ps. 145 *alt.* Ps. 41; ***42***; 43 Isa. ch. 35 Matt. 16. 1–12	Ps. 93; ***94*** *alt.* Ps. 45; ***46*** Isa. 49. 1–13 1 Thess. 4. 13–end **ct**
15 Sunday	**THE THIRD SUNDAY OF ADVENT**			
P		Isa. 35. 1–10 Ps. 146. 4–10 *or Canticle*: Magnificat Jas. 5. 7–10 Matt. 11. 2–11	Ps. 68. 1–19 Zeph. 3. 14–end Phil. 4. 4–7	Ps. 12; [14] Isa. 5. 8–end Acts 13. 13–41 *Gospel*: John 5. 31–40
16 Monday				
P		Num. 24. 2–7, 15–17 Ps. 25. 3–8 Matt. 21. 23–27	Ps. 40 *alt.* Ps. 44 Isa. 38. 1–8, 21–22 Matt. 16. 13–end	Ps. 25; ***26*** *alt.* Ps. ***47***; 49 Isa. 49. 14–25 1 Thess. 5. 1–11

*For Ember Day provision, see p. 11.

	Calendar and Holy Communion	Morning Prayer	Evening Prayer
P		Isa. 30. 1–18 Matt. 14. 1–12	Isa. 45. 14–end 1 Thess. ch. 1
P		Isa. 30. 19–end Matt. 14. 13–end	Isa. ch. 46 1 Thess. 2. 1–12
P		Isa. ch. 31 Matt. 15. 1–20	Isa. ch. 47 1 Thess. 2. 13–end
P		Isa. ch. 32 Matt. 15. 21–28	Isa. 48. 1–11 1 Thess. ch. 3
	Lucy, Martyr at Syracuse, 304		
Pr	Com. Virgin Martyr	Isa. 33. 1–22 Matt. 15. 29–end	Isa. 48. 12–end 1 Thess. 4. 1–12
P		Isa. ch. 35 Matt. 16. 1–12	Isa. 49. 1–13 1 Thess. 4. 13–end
			ct
	THE THIRD SUNDAY IN ADVENT		
P	Isa. ch. 35 Ps. 80. 1–7 1 Cor. 4. 1–5 Matt. 11. 2–10	Ps. 68. 1–19 Zeph. 3. 14–end Jas. 5. 7–10	Ps. 12; [14] Isa. 5. 8–end Acts 13. 13–41
	O Sapientia		
P		Isa. 38. 1–8, 21–22 Matt. 16. 13–end	Isa. 49. 14–25 1 Thess. 5. 1–11

NOTES

		Sunday Principal Service Weekday Eucharist	Third Service Morning Prayer	Second Service Evening Prayer
17 Tuesday	O Sapientia* *Eglantyne Jebb, Social Reformer, Founder of 'Save the Children', 1928*			
P		Gen. 49. 2, 8–10 Ps. 72. 1–5, 18–19 Matt. 1. 1–17	Ps. ***70***; 74 *alt.* Ps. **48**; 52 Isa. 38. 9–20 Matt. 17. 1–13	Ps. ***50***; 54 *alt.* Ps. 50 Isa. ch. 50 1 Thess. 5. 12–end
18 Wednesday				
P		Jer. 23. 5–8 Ps. 72. 1–2, 12–13, 18–end Matt. 1. 18–24	Ps. ***75***; 96 *alt.* Ps. 119. 57–80 Isa. ch. 39 Matt. 17. 14–21	Ps. 25; ***82*** *alt.* Ps. ***59***; 60; (67) Isa. 51. 1–8 2 Thess. ch. 1
19 Thursday				
P		Judg. 13. 2–7, 24–end Ps. 71. 3–8 Luke 1. 5–25	Ps. 144; ***146*** Zeph. 1.1 – 2.3 Matt. 17. 22–end	Ps. 10; ***57*** Isa. 51. 9–16 2 Thess. ch. 2
20 Friday				
P		Isa. 7. 10–14 Ps. 24. 1–6 Luke 1. 26–38	Ps. ***46***; 95 Zeph. 3. 1–13 Matt. 18. 1–20	Ps. ***4***; 9 Isa. 51. 17–end 2 Thess. ch. 3
21 Saturday**				
P		Zeph. 3. 14–18 Ps. 33. 1–4, 11–12, 20–end Luke 1. 39–45	Ps. ***121***; 122; 123 Zeph. 3. 14–end Matt. 18. 21–end	Ps. 80; ***84*** Isa. 52. 1–12 Jude **ct**
22 Sunday	**THE FOURTH SUNDAY OF ADVENT**			
P		Isa. 7. 10–16 Ps. 80. 1–8, 18–20 (*or* 80. 1–8) Rom. 1. 1–7 Matt. 1. 18–end	Ps. 144 Mic. 5. 2–5a Luke 1. 26–38	Ps. 113; [126] 1 Sam. 1. 1–20 Rev. 22. 6–end *Gospel*: Luke 1. 39–45
23 Monday				
P		Mal. 3. 1–4; 4. 5–end Ps. 25. 3–9 Luke 1. 57–66	Ps. 128; 129; ***130***; 131 Mal. 1. 1, 6–end Matt. 19. 1–12	Ps. 89. 1–37 Isa. 52.13 – 53.end 2 Pet. 1. 1–15
24 Tuesday	**CHRISTMAS EVE**			
P		*Morning Eucharist* 2 Sam. 7. 1–5, 8–11, 16 Ps. 89. 2, 19–27 Acts 13. 16–26 Luke 1. 67–79	Ps. ***45***; 113 Mal. 2. 1–16 Matt. 19. 13–15	Ps. 85 Zech. ch. 2 Rev. 1. 1–8

*The Evening Prayer readings from the Additional Weekday Lectionary (see p. 116) may be used from 17 to 23 December.
**Thomas the Apostle may be celebrated on 21 December instead of 3 July.

	Calendar and Holy Communion	Morning Prayer	Evening Prayer	NOTES
P		Isa. 38. 9–20 Matt. 17. 1–13	Isa. ch. 50 1 Thess. 5. 12–end	
	Ember Day			
P	Ember CEG	Isa. ch. 39 Matt. 17. 14–21	Isa. 51. 1–8 2 Thess. ch. 1	
P		Zeph. 1.1 – 2.3 Matt. 17. 22–end	Isa. 51. 9–16 2 Thess. ch. 2	
	Ember Day			
P	Ember CEG	Zeph. 3. 1–13 Matt. 18. 1–20	Isa. 51. 17–end 2 Thess. ch. 3 *or First EP of Thomas* (Ps. 27) Isa. ch. 35 Heb. 10.35 – 11.1 **R ct**	
	THOMAS THE APOSTLE Ember Day			
R	Job 42. 1–6 Ps. 139. 1–11 Eph. 2. 19–end John 20. 24–end	(Ps. 92; 146) 2 Sam. 15. 17–21 *or* Ecclus. ch. 2 John 11. 1–16	(Ps. 139) Hab. 2. 1–4 1 Pet. 1. 3–12	
	THE FOURTH SUNDAY IN ADVENT			
P	Isa. 40. 1–9 Ps. 145. 17–end Phil. 4. 4–7 John 1. 19–28	Ps. 144 Mic. 5. 2–5a Luke 1. 26–38	Ps. 113; [126] 1 Sam. 1. 1–20 Rev. 22. 6–end	
P		Mal. 1. 1, 6–end Matt. 19. 1–12	Isa. 52.13 – 53.end 2 Pet. 1. 1–15	
	CHRISTMAS EVE			
P	Collect (1) Christmas Eve (2) Advent 1 Mic. 5. 2–5a Ps. 24 Titus 3. 3–7 Luke 2. 1–14	Mal. 2. 1–16 Matt. 19. 13–15	Zech. ch. 2 Rev. 1. 1–8	

		Sunday Principal Service Weekday Eucharist	Third Service Morning Prayer	Second Service Evening Prayer
25 Wednesday	**CHRISTMAS DAY**			
𝔚	*Any of the following sets of readings may be used on the evening of Christmas Eve and on Christmas Day. Set III should be used at some service during the celebration.*	*I* Isa. 9. 2–7 Ps. 96 Titus 2. 11–14 Luke 2. 1–14 [15–20] *II* Isa. 62. 6–end Ps. 97 Titus 3. 4–7 Luke 2. [1–7] 8–20 *III* Isa. 52. 7–10 Ps. 98 Heb. 1. 1–4 [5–12] John 1. 1–14	*MP*: Ps. ***110***; 117 Isa. 62. 1–5 Matt. 1. 18–end	*EP*: Ps. 8 Isa. 65. 17–25 Phil. 2. 5–11 *or* Luke 2. 1–20 *if it has not been used at the principal service of the day*
26 Thursday	**STEPHEN, DEACON, FIRST MARTYR**			
R		2 Chron. 24. 20–22 *or* Acts 7. 51–end Ps. 119. 161–168 Acts 7. 51–end *or* Gal. 2. 16b–20 Matt. 10. 17–22	*MP*: Ps. ***13***; 31. 1–8; 150 Jer. 26. 12–15 Acts ch. 6	*EP*: Ps. 57; ***86*** Gen. 4. 1–10 Matt. 23. 34–end
27 Friday	**JOHN, APOSTLE AND EVANGELIST**			
W		Exod. 33. 7–11a Ps. 117 1 John ch. 1 John 21. 19b–end	*MP*: Ps. ***21***; 147. 13–end Exod. 33. 12–end 1 John 2. 1–11	*EP*: Ps. 97 Isa. 6. 1–8 1 John 5. 1–12
28 Saturday	**THE HOLY INNOCENTS**			
R		Jer. 31. 15–17 Ps. 124 1 Cor. 1. 26–29 Matt. 2. 13–18	*MP*: Ps. ***36***; 146 Baruch 4. 21–27 *or* Gen. 37. 13–20 Matt. 18. 1–10	*EP*: Ps. 123; ***128*** Isa. 49. 14–25 Mark 10. 13–16
29 Sunday	**THE FIRST SUNDAY OF CHRISTMAS**			
W		Isa. 63. 7–9 Ps. 148 (*or* 148. 7–end) Heb. 2. 10–end Matt. 2. 13–end	Ps. 105. 1–11 Isa. 35. 1–6 Gal. 3. 23–end	Ps. 132 Isa. 49. 7–13 Phil. 2. 1–11 *Gospel*: Luke 2. 41–52
30 Monday				
W		1 John 2. 12–17 Ps. 96. 7–10 Luke 2. 36–40	Ps. 111; 112; ***113*** Jonah ch. 2 Col. 1. 15–23	Ps. ***65***; 84 Isa. 59. 1–15a John 1. 19–28

	Calendar and Holy Communion	Morning Prayer	Evening Prayer	NOTES
	CHRISTMAS DAY			
𝔚	Isa. 9. 2–7 Ps. 98 Heb. 1. 1–12 John 1. 1–14	Ps. 110; 117 Isa. 62. 1–5 Matt. 1. 18–end	Ps. 8 Isa. 65. 17–25 Phil. 2. 5–11 *or* Luke 2. 1–20	
	STEPHEN, DEACON, FIRST MARTYR			
R	Collect (1) Stephen (2) Christmas 2 Chron. 24. 20–22 Ps. 119. 161–168 Acts 7. 55–end Matt. 23. 34–end	(Ps. 13; 31. 1–8; 150) Jer. 26. 12–15 Acts ch. 6	(Ps. 57; 86) Gen. 4. 1–10 Matt. 10. 17–22	
	JOHN, APOSTLE AND EVANGELIST			
W	Collect (1) John (2) Christmas Exod. 33. 18–end Ps. 92. 11–end 1 John ch. 1 John 21. 19b–end	(Ps. 21; 147. 13–end) Exod. 33. 7–11a 1 John 2. 1–11	(Ps. 97) Isa. 6. 1–8 1 John 5. 1–12	
	THE HOLY INNOCENTS			
R	Collect (1) Innocents (2) Christmas Jer. 31. 10–17 Ps. 123 Rev. 14. 1–5 Matt. 2. 13–18	(Ps. 36; 146) Baruch 4. 21–27 *or* Gen. 37. 13–20 Matt. 18. 1–10	(Ps. 124; 128) Isa. 49. 14–25 Mark 10. 13–16	
	THE SUNDAY AFTER CHRISTMAS DAY			
W	Isa. 62. 10–12 Ps. 45. 1–7 Gal. 4. 1–7 Matt. 1. 18–end	Ps. 105. 1–11 Isa. 35. 1–6 Gal. 3. 23–end	Ps. 132 Isa. 49. 7–13 Phil. 2. 1–11	
W		Jonah ch. 2 Col. 1. 15–23	Isa. 59. 1–15a John 1. 19–28	

		Sunday Principal Service Weekday Eucharist	Third Service Morning Prayer	Second Service Evening Prayer
31 Tuesday	*John Wyclif, Reformer, 1384*			
W		1 John 2. 18–21 Ps. 96. 1, 11–end John 1. 1–18	Ps. 102 Jonah chs 3 & 4 Col. 1.24 – 2.7	Ps. ***90***; 148 Isa. 59. 15b–end John 1. 29–34 *or First EP of The Naming of Jesus* Ps. 148 Jer. 23. 1–6 Col. 2. 8–15 **ct**

January 2020

		Sunday Principal Service Weekday Eucharist	Third Service Morning Prayer	Second Service Evening Prayer
1 Wednesday	**THE NAMING AND CIRCUMCISION OF JESUS**			
W		Num. 6. 22–end Ps. 8 Gal. 4. 4–7 Luke 2. 15–21	*MP*: Ps. ***103***; 150 Gen. 17. 1–13 Rom. 2. 17–end	*EP*: Ps. 115 Deut. 30. [1–10] 11–end Acts 3. 1–16
2 Thursday	**Basil the Great and Gregory of Nazianzus, Bishops, Teachers, 379 and 389** *Seraphim, Monk of Sarov, Spiritual Guide, 1833; Vedanayagam Samuel Azariah, Bishop in South India, Evangelist, 1945*			
W	Com. Teacher *or* *esp.* 2 Tim. 4. 1–8 Matt. 5. 13–19	1 John 2. 22–28 Ps. 98. 1–4 John 1. 19–28	Ps. 18. 1–30 Ruth ch. 1 Col. 2. 8–end	Ps. 45; ***46*** Isa. 60. 1–12 John 1. 35–42
3 Friday				
W		1 John 2.29 – 3.6 Ps. 98. 2–7 John 1. 29–34	Ps. ***127***; 128; 131 Ruth ch. 2 Col. 3. 1–11	Ps. ***2***; 110 Isa. 60. 13–end John 1. 43–end
4 Saturday				
W		1 John 3. 7–10 Ps. 98. 1, 8–end John 1. 35–42	Ps. 89. 1–37 Ruth ch. 3 Col. 3.12 – 4.1	Ps. 85; ***87*** Isa. ch. 61 John 2. 1–12 **ct** *or First EP of The Epiphany* Ps. 96; ***97*** Isa. 49. 1–13 John 4. 7–26 **𝔚 ct**
5 Sunday	**THE SECOND SUNDAY OF CHRISTMAS** *or* The Epiphany (see provision on 6 January)			
W		Jer. 31. 7–14 *or* Ecclus. 24. 1–12 Ps. 147. 13–end *or Canticle*: Wisd. 10. 15–end Eph. 1. 3–14 John 1. [1–9] 10–18	Ps. 87 Jer. 31. 15–17 2 Cor. 1. 3–12	*First EP of The Epiphany* Ps. 96; ***97*** Isa. 49. 1–13 John 4. 7–26 **𝔚 ct**

	Calendar and Holy Communion	Morning Prayer	Evening Prayer	NOTES
	Silvester, Bishop of Rome, 335			
W	Com. Bishop	Jonah chs 3 & 4 Col. 1.24 - 2.7	Isa. 59. 15b–end John 1. 29–34 *or First EP of The Circumcision of Christ* (Ps. 148) Jer. 23. 1–6 Col. 2. 8–15 **ct**	
	THE CIRCUMCISION OF CHRIST			
W	Additional collect Gen. 17. 3b–10 Ps. 98 Rom. 4. 8–13 *or* Eph. 2. 11–18 Luke 2. 15–21	(Ps. 103; 150) Gen. 17. 1–13 Rom. 2. 17–end	(Ps. 115) Deut. 30. [1–10] 11–end Acts 3. 1–16	
W		Ruth ch. 1 Col. 2. 8–end	Isa. 60. 1–12 John 1. 35–42	
W		Ruth ch. 2 Col. 3. 1–11	Isa. 60. 13–end John 1. 43–end	
W		Ruth ch. 3 Col. 3.12 - 4.1	Isa. ch. 61 John 2. 1–12 **ct**	
	THE SECOND SUNDAY AFTER CHRISTMAS DAY			
W	Exod. 24. 12–18 Ps. 93 2 Cor. 8. 9 John 1. 14–18	Ps. 87 Jer. 31. 15–17 2 Cor. 1. 3–12	*First EP of The Epiphany* Ps. 96; **97** Isa. 49. 1–13 John 4. 7–26 𝔚 **ct**	

		Sunday Principal Service Weekday Eucharist	Third Service Morning Prayer	Second Service Evening Prayer
6 Monday	**THE EPIPHANY**			
𝔚		Isa. 60. 1–6 Ps. 72. [1–9] 10–15 Eph. 3. 1–12 Matt. 2. 1–12	*MP*: Ps. ***132***; 113 Jer. 31. 7–14 John 1. 29–34	*EP*: Ps. ***98***; 100 Baruch 4.36 – 5.end *or* Isa. 60. 1–9 John 2. 1–11
	or, if The Epiphany is celebrated on 5 January:			
W		1 John 3.22 – 4.6 Ps. 2. 7–end Matt. 4. 12–17, 23–end	Ps. 8; ***48*** *alt*. Ps. 71 Ruth 4. 1–17 Col. 4. 2–end	Ps. 96; ***97*** *alt*. Ps. ***72***; 75 Isa. ch. 62 John 2. 13–end
7 Tuesday				
W		1 John 3.22 – 4.6 Ps. 2. 7–end Matt. 4. 12–17, 23–end	Ps. ***99***; 147. 1–12 *alt*. Ps. 73 Baruch 1.15 – 2.10 *or* Jer. 23. 1–8 Matt. 20. 1–16	Ps. 118 *alt*. Ps. 74 Isa. 63. 7–end 1 John ch. 3
	or, if The Epiphany is celebrated on 5 January:			
		1 John 4. 7–10 Ps. 72. 1–8 Mark 6. 34–44	Ps. ***99***; 147. 1–12 *alt*. Ps. 73 Baruch 1.15 – 2.10 *or* Jer. 23. 1–8 Matt. 20. 1–16	Ps. 118 *alt*. Ps. 74 Isa. 63. 7–end 1 John ch. 3
8 Wednesday				
W		1 John 4. 7–10 Ps. 72. 1–8 Mark 6. 34–44	Ps. ***46***; 147. 13–end *alt*. Ps. 77 Baruch 2. 11–end *or* Jer. 30. 1–17 Matt. 20. 17–28	Ps. 145 *alt*. Ps. 119. 81–104 Isa. ch. 64 1 John 4. 7–end
	or, if The Epiphany is celebrated on 5 January:			
		1 John 4. 11–18 Ps. 72. 1, 10–13 Mark 6. 45–52	Ps. ***46***; 147. 13–end *alt*. Ps. 77 Baruch 2. 11–end *or* Jer. 30. 1–17 Matt. 20. 17–28	Ps. 145 *alt*. Ps. 119. 81–104 Isa. ch. 64 1 John 4. 7–end
9 Thursday				
W		1 John 4. 11–18 Ps. 72. 1, 10–13 Mark 6. 45–52	Ps. 2; ***148*** *alt*. Ps. 78. 1–39† Baruch 3. 1–8 *or* Jer. 30.18 – 31.9 Matt. 20. 29–end	Ps. ***67***; 72 *alt*. Ps. 78. 40–end† Isa. 65. 1–16 1 John 5. 1–12
	or, if The Epiphany is celebrated on 5 January:			
		1 John 4.19 – 5.4 Ps. 72. 1, 17–end Luke 4. 14–22	Ps. 2; ***148*** *alt*. Ps. 78. 1–39† Baruch 3. 1–8 *or* Jer. 30.18 – 31.9 Matt. 20. 29–end	Ps. ***67***; 72 *alt*. Ps. 78. 40–end† Isa. 65. 1–16 1 John 5. 1–12

	Calendar and Holy Communion	Morning Prayer	Evening Prayer	NOTES
	THE EPIPHANY			
𝔚	Isa. 60. 1–9 Ps. 100 Eph. 3. 1–12 Matt. 2. 1–12	Ps. 132; 113 Jer. 31. 7–14 John 1. 29–34	Ps. 72; 98 Baruch 4.36 - 5.end *or* Isa. 60. 1–9 John 2. 1–11	
W *or* **G**		Baruch 1.15 - 2.10 *or* Jer. 23. 1–8 Matt. 20. 1–16	Isa. 63. 7–end 1 John ch. 3	
	Lucian, Priest and Martyr, 290			
Wr *or* **Gr**	Com. Martyr	Baruch 2. 11–end *or* Jer. 30. 1–17 Matt. 20. 17–28	Isa. ch. 64 1 John 4. 7–end	
W *or* **G**		Baruch 3. 1–8 *or* Jer. 30.18 - 31.9 Matt. 20. 29–end	Isa. 65. 1–16 1 John 5. 1–12	

		Sunday Principal Service Weekday Eucharist	Third Service Morning Prayer	Second Service Evening Prayer
10 Friday	*William Laud, Archbishop of Canterbury, 1645*			
W		1 John 4.19 - 5.4 Ps. 72. 1, 17–end Luke 4. 14–22	Ps. 97; ***149*** *alt.* Ps. 55 Baruch 3.9 - 4.4 *or* Jer. 31. 10–17 Matt. 23. 1–12	Ps. 27; ***29*** *alt.* Ps. 69 Isa. 65. 17–end 1 John 5. 13–end
	or, if The Epiphany is celebrated on 5 January:	1 John 5. 5–13 Ps. 147. 13–end Luke 5. 12–16	Ps. 97; ***149*** *alt.* Ps. 55 Baruch 3.9 - 4.4 *or* Jer. 31. 10–17 Matt. 23. 1–12	Ps. 27; ***29*** *alt.* Ps. 69 Isa. 65. 17–end 1 John 5. 13–end
11 Saturday	*Mary Slessor, Missionary in West Africa, 1915*			
W		1 John 5. 5–13 Ps. 147. 13–end Luke 5. 12–16	Ps. 98; ***150*** *alt.* Ps. ***76***; 79 Baruch 4. 21–30 *or* Jer. 33. 14–end Matt. 23. 13–28	*First EP of The Baptism* Ps. 36 Isa. ch. 61 Titus 2. 11–14; 3. 4–7 **𝔚 ct**
	or, if The Epiphany is celebrated on 5 January:	1 John 5. 14–end Ps. 149. 1–5 John 3. 22–30	Ps. 98; ***150*** *alt.* Ps. ***76***; 79 Baruch 4. 21–30 *or* Jer. 33. 14–end Matt. 23. 13–28	*First EP of The Baptism* Ps. 36 Isa. ch. 61 Titus 2. 11–14; 3. 4–7 **𝔚 ct**
12 Sunday	**THE BAPTISM OF CHRIST (THE FIRST SUNDAY OF EPIPHANY)**			
𝔚		Isa. 42. 1–9 Ps. 29 Acts 10. 34–43 Matt. 3. 13–end	Ps. 89. 19–29 Exod. 14. 15–22 1 John 5. 6–9	Ps. 46; 47 Josh. 3. 1–8, 14–end Heb. 1. 1–12 *Gospel*: Luke 3. 15–22
13 Monday	**Hilary, Bishop of Poitiers, Teacher, 367** *Kentigern (Mungo), Missionary Bishop in Strathclyde and Cumbria, 603; George Fox, Founder of the Society of Friends (the Quakers), 1691*			
W **DEL 1**	Com. Teacher *or* *also* 1 John 2. 18–25 John 8. 25–32	1 Sam. 1. 1–8 Ps. 116. 10–15 Mark 1. 14–20	Ps. ***2***; 110 *alt.* Ps. ***80***; 82 Gen. 1. 1–19 Matt. 21. 1–17	Ps. ***34***; 36 *alt.* Ps. ***85***; 86 Amos ch. 1 1 Cor. 1. 1–17
14 Tuesday				
W		1 Sam. 1. 9–20 *Canticle*: 1 Sam. 2. 1, 4–8 *or* Magnificat Mark 1. 21–28	Ps. 8; ***9*** *alt.* Ps. 87; ***89. 1–18*** Gen. 1.20 - 2.3 Matt. 21. 18–32	Ps. ***45***; 46 *alt.* Ps. 89. 19–end Amos ch. 2 1 Cor. 1. 18–end
15 Wednesday				
W		1 Sam. 3. 1–10, 19–20 Ps. 40. 1–4, 7–10 Mark 1. 29–39	Ps. 19; ***20*** *alt.* Ps. 119. 105–128 Gen. 2. 4–end Matt. 21. 33–end	Ps. ***47***; 48 *alt.* Ps. ***91***; 93 Amos ch. 3 1 Cor. ch. 2

	Calendar and Holy Communion	Morning Prayer	Evening Prayer
W *or* **G**		Baruch 3.9 - 4.4 *or* Jer. 31. 10-17 Matt. 23. 1-12	Isa. 65. 17-end 1 John 5. 13-end
W *or* **G**		Baruch 4. 21-30 *or* Jer. 33. 14-end Matt. 23. 13-28	Isa. 66. 1-11 2 John **ct**
	THE FIRST SUNDAY AFTER THE EPIPHANY To celebrate The Baptism of Christ, see *Common Worship* provision.		
W *or* **G**	Zech. 8. 1-8 Ps. 72. 1-8 Rom. 12. 1-5 Luke 2. 41-end	Ps. 89. 19-29 Exod. 14. 15-22 1 John 5. 6-9	Ps. 46; 47 Josh. 3. 1-8, 14-end Heb. 1. 1-12
	Hilary, Bishop of Poitiers, Teacher, 367		
W *or* **Gw**	Com. Doctor	Gen. 1. 1-19 Matt. 21. 1-17	Amos ch. 1 1 Cor. 1. 1-17
W *or* **G**		Gen. 1.20 - 2.3 Matt. 21. 18-32	Amos ch. 2 1 Cor. 1. 18-end
W *or* **G**		Gen. 2. 4-end Matt. 21. 33-end	Amos ch. 3 1 Cor. ch. 2

NOTES

		Sunday Principal Service Weekday Eucharist	Third Service Morning Prayer	Second Service Evening Prayer
16 Thursday				
W		1 Sam. 4. 1–11 Ps. 44. 10–15, 24–25 Mark 1. 40–end	Ps. ***21***; 24 *alt.* Ps. 90; ***92*** Gen. ch. 3 Matt. 22. 1–14	Ps. ***61***; 65 *alt.* Ps. 94 Amos ch. 4 1 Cor. ch. 3
17 Friday	**Antony of Egypt, Hermit, Abbot, 356** *Charles Gore, Bishop, Founder of the Community of the Resurrection, 1932*			
W	Com. Religious *or* *esp.* Phil. 3. 7–14 *also* Matt. 19. 16–26	1 Sam. 8. 4–7, 10–end Ps. 89. 15–18 Mark 2. 1–12	Ps. ***67***; 72 *alt.* Ps. ***88***; (95) Gen. 4. 1–16, 25–26 Matt. 22. 15–33	Ps. 68 *alt.* Ps. 102 Amos 5. 1–17 1 Cor. ch. 4
18 Saturday	*Amy Carmichael, Founder of the Dohnavur Fellowship, Spiritual Writer, 1951* The Week of Prayer for Christian Unity until 25 January			
W		1 Sam. 9. 1–4, 17–19; 10. 1a Ps. 21. 1–6 Mark 2. 13–17	Ps. 29; ***33*** *alt.* Ps. 96; ***97***; 100 Gen. 6. 1–10 Matt. 22. 34–end	Ps. 84; ***85*** *alt.* Ps. 104 Amos 5. 18–end 1 Cor. ch. 5 **ct**
19 Sunday	**THE SECOND SUNDAY OF EPIPHANY**			
W		Isa. 49. 1–7 Ps. 40. 1–12 1 Cor. 1. 1–9 John 1. 29–42	Ps. 145. 1–12 Jer. 1. 4–10 Mark 1. 14–20	Ps. 96 Ezek. 2.1 - 3.4 Gal. 1. 11–end *Gospel*: John 1. 43–end
20 Monday	*Richard Rolle of Hampole, Spiritual Writer, 1349*			
W **DEL 2**		1 Sam. 15. 16–23 Ps. 50. 8–10, 16–17, 24 Mark 2. 18–22	Ps. 145; ***146*** *alt.* Ps. ***98***; 99; 101 Gen. 6.11 - 7.10 Matt. 24. 1–14	Ps. 71 *alt.* Ps. 105† (*or* 103) Amos ch. 6 1 Cor. 6. 1–11
21 Tuesday	**Agnes, Child Martyr at Rome, 304**			
Wr	Com. Martyr *or* *also* Rev. 7. 13–end	1 Sam. 16. 1–13 Ps. 89. 19–27 Mark 2. 23–end	Ps. ***132***; 147. 1–12 *alt.* Ps. 106† (*or* 103) Gen. 7. 11–end Matt. 24. 15–28	Ps. 89. 1–37 *alt.* Ps. 107† Amos ch. 7 1 Cor. 6. 12–end
22 Wednesday	*Vincent of Saragossa, Deacon, first Martyr of Spain, 304*			
W		1 Sam. 17. 32–33, 37, 40–51 Ps. 144. 1–2, 9–10 Mark 3. 1–6	Ps. ***81***; 147. 13–end *alt.* Ps. 110; ***111***; 112 Gen. 8. 1–14 Matt. 24. 29–end	Ps. ***97***; 98 *alt.* Ps. 119. 129–152 Amos ch. 8 1 Cor. 7. 1–24
23 Thursday				
W		1 Sam. 18. 6–9; 19. 1–7 Ps. 56. 1–2, 8–end Mark 3. 7–12	Ps. ***76***; 148 *alt.* Ps. 113; ***115*** Gen. 8.15 - 9.7 Matt. 25. 1–13	Ps. 99; 100; ***111*** *alt.* Ps. 114; ***116***; 117 Amos ch. 9 1 Cor. 7. 25–end

	Calendar and Holy Communion	Morning Prayer	Evening Prayer
W *or* **G**		Gen. ch. 3 Matt. 22. 1–14	Amos ch. 4 1 Cor. ch. 3
W *or* **G**		Gen. 4. 1–16, 25–26 Matt. 22. 15–33	Amos 5. 1–17 1 Cor. ch. 4
	Prisca, Martyr at Rome, c. 265 For the Week of Prayer for Christian Unity, see *Common Worship* provision.		
Wr *or* **Gr**	Com. Virgin Martyr	Gen. 6. 1–10 Matt. 22. 34–end	Amos 5. 18–end 1 Cor. ch. 5 **ct**
	THE SECOND SUNDAY AFTER THE EPIPHANY		
W *or* **G**	2 Kings 4. 1–17 Ps. 107. 13–22 Rom. 12. 6–16a John 2. 1–11	Ps. 145. 1–12 Jer. 1. 4–10 Mark 1. 14–20	Ps. 96 Ezek. 2.1 - 3.4 Gal. 1. 11–end
	Fabian, Bishop of Rome, Martyr, 250		
Wr *or* **Gr**	Com. Martyr	Gen. 6.11 - 7.10 Matt. 24. 1–14	Amos ch. 6 1 Cor. 6. 1–11
	Agnes, Child Martyr at Rome, 304		
Wr *or* **Gr**	Com. Virgin Martyr	Gen. 7. 11–end Matt. 24. 15–28	Amos ch. 7 1 Cor. 6. 12–end
	Vincent of Saragossa, Deacon, first Martyr of Spain, 304		
Wr *or* **Gr**	Com. Martyr	Gen. 8. 1–14 Matt. 24. 29–end	Amos ch. 8 1 Cor. 7. 1–24
W *or* **G**		Gen. 8.15 - 9.7 Matt. 25. 1–13	Amos ch. 9 1 Cor. 7. 25–end

NOTES

		Sunday Principal Service Weekday Eucharist	Third Service Morning Prayer	Second Service Evening Prayer
24 Friday	**Francis de Sales, Bishop of Geneva, Teacher, 1622**			
W	Com. Teacher *or* *also* Prov. 3. 13–18 John 3. 17–21	1 Sam. 24. 3–22a Ps. 57. 1–2, 8–end Mark 3. 13–19	Ps. ***27***; 149 *alt.* Ps. 139 Gen. 9. 8–19 Matt. 25. 14–30	Ps. 73 *alt.* Ps. ***130***; 131; 137 Hos. 1.1 - 2.1 1 Cor. ch. 8 *or First EP of The Conversion of Paul* Ps. 149 Isa. 49. 1–13 Acts 22. 3–16 **ct**
25 Saturday	**THE CONVERSION OF PAUL**			
W		Jer. 1. 4–10 *or* Acts 9. 1–22 Ps. 67 Acts 9. 1–22 *or* Gal. 1. 11–16a Matt. 19. 27–end	*MP*: Ps. 66; 147. 13–end Ezek. 3. 22–end Phil. 3. 1–14	*EP*: Ps. 119. 41–56 Ecclus. 39. 1–10 *or* Isa. 56. 1–8 Col. 1.24 - 2.7
26 Sunday	**THE THIRD SUNDAY OF EPIPHANY**			
W		Isa. 9. 1–4 Ps. 27. 1, 4–12 (*or* 27. 1–11) 1 Cor. 1. 10–18 Matt. 4. 12–23	Ps. 113 Amos 3. 1–8 1 John 1. 1–4	Ps. 33 (*or* 33. 1–12) Eccles. 3. 1–11 1 Pet. 1. 3–12 *Gospel*: Luke 4. 14–21
27 Monday				
W **DEL 3**		2 Sam. 5. 1–7, 10 Ps. 89. 19–27 Mark 3. 22–30	Ps. 40; ***108*** *alt.* Ps. 123; 124; 125; ***126*** Gen. 11.27 - 12.9 Matt. 26. 1–16	Ps. ***138***; 144 *alt.* Ps. ***127***; 128; 129 Hos. 2.18 - 3.end 1 Cor. 9. 15–end
28 Tuesday	**Thomas Aquinas, Priest, Philosopher, Teacher, 1274**			
W	Com. Teacher *or* *esp.* Wisd. 7. 7–10, 15–16 1 Cor. 2. 9–end John 16. 12–15	2 Sam. 6. 12–15, 17–19 Ps. 24. 7–end Mark 3. 31–end	Ps. 34; ***36*** *alt.* Ps. ***132***; 133 Gen. 13. 2–end Matt. 26. 17–35	Ps. 145 *alt.* Ps. (134); ***135*** Hos. 4. 1–16 1 Cor. 10. 1–13
29 Wednesday				
W		2 Sam. 7. 4–17 Ps. 89. 19–27 Mark 4. 1–20	Ps. 45; ***46*** *alt.* Ps. 119. 153–end Gen. ch. 14 Matt. 26. 36–46	Ps. 21; ***29*** *alt.* Ps. 136 Hos. 5. 1–7 1 Cor. 10.14 - 11.1
30 Thursday	**Charles, King and Martyr, 1649**			
Wr	Com. Martyr *or* *also* Ecclus. 2. 12–17 1 Tim. 6. 12–16	2 Sam. 7. 18–19, 24–end Ps. 132. 1–5, 11–15 Mark 4. 21–25	Ps. ***47***; 48 *alt.* Ps. ***143***; 146 Gen. ch. 15 Matt. 26. 47–56	Ps. ***24***; 33 *alt.* Ps. ***138***; 140; 141 Hos. 5.8 - 6.6 1 Cor. 11. 2–16
31 Friday	*John Bosco, Priest, Founder of the Salesian Teaching Order, 1888*			
W		2 Sam. 11. 1–10, 13–17 Ps. 51. 1–6, 9 Mark 4. 26–34	Ps. 61; ***65*** *alt.* Ps. 142; ***144*** Gen. ch. 16 Matt. 26. 57–end	Ps. ***67***; 77 *alt.* Ps. 145 Hos. 6.7 - 7.2 1 Cor. 11. 17–end

	Calendar and Holy Communion	Morning Prayer	Evening Prayer
W *or* **G**		Gen. 9. 8–19 Matt. 25. 14–30	Hos. 1.1 - 2.1 1 Cor. ch. 8 *or First EP of The Conversion of Paul* (Ps. 149) Isa. 49. 1-13 Acts 22. 3-16 **W ct**
	THE CONVERSION OF PAUL		
W	Josh. 5. 13–end Ps. 67 Acts 9. 1–22 Matt. 19. 27–end	(Ps. 66, 147. 13–end) Ezek. 3. 22–end Phil. 3. 1–14	(Ps. 119. 41–56) Ecclus. 39. 1–10 *or* Isa. 56. 1–8 Col. 1.24 - 2.7
	THE THIRD SUNDAY AFTER THE EPIPHANY		
W *or* **G**	2 Kings 6. 14b–23 Ps. 102. 15–22 Rom. 12. 16b–end Matt. 8. 1–13	Ps. 113 Amos 3. 1–8 1 John 1. 1–4	Ps. 33 (*or* 33. 1–12) Eccles. 3. 1–11 1 Pet. 1. 3–12
W *or* **G**		Gen. 11.27 - 12.9 Matt. 26. 1–16	Hos. 2.18 - 3.end 1 Cor. 9. 15–end
W *or* **G**		Gen. 13. 2–end Matt. 26. 17–35	Hos. 4. 1–16 1 Cor. 10. 1–13
W *or* **G**		Gen. ch. 14 Matt. 26. 36–46	Hos. 5. 1–7 1 Cor. 10.14 - 11.1
	Charles, King and Martyr, 1649		
Wr *or* **Gr**	Com. Martyr	Gen. ch. 15 Matt. 26. 47–56	Hos. 5.8 - 6.6 1 Cor. 11. 2–16
W *or* **G**		Gen. ch. 16 Matt. 26. 57–end	Hos. 6.7 - 7.2 1 Cor. 11. 17–end

NOTES

		Sunday Principal Service Weekday Eucharist	Third Service Morning Prayer	Second Service Evening Prayer
February 2020				
1 Saturday	*Brigid, Abbess of Kildare, c. 525*			
W		2 Sam. 12. 1–7, 10–17 Ps. 51. 11–16 Mark 4. 35–end	Ps. 68 *alt.* Ps. 147 Gen. 17. 1–22 Matt. 27. 1–10	*First EP of The Presentation* Ps. 118 1 Sam. 1. 19b–end Heb. 4. 11–end **𝔚 ct**
2 Sunday	**THE PRESENTATION OF CHRIST IN THE TEMPLE (CANDLEMAS)**			
𝔚		Mal. 3. 1–5 Ps. 24 (*or* 24. 7–end) Heb. 2. 14–end Luke 2. 22–40	*MP*: Ps. ***48***; 146 Exod. 13. 1–16 Rom. 12. 1–5	*EP*: Ps. 122; ***132*** Hag. 2. 1–9 John 2. 18–22
3 Monday	**Anskar, Archbishop of Hamburg, Missionary in Denmark and Sweden, 865** Ordinary Time starts today*			
Gw **DEL 4**	Com. Missionary *or* *esp.* Isa. 52. 7–10 *also* Rom. 10. 11–15	2 Sam. 15. 13–14, 30; 16. 5–13 Ps. 3 Mark 5. 1–20	Ps. ***1***; 2; 3 Lev. 19. 1–18, 30–end 1 Tim. 1. 1–17	Ps. ***4***; 7 Joel 1. 1–14 John 15. 1–11
4 Tuesday	*Gilbert of Sempringham, Founder of the Gilbertine Order, 1189*			
G		2 Sam. 18.9–10, 14, 24–25, 30 – 19.3 Ps. 86. 1–6 Mark. 5. 21–end	Ps. ***5***; 6; (8) Lev. 23. 1–22 1 Tim. 1.18 – 2.end	Ps. ***9***; 10† Joel 1. 15–end John 15. 12–17
5 Wednesday				
G		2 Sam. 24. 2, 9–17 Ps. 32. 1–8 Mark 6. 1–6a	Ps. 119. 1–32 Lev. 23. 23–end 1 Tim. ch. 3	Ps. ***11***; 12; 13 Joel 2. 1–17 John 15. 18–end
6 Thursday	*The Martyrs of Japan, 1597* (The Accession of Queen Elizabeth II may be observed on 6 February, and Collect, Readings and Post-Communion for the Sovereign used.)			
G		1 Kings 2. 1–4, 10–12 *Canticle*: 1 Chron. 29. 10–12 *or* Ps. 145. 1–5 Mark 6. 7–13	Ps. 14; ***15***; 16 Lev. 24. 1–9 1 Tim. ch. 4	Ps. 18† Joel 2. 18–27 John 16. 1–15
7 Friday				
G		Ecclus. 47. 2–11 Ps. 18. 31–36, 50–end Mark 6. 14–29	Ps. 17; ***19*** Lev. 25. 1–24 1 Tim. 5. 1–16	Ps. 22 Joel 2. 28–end John 16. 16–22
8 Saturday				
G		1 Kings 3. 4–13 Ps. 119. 9–16 Mark 6. 30–34	Ps. 20; 21; ***23*** Num. 6. 1–5, 21–end 1 Tim. 5. 17–end	Ps. ***24***; 25 Joel 3. 1–3, 9–end John 16. 23–end **ct**
9 Sunday	**THE THIRD SUNDAY BEFORE LENT (Proper 1)**			
G		Isa. 58. 1–9a [9b–12] Ps. 112 (*or* 112. 1–9) 1 Cor. 2. 1–12 [13–end] Matt. 5. 13–20	Ps. 5; 6 Jer. 26. 1–16 Acts 3. 1–10	Ps. [1; 3] 4 Amos 2. 4–end Eph. 4. 17–end *Gospel*: Mark 1. 29–39

*The Collect of 4 before Lent is used.

	Calendar and Holy Communion	Morning Prayer	Evening Prayer	NOTES
W *or* **G**		Gen. 17. 1–22 Matt. 27. 1–10	*First EP of The Presentation* Ps. 118 1 Sam. 1. 19b–end Heb. 4. 11–end **𝔚 ct**	
	THE PRESENTATION OF CHRIST IN THE TEMPLE			
𝔚	Mal. 3. 1–5 Ps. 48. 1–7 Gal. 4. 1–7 Luke 2. 22–40	Ps. 48; 146 Exod. 13. 1–16 Rom. 12. 1–5	Ps. 122; 132 Hag. 2. 1–9 John 2. 18–22	
	Blasius, Bishop of Sebastopol, Martyr, c. 316			
Gr	Com. Martyr	Lev. 19. 1–18, 30–end 1 Tim. 1. 1–17	Joel 1. 1–14 John 15. 1–11	
G		Lev. 23. 1–22 1 Tim. 1.18 – 2.end	Joel 1. 15–end John 15. 12–17	
	Agatha, Martyr in Sicily, 251			
Gr	Com. Virgin Martyr	Lev. 23. 23–end 1 Tim. ch. 3	Joel 2. 1–17 John 15. 18–end	
	The Accession of Queen Elizabeth II, 1952			
G	*For Accession Service*: Ps. 20; 101; 121; Josh. 1. 1–9; Prov. 8. 1–16, Rom. 13. 1–10; Rev. 21.22 – 22.4 *For The Accession*: 1 Pet. 2. 11–17 Matt. 22. 16–22	Lev. 24. 1–9 1 Tim. ch. 4	Joel 2. 18–27 John 16. 1–15	
G		Lev. 25. 1–24 1 Tim. 5. 1–16	Joel 2. 28–end John 16. 16–22	
G		Num. 6. 1–5, 21–end 1 Tim. 5. 17–end	Joel 3. 1–3, 9–end John 16. 23–end **ct**	
	SEPTUAGESIMA			
G	Gen. 1. 1–5 Ps. 9. 10–20 1 Cor. 9. 24–end Matt. 20. 1–16	Ps. 5; 6 Jer. 26. 1–16 Acts 3. 1–10	Ps. [1; 3] 4 Amos 2. 4–end Eph. 4. 17–end	

		Sunday Principal Service Weekday Eucharist	Third Service Morning Prayer	Second Service Evening Prayer
10 Monday	*Scholastica, sister of Benedict, Abbess of Plombariola, c. 543*			
G **DEL 5**		1 Kings 8. 1–7, 9–13 Ps. 132. 1–9 Mark 6. 53–end	Ps. 27; ***30*** Gen. 24. 1–28 1 Tim. 6. 1–10	Ps. 26; ***28***; 29 Eccles. ch. 1 John 17. 1–5
11 Tuesday				
G		1 Kings 8. 22–23, 27–30 Ps. 84. 1–10 Mark 7. 1–13	Ps. 32; ***36*** Gen. 24. 29–end 1 Tim. 6. 11–end	Ps. 33 Eccles. ch. 2 John 17. 6–19
12 Wednesday				
G		1 Kings 10. 1–10 Ps. 37. 3–6, 30–32 Mark 7. 14–23	Ps. 34 Gen. 25. 7–11, 19–end 2 Tim. 1. 1–14	Ps. 119. 33–56 Eccles. 3. 1–15 John 17. 20–end
13 Thursday				
G		1 Kings 11. 4–13 Ps. 106. 3, 35–41 Mark 7. 24–30	Ps. 37† Gen. 26.34 – 27.40 2 Tim. 1.15 – 2.13	Ps. 39; ***40*** Eccles. 3.16 – 4.end John 18. 1–11
14 Friday	**Cyril and Methodius, Missionaries to the Slavs, 869 and 885** *Valentine, Martyr at Rome, c. 269*			
Gw	Com. Missionaries *or* *esp.* Isa. 52. 7–10 *also* Rom. 10. 11–15	1 Kings 11. 29–32; 12. 19 Ps. 81. 8–14 Mark 7. 31–end	Ps. 31 Gen. 27.41 – 28.end 2 Tim. 2. 14–end	Ps. 35 Eccles. ch. 5 John 18. 12–27
15 Saturday	*Sigfrid, Bishop, Apostle of Sweden, 1045; Thomas Bray, Priest, Founder of the SPCK and SPG, 1730*			
G		1 Kings 12. 26–32; 13. 33–end Ps. 106. 6–7, 20–23 Mark 8. 1–10	Ps. 41; ***42***; 43 Gen. 29. 1–30 2 Tim. ch. 3	Ps. 45; ***46*** Eccles. ch. 6 John 18. 28–end **ct**
16 Sunday	**THE SECOND SUNDAY BEFORE LENT (Proper 2)**			
G		Gen. 1.1 – 2.3 Ps. 136 (*or* 136. 1–9, 23–end) Rom. 8. 18–25 Matt. 6. 25–end	Ps. 100; 150 Job 38. 1–21 Col. 1. 15–20	Ps. 148 Prov. 8. 1, 22–31 Rev. ch. 4 *Gospel*: Luke 12. 16–31
17 Monday	**Janani Luwum, Archbishop of Uganda, Martyr, 1977**			
Gr **DEL 6**	Com. Martyr *or* *also* Ecclus. 4. 20–28 John 12. 24–32	Jas. 1. 1–11 Ps. 119. 65–72 Mark 8. 11–13	Ps. 44 Gen. 29.31 – 30.24 2 Tim. 4. 1–8	Ps. ***47***; 49 Eccles. 7. 1–14 John 19. 1–16
18 Tuesday				
G		Jas. 1. 12–18 Ps. 94. 12–18 Mark 8. 14–21	Ps. ***48***; 52 Gen. 31. 1–24 2 Tim. 4. 9–end	Ps. 50 Eccles. 7. 15–end John 19. 17–30
19 Wednesday				
G		Jas. 1. 19–end Ps. 15 Mark 8. 22–26	Ps. 119. 57–80 Gen. 31.25 – 32.2 Titus ch. 1	Ps. ***59***; 60; (67) Eccles. ch. 8 John 19. 31–end

	Calendar and Holy Communion	Morning Prayer	Evening Prayer	NOTES
G		Gen. 24. 1–28 1 Tim. 6. 1–10	Eccles. ch. 1 John 17. 1–5	
G		Gen. 24. 29–end 1 Tim. 6. 11–end	Eccles. ch. 2 John 17. 6–19	
G		Gen. 25. 7–11, 19–end 2 Tim. 1. 1–14	Eccles. 3. 1–15 John 17. 20–end	
G		Gen. 26.34 – 27.40 2 Tim. 1.15 – 2.13	Eccles. 3.16 – 4.end John 18. 1–11	
	Valentine, Martyr at Rome, c. 269			
Gr	Com. Martyr	Gen. 27.41 – 28.end 2 Tim. 2. 14–end	Eccles. ch. 5 John 18. 12–27	
G		Gen. 29. 1–30 2 Tim. ch. 3	Eccles. ch. 6 John 18. 28–end **ct**	
	SEXAGESIMA			
	Gen. 3. 9–19 Ps. 83. 1–2, 13–end 2 Cor. 11. 19–31 Luke 8. 4–15	Ps. 100; 150 Job 38. 1–21 Col. 1. 15–20	Ps. 148 Prov. 8. 1, 22–31 Rev. ch. 4	
G		Gen. 29.31 – 30.24 2 Tim. 4. 1–8	Eccles. 7. 1–14 John 19. 1–16	
G		Gen. 31. 1–24 2 Tim. 4. 9–end	Eccles. 7. 15–end John 19. 17–30	
G		Gen. 31.25 – 32.2 Titus ch. 1	Eccles. ch. 8 John 19. 31–end	

		Sunday Principal Service Weekday Eucharist	Third Service Morning Prayer	Second Service Evening Prayer
20 Thursday				
G		Jas. 2. 1–9 Ps. 34. 1–7 Mark 8. 27–33	Ps. 56; ***57***; (63†) Gen. 32. 3–30 Titus ch. 2	Ps. 61; ***62***; 64 Eccles. ch. 9 John 20. 1–10
21 Friday				
G		Jas. 2. 14–24, 26 Ps. 112 Mark 8.34 – 9.1	Ps. ***51***; 54 Gen. 33. 1–17 Titus ch. 3	Ps. 38 Eccles. 11. 1–8 John 20. 11–18
22 Saturday				
G		Jas. 3. 1–10 Ps. 12. 1–7 Mark 9. 2–13	Ps. 68 Gen. ch. 35 Philem.	Ps. 65; ***66*** Eccles. 11.9 – 12.end John 20. 19–end **ct**
23 Sunday	**THE SUNDAY NEXT BEFORE LENT**			
G		Exod. 24. 12–end Ps. 2 *or* Ps. 99 2 Pet. 1. 16–end Matt. 17. 1–9	Ps. 72 Exod. 34. 29–end 2 Cor. 4. 3–6	Ps. 84 Ecclus. 48. 1–10 *or* 2 Kings 2. 1–12 Matt. 17. 9–23 (*or* 1–23)
24 Monday*				
G **DEL 7**		Jas. 3. 13–end Ps. 19. 7–end Mark 9. 14–29	Ps. 71 Gen. 37. 1–11 Gal. ch. 1	Ps. ***72***; 75 Jer. ch. 1 John 3. 1–21
25 Tuesday				
G		Jas. 4. 1–10 Ps. 55. 7–9, 24 Mark 9. 30–37	Ps. 73 Gen. 37. 12–end Gal. 2. 1–10	Ps. 74 Jer. 2. 1–13 John 3. 22–end
26 Wednesday	**ASH WEDNESDAY**			
P		Joel 2. 1–2, 12–17 *or* Isa. 58. 1–12 Ps. 51. 1–18 2 Cor. 5.20b – 6.10 Matt. 6. 1–6, 16–21 *or* John 8. 1–11	*MP*: Ps. 38 Dan. 9. 3–6, 17–19 1 Tim. 6. 6–19	*EP*: Ps. ***51*** *or* Ps. 102 (*or* 102. 1–18) Isa. 1. 10–18 Luke 15. 11–end
27 Thursday	**George Herbert, Priest, Poet, 1633**			
Pw	Com. Pastor *or* *esp*. Mal. 2. 5–7 Matt. 11. 25–end *also* Rev. 19. 5–9	Deut. 30. 15–end Ps. 1 Luke 9. 22–25	Ps. 77 *alt*. Ps. 78. 1–39† Gen. ch. 39 Gal. 2. 11–end	Ps. 74 *alt*. Ps. 78. 40–end† Jer. 2. 14–32 John 4. 1–26
28 Friday				
P		Isa. 58. 1–9a Ps. 51. 1–5, 17–18 Matt. 9. 14–15	Ps. ***3***; 7 *alt*. Ps. 55 Gen. ch. 40 Gal. 3. 1–14	Ps. 31 *alt*. Ps. 69 Jer. 3. 6–22 John 4. 27–42

*Matthias may be celebrated on 24 February instead of 14 May.

	Calendar and Holy Communion	Morning Prayer	Evening Prayer	NOTES
G		Gen. 32. 3–30 Titus ch. 2	Eccles. ch. 9 John 20. 1–10	
G		Gen. 33. 1–17 Titus ch. 3	Eccles. 11. 1–8 John 20. 11–18	
G		Gen. ch. 35 Philem.	Eccles. 11.9 - 12.end John 20. 19–end **ct**	
	QUINQUAGESIMA			
G	Gen. 9. 8–17 Ps. 77. 11–end 1 Cor. ch. 13 Luke 18. 31–43	Ps. 72 Exod. 34. 29–end 2 Cor. 4. 3–6	Ps. 84 Ecclus. 48. 1–10 *or* 2 Kings 2. 1–12 Matt. 17. 9–23 (*or* 1–23) *or First EP of Matthias* Ps. 147 Isa. 22. 15–22 Phil. 3.13b - 14.1 **R ct**	
	MATTHIAS THE APOSTLE			
R	1 Sam. 2. 27–35 Ps. 16. 1–7 Acts 1. 15–end Matt. 11. 25–end	(Ps. 15) Jonah 1. 1–9 Acts 2. 37–end	(Ps. 80) 1 Sam. 16. 1–13a Matt. 7. 15–27	
G		Gen. 37. 12–end Gal. 2. 1–10	Jer. 2. 1–13 John 3. 22–end	
	ASH WEDNESDAY			
P	Ash Wed. Collect until 11 April Commination Joel 2. 12–17 Ps. 57 Jas. 4. 1–10 Matt. 6. 16–21	 Ps. 38 Dan. 9. 3–6, 17–19 1 Tim. 6. 6–19	Ps. 51 *or* Ps. 102 (*or* 102. 1–18) Isa. 1. 10–18 Luke 15. 11–end	
P	Exod. 24. 12–end Matt. 8. 5–13	Gen. ch. 39 Gal. 2. 11–end	Jer. 2. 14–32 John 4. 1–26	
P	1 Kings 19. 3b–8 Matt. 5.43 - 6.6	Gen. ch. 40 Gal. 3. 1–14	Jer. 3. 6–22 John 4. 27–42	

		Sunday Principal Service Weekday Eucharist	Third Service Morning Prayer	Second Service Evening Prayer
29 Saturday				
P		Isa. 58. 9b–end Ps. 86. 1–7 Luke 5. 27–32	Ps. 71 *alt.* Ps. ***76***; 79 Gen. 41. 1–24 Gal. 3. 15–22	Ps. 73 *alt.* Ps. 81; ***84*** Jer. 4. 1–18 John 4. 43–end **ct**

March 2020

		Sunday Principal Service Weekday Eucharist	Third Service Morning Prayer	Second Service Evening Prayer
1 Sunday	**THE FIRST SUNDAY OF LENT**			
P		Gen. 2. 15–17; 3. 1–7 Ps. 32 Rom. 5. 12–19 Matt. 4. 1–11	Ps. 119. 1–16 Jer. 18. 1–11 Luke 18. 9–14	Ps. 50. 1–15 Deut. 6. 4–9, 16–end Luke 15. 1–10
2 Monday	**Chad, Bishop of Lichfield, Missionary, 672***			
Pw	Com. Missionary *or* *also* 1 Tim. 6. 11b–16	Lev. 19. 1–2, 11–18 Ps. 19. 7–end Matt. 25. 31–end	Ps. 10; ***11*** *alt.* Ps. ***80***; 82 Gen. 41. 25–45 Gal. 3.23 - 4.7	Ps. 12; ***13***; 14 *alt.* Ps. ***85***; 86 Jer. 4. 19–end John 5. 1–18
3 Tuesday				
P		Isa. 55. 10–11 Ps. 34. 4–6, 21–22 Matt. 6. 7–15	Ps. 44 *alt.* Ps. 87; ***89. 1–18*** Gen. 41.46 - 42.5 Gal. 4. 8–20	Ps. 46; ***49*** *alt.* Ps. 89. 19–end Jer. 5. 1–19 John 5. 19–29
4 Wednesday	Ember Day**			
P		Jonah ch. 3 Ps. 51. 1–5, 17–18 Luke 11. 29–32	Ps. ***6***; 17 *alt.* Ps. 119. 105–128 Gen. 42. 6–17 Gal. 4.21 - 5.1	Ps. 9; ***28*** *alt.* Ps. ***91***; 93 Jer. 5. 20–end John 5. 30–end
5 Thursday				
P		Esth. 14. 1–5, 12–14 *or* Isa. 55. 6–9 Ps. 138 Matt. 7. 7–12	Ps. ***42***; 43 *alt.* Ps. 90; ***92*** Gen. 42. 18–28 Gal. 5. 2–15	Ps. 137; 138; ***142*** *alt.* Ps. 94 Jer. 6. 9–21 John 6. 1–15
6 Friday	Ember Day**			
P		Ezek. 18. 21–28 Ps. 130 Matt. 5. 20–26	Ps. 22 *alt.* Ps. ***88***; (95) Gen. 42. 29–end Gal. 5. 16–end	Ps. 54; ***55*** *alt.* Ps. 102 Jer. 6. 22–end John 6. 16–27
7 Saturday	**Perpetua, Felicity and their Companions, Martyrs at Carthage, 203** Ember Day**			
Pr	Com. Martyr *or* *esp.* Rev. 12. 10–12a *also* Wisd. 3. 1–7	Deut. 26. 16–end Ps. 119. 1–8 Matt. 5. 43–end	Ps. 59; ***63*** *alt.* Ps. 96; ***97***; 100 Gen. 43. 1–15 Gal. ch. 6	Ps. ***4***; 16 *alt.* Ps. 104 Jer. 7. 1–20 John 6. 27–40 **ct**

*Chad may be celebrated with Cedd on 26 October instead of 2 March.
**For Ember Day provision, see p. 11.

	Calendar and Holy Communion	Morning Prayer	Evening Prayer	NOTES
P	Isa. 38. 1–6a Mark 6. 45–end	Gen. 41. 1–24 Gal. 3. 15–22	Jer. 4. 1–18 John 4. 43–end **ct**	
	THE FIRST SUNDAY IN LENT			
P	Collect (1) Lent 1 (2) Ash Wednesday Ember until 7 March Gen. 3. 1–6 Ps. 91. 1–12 2 Cor. 6. 1–10 Matt. 4. 1–11	Ps. 119. 1–16 Jer. 18. 1–11 Luke 18. 9–14	Ps. 50. 1–15 Deut. 6. 4–9, 16–end Luke 15. 1–10	
	Chad, Bishop of Lichfield, Missionary, 672			
Pw	Com. Bishop *or* Ezek. 34. 11–16a Matt. 25. 31–end	Gen. 41. 25–45 Gal. 3.23 – 4.7	Jer. 4. 19–end John 5. 1–18	
P	Isa. 55. 6–11 Matt. 21. 10–16	Gen. 41.46 – 42.5 Gal. 4. 8–20	Jer. 5. 1–19 John 5. 19–29	
	Ember Day			
P	Ember CEG *or* Isa. 58. 1–9a Matt. 12. 38–end	Gen. 42. 6–17 Gal. 4.21 – 5.1	Jer. 5. 20–end John 5. 30–end	
P	Isa. 58. 9b–end John 8. 31–45	Gen. 42. 18–28 Gal. 5. 2–15	Jer. 6. 9–21 John 6. 1–15	
	Ember Day			
P	Ember CEG *or* Ezek. 18. 20–25 John 5. 2–15	Gen. 42. 29–end Gal. 5. 16–end	Jer. 6. 22–end John 6. 16–27	
	Perpetua, Felicity and their Companions, Martyrs at Carthage, 203 Ember Day			
Pr	Ember CEG *or* Com. Martyr *or* Ezek. 18. 26–end Matt. 17. 1–9 *or* Luke 4. 16–21 *or* John 10. 1–16	Gen. 43. 1–15 Gal. ch. 6	Jer. 7. 1–20 John 6. 27–40 **ct**	

		Sunday Principal Service Weekday Eucharist	Third Service Morning Prayer	Second Service Evening Prayer
8 Sunday	**THE SECOND SUNDAY OF LENT**			
P		Gen. 12. 1–4a Ps. 121 Rom. 4. 1–5, 13–17 John 3. 1–17	Ps. 74 Jer. 22. 1–9 Matt. 8. 1–13	Ps. 135 (*or* 135. 1–14) Num. 21. 4–9 Luke 14. 27–33
9 Monday				
P		Dan. 9. 4–10 Ps. 79. 8–9, 12, 14 Luke 6. 36–38	Ps. 26; ***32*** *alt.* Ps. 98; ***99***; 101 Gen. 43. 16–end Heb. ch. 1	Ps. 70; ***74*** *alt.* Ps. ***105***† (*or* 103) Jer. 7. 21–end John 6. 41–51
10 Tuesday				
P		Isa. 1. 10, 16–20 Ps. 50. 8, 16–end Matt. 23. 1–12	Ps. 50 *alt.* Ps. ***106***† (*or* 103) Gen. 44. 1–17 Heb. 2. 1–9	Ps. ***52***; 53; 54 *alt.* Ps. 107† Jer. 8. 1–15 John 6. 52–59
11 Wednesday				
P		Jer. 18. 18–20 Ps. 31. 4–5, 14–18 Matt. 20. 17–28	Ps. 35 *alt.* Ps. 110; ***111***; 112 Gen. 44. 18–end Heb. 2. 10–end	Ps. ***3***; 51 *alt.* Ps. 119. 129–152 Jer. 8.18 – 9.11 John 6. 60–end
12 Thursday				
P		Jer. 17. 5–10 Ps. 1 Luke 16. 19–end	Ps. 34 *alt.* Ps. 113; ***115*** Gen. 45. 1–15 Heb. 3. 1–6	Ps. 71 *alt.* Ps. 114; ***116***; 117 Jer. 9. 12–24 John 7. 1–13
13 Friday				
P		Gen. 37. 3–4, 12–13, 17–28 Ps. 105. 16–22 Matt. 21. 33–43, 45–46	Ps. 40; ***41*** *alt.* Ps. 139 Gen. 45. 16–end Heb. 3. 7–end	Ps. ***6***; 38 *alt.* Ps. ***130***; 131; 137 Jer. 10. 1–16 John 7. 14–24
14 Saturday				
P		Mic. 7. 14–15, 18–20 Ps. 103. 1–4, 9–12 Luke 15. 1–3, 11–end	Ps. 3; ***25*** *alt.* Ps. 120; ***121***; 122 Gen. 46. 1–7, 28–end Heb. 4. 1–13	Ps. ***23***; 27 *alt.* Ps. 118 Jer. 10. 17–24 John 7. 25–36 **ct**
15 Sunday	**THE THIRD SUNDAY OF LENT**			
P		Exod. 17. 1–7 Ps. 95 Rom. 5. 1–11 John 4. 5–42	Ps. 46 Amos 7. 10–end 2 Cor. 1. 1–11	Ps. 40 Josh. 1. 1–9 Eph. 6. 10–20 *Gospel*: John 2. 13–22
16 Monday*				
P		2 Kings 5. 1–15 Ps. 42. 1–2; 43. 1–4 Luke 4. 24–30	Ps. ***5***; 7 *alt.* Ps. 123; 124; 125; ***126*** Gen. 47. 1–27 Heb. 4.14 – 5.10	Ps. 11; ***17*** *alt.* Ps. ***127***; 128; 129 Jer. 11. 1–17 John 7. 37–52

*The following readings may replace those provided for Holy Communion on any day (except Joseph of Nazareth) during the Third Week of Lent: Exod. 17. 1–7; Ps. 95. 1–2, 6–end; John 4. 5–42.

	Calendar and Holy Communion	Morning Prayer	Evening Prayer	NOTES
	THE SECOND SUNDAY IN LENT			
P	Jer. 17. 5–10 Ps. 25. 13–end 1 Thess. 4. 1–8 Matt. 15. 21–28	Ps. 74 Jer. 22. 1–9 Matt. 8. 1–13	Ps. 135 (*or* 135. 1–14) Num. 21. 4–9 Luke 14. 27–33	
P	Heb. 2. 1–10 John 8. 21–30	Gen. 43. 16–end Heb. ch. 1	Jer. 7. 21–end John 6. 41–51	
P	Heb. 2. 11–end Matt. 23. 1–12	Gen. 44. 1–17 Heb. 2. 1–9	Jer. 8. 1–15 John 6. 52–59	
P	Heb. 3. 1–6 Matt. 20. 17–28	Gen. 44. 18–end Heb. 2. 10–end	Jer. 8.18 – 9.11 John 6. 60–end	
	Gregory the Great, Bishop of Rome, 604			
Pw	Com. Doctor *or* Heb. 3. 7–end John 5. 30–end	Gen. 45. 1–15 Heb. 3. 1–6	Jer. 9. 12–24 John 7. 1–13	
P	Heb. ch. 4 Matt. 21. 33–end	Gen. 45. 16–end Heb. 3. 7–end	Jer. 10. 1–16 John 7. 14–24	
P	Heb. ch. 5 Luke 15. 11–end	Gen. 46. 1–7, 28–end Heb. 4. 1–13	Jer. 10. 17–24 John 7. 25–36 **ct**	
	THE THIRD SUNDAY IN LENT			
P	Num. 22. 21–31 Ps. 9. 13–end Eph. 5. 1–14 Luke 11. 14–28	Ps. 46 Amos 7. 10–end 2 Cor. 1. 1–11	Ps. 40 Josh. 1. 1–9 Eph. 6. 10–20	
P	Heb. 6. 1–10 Luke 4. 23–30	Gen. 47. 1–27 Heb. 4.14 – 5.10	Jer. 11. 1–17 John 7. 37–52	

		Sunday Principal Service Weekday Eucharist	Third Service Morning Prayer	Second Service Evening Prayer
17 Tuesday	**Patrick, Bishop, Missionary, Patron of Ireland, c. 460**			
Pw	Com. Missionary *or* *also* Ps. 91. 1–4, 13–end Luke 10. 1–12, 17–20	Song of the Three 2, 11–20 *or* Dan. 2. 20–23 Ps. 25. 3–10 Matt. 18. 21–end	Ps. 6; ***9*** *alt.* Ps. ***132***; 133 Gen. 47.28 – 48.end Heb. 5.11 – 6.12	Ps. 61; 62; ***64*** *alt.* Ps. (134); ***135*** Jer. 11.18 – 12.6 John 7.53 – 8.11
18 Wednesday	*Cyril, Bishop of Jerusalem, Teacher, 386*			
P		Deut. 4. 1, 5–9 Ps. 147. 13–end Matt. 5. 17–19	Ps. 38 *alt.* Ps. 119. 153–end Gen. 49. 1–32 Heb. 6. 13–end	Ps. 36; ***39*** *alt.* Ps. 136 Jer. 13. 1–11 John 8. 12–30 *or First EP of Joseph* Ps. 132 Hos. 11. 1–9 Luke 2. 41–end **W ct**
19 Thursday	**JOSEPH OF NAZARETH**			
W		2 Sam. 7. 4–16 Ps. 89. 26–36 Rom. 4. 13–18 Matt. 1. 18–end	*MP*: Ps. 25; 147. 1–12 Isa. 11. 1–10 Matt. 13. 54–end	*EP*: Ps. 1; 112 Gen. 50. 22–end Matt. 2. 13–end
20 Friday	**Cuthbert, Bishop of Lindisfarne, Missionary, 687***			
Pw	Com. Missionary *or* *esp.* Ezek. 34. 11–16 *also* Matt. 18. 12–14	Hos. ch. 14 Ps. 81. 6–10, 13, 16 Mark 12. 28–34	Ps. 22 *alt.* Ps. 142; ***144*** Exod. 1. 1–14 Heb. 7. 11–end	Ps. 69 *alt.* Ps. 145 Jer. 15. 10–end John 8. 48–end
21 Saturday	**Thomas Cranmer, Archbishop of Canterbury, Reformation Martyr, 1556**			
Pr	Com. Martyr *or*	Hos. 5.15 – 6.6 Ps. 51. 1–2, 17–end Luke 18. 9–14	Ps. 31 *alt.* Ps. 147 Exod. 1.22 – 2.10 Heb. ch. 8	Ps. ***116***; 130 *alt.* Ps. ***148***; 149; 150 Jer. 16.10 – 17.4 John 9. 1–17 **ct**
22 Sunday	**THE FOURTH SUNDAY OF LENT** (Mothering Sunday)			
P		1 Sam. 16. 1–13 Ps. 23 Eph. 5. 8–14 John ch. 9	Ps. 19 Isa. 43. 1–7 Eph. 2. 8–14	Ps. 31. 1–16 (*or* 31. 1–8) Mic. ch. 7 *or* Prayer of Manasseh Jas. ch. 5 *Gospel*: John 3. 14–21 *If the Principal Service readings for The Fourth Sunday of Lent are displaced by Mothering Sunday provisions, they may be used at the Second Service.* (*continued overleaf*)

*Cuthbert may be celebrated on 4 September instead of 20 March.

	Calendar and Holy Communion	Morning Prayer	Evening Prayer
P	Heb. 6. 11–end Matt. 18. 15–22	Gen. 47.28 – 48.end Heb. 5.11 – 6.12	Jer. 11.18 – 12.6 John 7.53 – 8.11
	Edward, King of the W. Saxons, 978		
Pr	Com. Martyr *or* Heb. 7. 1–10 Matt. 15. 1–20	Gen. 49. 1–32 Heb. 6. 13–end	Jer. 13. 1–11 John 8. 12–30
	To celebrate Joseph, see *Common Worship* provision.		
P	Heb. 7. 11–25 John 6. 26–35	Gen. 49.33 – 50.end Heb. 7. 1–10	Jer. ch. 14 John 8. 31–47
P	Heb. 7. 26–end John 4. 5–26	Exod. 1. 1–14 Heb. 7. 11–end	Jer. 15. 10–end John 8. 48–end
	Benedict, Abbot of Monte Cassino, c. 550		
Pw	Com. Abbot *or* Heb. 8. 1–6 John 8. 1–11	Exod. 1.22 – 2.10 Heb. ch. 8	Jer. 16.10 – 17.4 John 9. 1–17 **ct**
	THE FOURTH SUNDAY IN LENT To celebrate Mothering Sunday, see *Common Worship* provision.		
P	Exod. 16. 2–7a Ps. 122 Gal. 4. 21–end *or* Heb. 12. 22–24 John 6. 1–14	Ps. 19 Isa. 43. 1–7 Eph. 2. 8–14	Ps. 31. 1–16 (*or* 31. 1–8) Mic. ch. 7 *or* Prayer of Manasseh Jas. ch. 5

NOTES

		Sunday Principal Service Weekday Eucharist	Third Service Morning Prayer	Second Service Evening Prayer
22 Sunday	**THE FOURTH SUNDAY OF LENT** *(continued)* (Mothering Sunday)			
	or, for Mothering Sunday:			
P		Exod. 2. 1–10 *or* 1 Sam. 1. 20–end Ps. 34. 11–20 *or* Ps. 127. 1–4 2 Cor. 1. 3–7 *or* Col. 3. 12–17 Luke 2. 33–35 *or* John 19. 25b–27		
23 Monday*				
P		Isa. 65. 17–21 Ps. 30. 1–5, 8, 11–end John 4. 43–end	Ps. 70; ***77*** *alt.* Ps. ***1***; 2; 3 Exod. 2. 11–22 Heb. 9. 1–14	Ps. ***25***; 28 *alt.* Ps. ***4***; 7 Jer. 17. 5–18 John 9. 18–end
24 Tuesday	*Walter Hilton of Thurgarton, Augustinian Canon, Mystic, 1396; Paul Couturier, Priest, Ecumenist, 1953; Oscar Romero, Archbishop of San Salvador, Martyr, 1980*			
P		Ezek. 47. 1–9, 12 Ps. 46. 1–8 John 5. 1–3, 5–16	Ps. 54; ***79*** *alt.* Ps. ***5***; 6; (8) Exod. 2.23 - 3.20 Heb. 9. 15–end	*First EP of The Annunciation* Ps. 85 Wisd. 9. 1–12 *or* Gen. 3. 8–15 Gal. 4. 1–5 **W ct**
25 Wednesday	**THE ANNUNCIATION OF OUR LORD TO THE BLESSED VIRGIN MARY**			
W		Isa. 7. 10–14 Ps. 40. 5–11 Heb. 10. 4–10 Luke 1. 26–38	*MP*: Ps. 111; 113 1 Sam. 2. 1–10 Rom. 5. 12–end	*EP*: Ps. 131; 146 Isa. 52. 1–12 Heb. 2. 5–end
26 Thursday	*Harriet Monsell, Founder of the Community of St John the Baptist, Clewer, 1883*			
P		Exod. 32. 7–14 Ps. 106. 19–23 John 5. 31–end	Ps. 53; ***86*** *alt.* Ps. 14; ***15***; 16 Exod. 4.27 - 6.1 Heb. 10. 19–25	Ps. 94 *alt.* Ps. 18† Jer. 19. 1–13 John 10. 22–end
27 Friday				
P		Wisd. 2. 1, 12–22 *or* Jer. 26. 8–11 Ps. 34. 15–end John 7. 1–2, 10, 25–30	Ps. 102 *alt.* Ps. 17; ***19*** Exod. 6. 2–13 Heb. 10. 26–end	Ps. 13; ***16*** *alt.* Ps. 22 Jer. 19.14 - 20.6 John 11. 1–16
28 Saturday				
P		Jer. 11. 18–20 Ps. 7. 1–2, 8–10 John 7. 40–52	Ps. 32 *alt.* Ps. 20; 21; ***23*** Exod. 7. 8–end Heb. 11. 1–16	Ps. ***140***; 141; 142 *alt.* Ps. ***24***; 25 Jer. 20. 7–end John 11. 17–27 **ct**

* The following readings may replace those provided for Holy Communion on any day (except The Annunciation) during the Fourth Week of Lent: Mic. 7. 7–9; Ps. 27. 1, 9–10, 16–17; John ch. 9.

	Calendar and Holy Communion	Morning Prayer	Evening Prayer	NOTES
	THE FOURTH SUNDAY IN LENT			
P				
P	Heb. 11. 1–6 John 2. 13–end	Exod. 2. 11–22 Heb. 9. 1–14	Jer. 17. 5–18 John 9. 18–end	
P	Heb. 11. 13–16a John 7. 14–24	Exod. 2.23 – 3.20 Heb. 9. 15–end	*First EP of The Annunciation* Ps. 85 Wisd. 9. 1–12 *or* Gen. 3. 8–15 Gal. 4. 1–5 **𝔚 ct**	
	THE ANNUNCIATION OF THE BLESSED VIRGIN MARY			
𝔚	Isa. 7. 10–14 [15] Ps. 113 Rom. 5. 12–19 Luke 1. 26–38	Ps. 111 1 Sam. 2. 1–10 Heb. 10. 4–10	Ps. 131; 146 Isa. 52. 1–12 Heb. 2. 5–end	
P	Heb. 12. 12–17 John 5. 17–27	Exod. 4.27 – 6.1 Heb. 10. 19–25	Jer. 19. 1–13 John 10. 22–end	
P	Heb. 12. 22–end John 11. 33–46	Exod. 6. 2–13 Heb. 10. 26–end	Jer. 19.14 – 20.6 John 11. 1–16	
P	Heb. 13. 7–21 John 8. 12–20	Exod. 7. 8–end Heb. 11. 1–16	Jer. 20. 7–end John 11. 17–27 **ct**	

		Sunday Principal Service Weekday Eucharist	Third Service Morning Prayer	Second Service Evening Prayer
29 Sunday	**THE FIFTH SUNDAY OF LENT (Passiontide begins)**			
P		Ezek. 37. 1–14 Ps. 130 Rom. 8. 6–11 John 11. 1–45	Ps. 86 Jer. 31. 27–37 John 12. 20–33	Ps. 30 Lam. 3. 19–33 Matt. 20. 17–end
30 Monday*				
P		Susanna 1–9, 15–17, 19–30, 33–62 (*or* 41b–62) *or* Josh. 2. 1–14 Ps. 23 John 8. 1–11	Ps. ***73***; 121 *alt.* Ps. 27; ***30*** Exod. 8. 1–19 Heb. 11. 17–31	Ps. ***26***; 27 *alt.* Ps. 26; ***28***; 29 Jer. 21. 1–10 John 11. 28–44
31 Tuesday	*John Donne, Priest, Poet, 1631*			
P		Num. 21. 4–9 Ps. 102. 1–3, 16–23 John 8. 21–30	Ps. ***35***; 123 *alt.* Ps. 32; ***36*** Exod. 8. 20–end Heb. 11.32 - 12.2	Ps. ***61***; 64 *alt.* Ps. 33 Jer. 22. 1–5, 13–19 John 11. 45–end

April 2020

1 Wednesday	*Frederick Denison Maurice, Priest, Teacher, 1872*			
P		Dan. 3. 14–20, 24–25, 28 *Canticle*: Bless the Lord John 8. 31–42	Ps. ***55***; 124 *alt.* Ps. 34 Exod. 9. 1–12 Heb. 12. 3–13	Ps. 56; ***62*** *alt.* Ps. 119. 33–56 Jer. 22.20 - 23.8 John 12. 1–11
2 Thursday				
P		Gen. 17. 3–9 Ps. 105. 4–9 John 8. 51–end	Ps. ***40***; 125 *alt.* Ps. 37† Exod. 9. 13–end Heb. 12. 14–end	Ps. 42; ***43*** *alt.* Ps. 39; ***40*** Jer. 23. 9–32 John 12. 12–19
3 Friday				
P		Jer. 20. 10–13 Ps. 18. 1–6 John 10. 31–end	Ps. ***22***; 126 *alt.* Ps. 31 Exod. ch. 10 Heb. 13. 1–16	Ps. 31 *alt.* Ps. 35 Jer. ch. 24 John 12. 20–36a
4 Saturday				
P		Ezek. 37. 21–end *Canticle*: Jer. 31. 10–13 *or* Ps. 121 John 11. 45–end	Ps. ***23***; 127 *alt.* Ps. 41; ***42***; 43 Exod. ch. 11 Heb. 13. 17–end	Ps. 128; 129; ***130*** Ps. 45; ***46*** Jer. 25. 1–14 John 12. 36b–end **ct**
5 Sunday	**PALM SUNDAY**			
R	*Liturgy of the Palms* Matt. 21. 1–11 Ps. 118. 1–2, 19–end (*or* 118. 19–24)	*Liturgy of the Passion* Isa. 50. 4–9a Ps. 31. 9–16 (*or* 31. 9–18) Phil. 2. 5–11 Matt. 26.14 - 27.end *or* Matt. 27. 11–54	Ps. 61; 62 Zech. 9. 9–12 Luke 16. 19–end	Ps. 80 Isa. 5. 1–7 Matt. 21. 33–end

*The following readings may replace those provided for Holy Communion on any day during the Fifth Week of Lent: 2 Kings 4. 18–21, 32–37; Ps. 17. 1–8, 16; John 11. 1–45.

	Calendar and Holy Communion	Morning Prayer	Evening Prayer	NOTES
	THE FIFTH SUNDAY IN LENT			
P	Exod. 24. 4–8 Ps. 143 Heb. 9. 11–15 John 8. 46–end	Ps. 86 Jer. 31. 27–37 John 12. 20–33	Ps. 30 Lam. 3. 19–33 Matt. 20. 17–end	
P	Col. 1. 13–23a John 7. 1–13	Exod. 8. 1–19 Heb. 11. 17–31	Jer. 21. 1–10 John 11. 28–44	
P	Col. 2. 8–12 John 7. 32–39	Exod. 8. 20–end Heb. 11.32 – 12.2	Jer. 22. 1–5, 13–19 John 11. 45–end	
P	Col. 2. 13–19 John 7. 40–end	Exod. 9. 1–12 Heb. 12. 3–13	Jer. 22.20 – 23.8 John 12. 1–11	
P	Col. 3. 8–11 John 10. 22–38	Exod. 9. 13–end Heb. 12. 14–end	Jer. 23. 9–32 John 12. 12–19	
	Richard, Bishop of Chichester, 1253			
Pw	Com. Bishop *or* Col. 3. 12–17 John 11. 47–54	Exod. ch. 10 Heb. 13. 1–16	Jer. ch. 24 John 12. 20–36a	
	Ambrose, Bishop of Milan, 397			
Pw	Com. Doctor *or* Col. 4. 2–6 John 6. 53–end	Exod. ch. 11 Heb. 13. 17–end	Jer. 25. 1–14 John 12. 36b–end **et**	
	THE SUNDAY NEXT BEFORE EASTER (PALM SUNDAY)			
R	Zech. 9. 9–12 Ps. 73. 22–end Phil. 2. 5–11 Passion acc. to Matt. Matt. 27. 1–54 *or* Matt. 26.1 – 27.61 *or* Matt. 21. 1–13	Ps. 61; 62 Isa. 42. 1–9 Luke 16. 19–end	Ps. 80 Isa. 5. 1–7 Matt. 21. 33–end	

		Sunday Principal Service Weekday Eucharist	Third Service Morning Prayer	Second Service Evening Prayer
6 Monday	**MONDAY OF HOLY WEEK**			
R		Isa. 42. 1–9 Ps. 36. 5–11 Heb. 9. 11–15 John 12. 1–11	*MP*: Ps. 41 Lam. 1. 1–12a Luke 22. 1–23	*EP*: Ps. 25 Lam. 2. 8–19 Col. 1. 18–23
7 Tuesday	**TUESDAY OF HOLY WEEK**			
R		Isa. 49. 1–7 Ps. 71. 1–8 [9–14] 1 Cor. 1. 18–31 John 12. 20–36	*MP*: Ps. 27 Lam. 3. 1–18 Luke 22. [24–38] 39–53	*EP*: Ps. 55. 13–24 Lam. 3. 40–51 Gal. 6. 11–end
8 Wednesday	**WEDNESDAY OF HOLY WEEK**			
R		Isa. 50. 4–9a Ps. 70 Heb. 12. 1–3 John 13. 21–32	*MP*: Ps. 102 (*or* 102. 1–18) Wisd. 1.16 – 2.1, 12–22 *or* Jer. 11. 18–20 Luke 22. 54–end	*EP*: Ps. 88 Isa. 63. 1–9 Rev. 14.18 – 15.4
9 Thursday	**MAUNDY THURSDAY**			
W (HC) R		Exod. 12. 1–4 [5–10] 11–14 Ps. 116. 1, 10–end (*or* 116. 9–end) 1 Cor. 11. 23–26 John 13. 1–17, 31b–35	*MP*: Ps. 42; 43 Lev. 16. 2–24 Luke 23. 1–25	*EP*: Ps. 39 Exod. ch. 11 Eph. 2. 11–18
10 Friday	**GOOD FRIDAY**			
R		Isa. 52.13 – 53.end Ps. 22 (*or* 22. 1–11 *or* 22. 1–21) Heb. 10. 16–25 *or* Heb. 4. 14–16; 5. 7–9 John 18.1 – 19.end	*MP*: Ps. 69 Gen. 22. 1–18 *A part of* John 18 – 19 *if not read at the Principal Service* *or* Heb. 10. 1–10	*EP*: Ps. 130; 143 Lam. 5. 15–end *A part of* John 18 – 19 *if not read at the Principal Service, especially* John 19. 38–end *or* Col. 1. 18–23
11 Saturday	**EASTER EVE**			
	These readings are for use at services other than the Easter Vigil.	Job 14. 1–14 *or* Lam. 3. 1–9, 19–24 Ps. 31. 1–4, 15–16 (*or* 1–5) 1 Pet. 4. 1–8 Matt. 27. 57–end *or* John 19. 38–end	Ps. 142 Hos. 6. 1–6 John 2. 18–22	Ps. 116 Job 19. 21–27 1 John 5. 5–12
12 Sunday	**EASTER DAY**			
𝔚	*The following readings and psalms (or canticles) are provided for use at the Easter Vigil. A minimum of three Old Testament readings should be chosen. The reading from* Exodus ch. 14 *should always be used.*	Gen. 1.1 – 2.4a & Ps. 136. 1–9, 23–end Gen. 7. 1–5, 11–18; 8. 6–18; 9. 8–13 & Ps. 46 Gen. 22. 1–18 & Ps. 16 Exod. 14. 10–end; 15. 20–21 & *Canticle*: Exod. 15. 1b–13, 17–18 Isa. 55. 1–11 & *Canticle*: Isa. 12. 2–end Baruch 3.9–15, 32 – 4.4 & Ps. 19 *or* Prov. 8. 1–8, 19–21; 9. 4b–6 & Ps. 19 Ezek. 36. 24–28 & Ps. 42; 43 Ezek. 37. 1–14 & Ps. 143 Zeph. 3. 14–end & Ps. 98 Rom. 6. 3–11 & Ps. 114 Matt. 28. 1–10		

(continued overleaf)

	Calendar and Holy Communion	Morning Prayer	Evening Prayer	NOTES
	MONDAY IN HOLY WEEK			
R	Isa. 63. 1–19 Ps. 55. 1–8 Gal. 6. 1–11 Mark ch. 14	Ps. 41 Lam. 1. 1–12a John 12. 1–11	Ps. 25 Lam. 2. 8–19 Col. 1. 18–23	
	TUESDAY IN HOLY WEEK			
R	Isa. 50. 5–11 Ps. 13 Rom. 5. 6–19 Mark 15. 1–39	Ps. 27 Lam. 3. 1–18 John 12. 20–36	Ps. 55. 13–24 Lam. 3. 40–51 Gal. 6. 11–end	
	WEDNESDAY IN HOLY WEEK			
R	Isa. 49. 1–9a Ps. 54 Heb. 9. 16–end Luke ch. 22	Ps. 102 (*or* 102. 1–18) Wisd. 1.16 – 2.1, 12–22 *or* Jer. 11. 18–20 John 13. 21–32	Ps. 88 Isa. 63. 1–9 Rev. 14.18 – 15.4	
	MAUNDY THURSDAY			
W **(HC)** **R**	Exod. 12. 1–11 Ps. 43 1 Cor. 11. 17–end Luke 23. 1–49	Ps. 42; 43 Lev. 16. 2–24 John 13. 1–17, 31b–35	Ps. 39 Exod. ch. 11 Eph. 2. 11–18	
	GOOD FRIDAY			
R	Alt. Collect Passion acc. to John Alt. Gospel, if Passion is read Num. 21. 4–9 Ps. 140. 1–9 Heb. 10. 1–25 John 19. 1–37 *or* John 19. 38–end	Ps. 69 Gen. 22. 1–18 John ch. 18	Ps. 130; 143 Lam. 5. 15–end John 19. 38–end	
	EASTER EVE			
	Job 14. 1–14 1 Pet. 3. 17–22 Matt. 27. 57–end	Ps. 142 Hos. 6. 1–6 John 2. 18–22	Ps. 116 Job 19. 21–27 1 John 5. 5–12	
	EASTER DAY			
W	Exod. 12. 21–28 Ps. 111 Col. 3. 1–7 John 20. 1–10	Ps. 114; 117 Exod. 14.10–18, 26 – 15.2 Rev. 15. 2–4	Ps. 105 *or* Ps. 66. 1–11 Song of Sol. 3. 2–5; 8. 6–7 John 20. 11–18 *or* Rev. 1. 12–18	

		Sunday Principal Service Weekday Eucharist	Third Service Morning Prayer	Second Service Evening Prayer
12 Sunday	**EASTER DAY** *(continued)*			
𝔚	*Easter Day Services* *The reading from Acts must be used as either the first or second reading at the Principal Service.*	Acts 10. 34–43 *or* Jer. 31. 1–6 Ps. 118. 1–2, 14–24 (*or* 118. 14–24) Col. 3. 1–4 *or* Acts 10. 34–43 John 20. 1–18 *or* Matt. 28. 1–10	*MP*: Ps. 114; 117 Exod. 14.10–18, 26 – 15.2 Rev. 15. 2–4	*EP*: Ps. 105 *or* Ps. 66. 1–11 Song of Sol. 3. 2–5; 8. 6–7 John 20. 11–18 *if not used at the Principal Service* *or* Rev. 1. 12–18
13 Monday	**MONDAY OF EASTER WEEK**			
W		Acts 2. 14, 22–32 Ps. 16. 1–2, 6–end Matt. 28. 8–15	Ps. ***111***; 117; 146 Exod. 12. 1–14 1 Cor. 15. 1–11	Ps. 135 Song of Sol. 1.9 – 2.7 Mark 16. 1–8
14 Tuesday	**TUESDAY OF EASTER WEEK**			
W		Acts 2. 36–41 Ps. 33. 4–5, 18–end John 20. 11–18	Ps. ***112***; 147. 1–12 Exod. 12. 14–36 1 Cor. 15. 12–19	Ps. 136 Song of Sol. 2. 8–end Luke 24. 1–12
15 Wednesday	**WEDNESDAY OF EASTER WEEK**			
W		Acts 3. 1–10 Ps. 105. 1–9 Luke 24. 13–35	Ps. ***113***; 147. 13–end Exod. 12. 37–end 1 Cor. 15. 20–28	Ps. 105 Song of Sol. ch. 3 Matt. 28. 16–end
16 Thursday	**THURSDAY OF EASTER WEEK**			
W		Acts 3. 11–end Ps. 8 Luke 24. 35–48	Ps. ***114***; 148 Exod. 13. 1–16 1 Cor. 15. 29–34	Ps. 106 Song of Sol. 5.2 – 6.3 Luke 7. 11–17
17 Friday	**FRIDAY OF EASTER WEEK**			
W		Acts 4. 1–12 Ps. 118. 1–4, 22–26 John 21. 1–14	Ps. ***115***; 149 Exod. 13.17 – 14.14 1 Cor. 15. 35–50	Ps. 107 Song of Sol. 7.10 – 8.4 Luke 8. 41–end
18 Saturday	**SATURDAY OF EASTER WEEK**			
W		Acts 4. 13–21 Ps. 118. 1–4, 14–21 Mark 16. 9–15	Ps. ***116***; 150 Exod. 14. 15–end 1 Cor. 15. 51–end	Ps. 145 Song of Sol. 8. 5–7 John 11. 17–44 **ct**
19 Sunday	**THE SECOND SUNDAY OF EASTER**			
W	*The reading from Acts must be used as either the first or second reading at the Principal Service.*	Acts 2. 14a, 22–32 [*or* Exod. 14. 10–end; 15. 20–21] Ps. 16 1 Pet. 1. 3–9 John 20. 19–end	Ps. 81. 1–10 Exod. 12. 1–17 1 Cor. 5. 6b–8	Ps. 30. 1–5 Dan. 6. 1–23 (*or* 6. 6–23) Mark 15.46 – 16.8
20 Monday				
W		Acts 4. 23–31 Ps. 2. 1–9 John 3. 1–8	Ps. 2; ***19*** *alt.* Ps. ***1***; 2; 3 Exod. 15. 1–21 Col. 1. 1–14	Ps. 139 *alt.* Ps. ***4***; 7 Deut. 1. 3–18 John 20. 1–10

	Calendar and Holy Communion	Morning Prayer	Evening Prayer	NOTES
	MONDAY IN EASTER WEEK			
W	Hos. 6. 1–6 Easter Anthems Acts 10. 34–43 Luke 24. 13–35	Exod. 12. 1–14 1 Cor. 15. 1–11	Song of Sol. 1.9 – 2.7 Mark 16. 1–8	
	TUESDAY IN EASTER WEEK			
W	1 Kings 17. 17–end Ps. 16. 9–end Acts 13. 26–41 Luke 24. 36b–48	Exod. 12. 14–36 1 Cor. 15. 12–19	Song of Sol. 2. 8–end Luke 24. 1–12	
W	Isa. 42. 10–16 Ps. 111 Acts 3. 12–18 John 20. 11–18	Exod. 12. 37–end 1 Cor. 15. 20–28	Song of Sol. ch. 3 Matt. 28. 16–end	
W	Isa. 43. 16–21 Ps. 113 Acts 8. 26–end John 21. 1–14	Exod. 13. 1–16 1 Cor. 15. 29–34	Song of Sol. 5.2 – 6.3 Luke 7. 11–17	
W	Ezek. 37. 1–14 Ps. 116. 1–9 1 Pet. 3. 18–end Matt. 28. 16–end	Exod. 13.17 – 14.14 1 Cor. 15. 35–50	Song of Sol. 7.10 – 8.4 Luke 8. 41–end	
W	Zech. 8. 1–8 Ps. 118. 14–21 1 Pet. 2. 1–10 John 20. 24–end	Exod. 14. 15–end 1 Cor. 15. 51–end	Song of Sol. 8. 5–7 John 11. 17–44 **ct**	
	THE FIRST SUNDAY AFTER EASTER			
W	Ezek. 37. 1–10 Ps. 81. 1–4 1 John 5. 4–12 John 20. 19–23	Ps. 81. 1–10 Exod. 12. 1–17 1 Cor. 5. 6b–8	Ps. 30. 1–5 Dan. 6. 1–23 (*or* 6. 6–23) Mark 15.46 – 16.8	
W		Exod. 15. 1–21 Col. 1. 1–14	Deut. 1. 3–18 John 20. 1–10	

		Sunday Principal Service Weekday Eucharist	Third Service Morning Prayer	Second Service Evening Prayer
21 Tuesday	**Anselm, Abbot of Le Bec, Archbishop of Canterbury, Teacher, 1109**			
W	Com. Teacher *or* *also* Wisd. 9. 13–end Rom. 5. 8–11	Acts 4. 32–end Ps. 93 John 3. 7–15	Ps. ***8***; 20; 21 *alt.* Ps. ***5***; 6; (8) Exod. 15.22 – 16.10 Col. 1. 15–end	Ps. 104 *alt.* Ps. 9; ***10***† Deut. 1. 19–40 John 20. 11–18
22 Wednesday				
W		Acts 5. 17–26 Ps. 34. 1–8 John 3. 16–21	Ps. 16; ***30*** *alt.* Ps. 119. 1–32 Exod. 16. 11–end Col. 2. 1–15	Ps. 33 *alt.* Ps. ***11***; 12; 13 Deut. 3. 18–end John 20. 19–end *or First EP of George* Ps. 111; 116 Jer. 15. 15–21 Heb. 11.32 – 12.2 **R ct**
23 Thursday	**GEORGE, MARTYR, PATRON OF ENGLAND, c. 304**			
R		1 Macc. 2. 59–64 *or* Rev. 12. 7–12 Ps. 126 2 Tim. 2. 3–13 John 15. 18–21	*MP*: Ps. 5; 146 Josh. 1. 1–9 Eph. 6. 10–20	*EP*: Ps. 3; 11 Isa. 43. 1–7 John 15. 1–8
24 Friday	*Mellitus, Bishop of London, first Bishop at St Paul's, 624; The Seven Martyrs of the Melanesian Brotherhood, Solomon Islands, 2003*			
W		Acts 5. 34–42 Ps. 27. 1–5, 16–17 John 6. 1–15	Ps. 57; ***61*** *alt.* Ps. 17; ***19*** Exod. 18. 1–12 Col. 3.12 – 4.1	Ps. 118 *alt.* Ps. 22 Deut. 4. 15–31 John 21. 15–19 *or First EP of Mark* Ps. 19 Isa. 52. 7–10 Mark 1. 1–15 **R ct**
25 Saturday	**MARK THE EVANGELIST**			
R		Prov. 15. 28–end *or* Acts 15. 35–end Ps. 119. 9–16 Eph. 4. 7–16 Mark 13. 5–13	*MP*: Ps. 37. 23–end; 148 Isa. 62. 6–10 *or* Ecclus. 51. 13–end Acts 12.25 – 13.13	*EP*: Ps. 45 Ezek. 1. 4–14 2 Tim. 4. 1–11
26 Sunday	**THE THIRD SUNDAY OF EASTER**			
W	*The reading from Acts must be used as either the first or second reading at the Principal Service.*	Acts 2. 14a, 36–41 [or Zeph. 3. 14–end] Ps. 116. 1–3, 10–end (*or* 116. 1–7) 1 Pet. 1. 17–23 Luke 24. 13–35	Ps. 23 Isa. 40. 1–11 1 Pet. 5. 1–11	Ps. 48 Hag. 1.13 – 2.9 1 Cor. 3. 10–17 *Gospel*: John 2. 13–22
27 Monday	*Christina Rossetti, Poet, 1894*			
W		Acts 6. 8–15 Ps. 119. 17–24 John 6. 22–29	Ps. ***96***; 97 *alt.* Ps. 27; ***30*** Exod. ch. 19 Luke 1. 1–25	Ps. ***61***; 65 *alt.* Ps. 26; ***28***; 29 Deut. 5. 1–22 Eph. 1. 1–14

	Calendar and Holy Communion	Morning Prayer	Evening Prayer
W		Exod. 15.22 - 16.10 Col. 1. 15–end	Deut. 1. 19–40 John 20. 11–18
W		Exod. 16. 11–end Col. 2. 1–15	Deut. 3. 18–end John 20. 19–end
	George, Martyr, Patron of England, c. 304 To celebrate George, see *Common Worship* provision.		
Wr	Com. Martyr	Exod. ch. 17 Col. 2.16 - 3.11	Deut. 4. 1–14 John 21. 1–14
W		Exod. 18. 1–12 Col. 3.12 - 4.1	Deut. 4. 15–31 John 21. 15–19 *or First EP of Mark* (Ps. 19) Isa. 52. 7–10 Mark 1. 1–15 **R ct**
	MARK THE EVANGELIST		
R	Prov. 15. 28–end Ps. 119. 9–16 Eph. 4. 7–16 John 15. 1–11	(Ps. 37. 23–end; 148) Isa. 62. 6–10 *or* Ecclus. 51. 13–end Acts 12.25 - 13.13	(Ps. 45) Ezek. 1. 4–14 2 Tim. 4. 1–11
	THE SECOND SUNDAY AFTER EASTER		
W	Ezek. 34. 11–16a Ps. 23 1 Pet. 2. 19–end John 10. 11–16	Ps. 23 Isa. 40. 1–11 1 Pet. 5. 1–11	Ps. 48 Hag. 1.13 - 2.9 1 Cor. 3. 10–17
W		Exod. ch. 19 Luke 1. 1–25	Deut. 5. 1–22 Eph. 1. 1–14

NOTES

		Sunday Principal Service Weekday Eucharist	Third Service Morning Prayer	Second Service Evening Prayer
28 Tuesday	*Peter Chanel, Missionary in the South Pacific, Martyr, 1841*			
W		Acts 7.51 - 8.1a Ps. 31. 1-5, 16 John 6. 30-35	Ps. ***98***; 99; 100 *alt.* Ps. 32; ***36*** Exod. 20. 1-21 Luke 1. 26-38	Ps. 71 *alt.* Ps. 33 Deut. 5. 22-end Eph. 1. 15-end
29 Wednesday	**Catherine of Siena, Teacher, 1380**			
W	Com. Teacher *or* *also* Prov. 8. 1, 6-11 John 17. 12-26	Acts 8. 1b-8 Ps. 66. 1-6 John 6. 35-40	Ps. 105 *alt.* Ps. 34 Exod. ch. 24 Luke 1. 39-56	Ps. 67; ***72*** *alt.* Ps. 119. 33-56 Deut. ch. 6 Eph. 2. 1-10
30 Thursday	*Pandita Mary Ramabai, Translator of the Scriptures, 1922*			
W		Acts 8. 26-end Ps. 66. 7-8, 14-end John 6. 44-51	Ps. 136 *alt.* Ps. 37† Exod. 25. 1-22 Luke 1. 57-end	Ps. 73 *alt.* Ps. 39; ***40*** Deut. 7. 1-11 Eph. 2. 11-end *or First EP of Philip and James* Ps. 25 Isa. 40. 27-end John 12. 20-26 **R ct**

May 2020

		Sunday Principal Service Weekday Eucharist	Third Service Morning Prayer	Second Service Evening Prayer
1 Friday	**PHILIP AND JAMES, APOSTLES**			
R		Isa. 30. 15-21 Ps. 119. 1-8 Eph. 1. 3-10 John 14. 1-14	*MP*: Ps. 139; 146 Prov. 4. 10-18 Jas. 1. 1-12	*EP*: Ps. 149 Job 23. 1-12 John 1. 43-end
2 Saturday	**Athanasius, Bishop of Alexandria, Teacher, 373**			
W	Com. Teacher *or* *also* Ecclus. 4. 20-28 Matt. 10. 24-27	Acts 9. 31-42 Ps. 116. 10-15 John 6. 60-69	Ps. 108; ***110***; 111 *alt.* Ps. 41; ***42***; 43 Exod. 29. 1-9 Luke 2. 21-40	Ps. 23; ***27*** *alt.* Ps. 45; ***46*** Deut. ch. 8 Eph. 3. 14-end **ct**
3 Sunday	**THE FOURTH SUNDAY OF EASTER**			
W	*The reading from Acts must be used as either the first or second reading at the Principal Service.*	Acts 2. 42-end [*or* Gen. ch. 7] Ps. 23 1 Pet. 2. 19-end John 10. 1-10	Ps. 106. 6-24 Neh. 9. 6-15 1 Cor. 10. 1-13	Ps. 29. 1-10 Ezra 3. 1-13 Eph. 2. 11-end *Gospel*: Luke 19. 37-end
4 Monday	**English Saints and Martyrs of the Reformation Era**			
W	Isa. 43. 1-7 *or* *or* Ecclus. 2. 10-17 Ps. 87 2 Cor. 4. 5-12 John 12. 20-26	Acts 11. 1-18 Ps. 42. 1-2; 43. 1-4 John 10. 1-10 (*or* 11-18)	Ps. 103 *alt.* Ps. 44 Exod. 32. 1-14 Luke 2. 41-end	Ps. 112; 113; ***114*** *alt.* Ps. ***47***; 49 Deut. 9. 1-21 Eph. 4. 1-16
5 Tuesday				
W		Acts 11. 19-26 Ps. 87 John 10. 22-30	Ps. 139 *alt.* Ps. ***48***; 52 Exod. 32. 15-34 Luke 3. 1-14	Ps. 115; ***116*** *alt.* Ps. 50 Deut. 9.23 - 10.5 Eph. 4. 17-end

	Calendar and Holy Communion	Morning Prayer	Evening Prayer	NOTES
W		Exod. 20. 1–21 Luke 1. 26–38	Deut. 5. 22–end Eph. 1. 15–end	
W		Exod. ch. 24 Luke 1. 39–56	Deut. ch. 6 Eph. 2. 1–10	
W		Exod. 25. 1–22 Luke 1. 57–end	Deut. 7. 1–11 Eph. 2. 11–end *or First EP of Philip and James* (Ps. 119. 1–8) Isa. 40. 27–end John 12. 20–26 **R ct**	
	PHILIP AND JAMES, APOSTLES			
R	Prov. 4. 10–18 Ps. 25. 1–9 Jas. 1. [1] 2–12 John 14. 1–14	(Ps. 139; 146) Isa. 30. 1–5 John 12. 20–26	(Ps. 149) Job 23. 1–12 John 1. 43–end	
W		Exod. 29. 1–9 Luke 2. 21–40	Deut. ch. 8 Eph. 3. 14–end **ct**	
	THE THIRD SUNDAY AFTER EASTER			
W	Gen. 45. 3–10 Ps. 57 1 Pet. 2. 11–17 John 16. 16–22	Ps. 106. 6–24 Neh. 9. 6–15 1 Cor. 10. 1–13	Ps. 29. 1–10 Ezra 3. 1–13 Eph. 2. 11–end	
W		Exod. 32. 1–14 Luke 2. 41–end	Deut. 9. 1–21 Eph. 4. 1–16	
W		Exod. 32. 15–34 Luke 3. 1–14	Deut. 9.23 – 10.5 Eph. 4. 17–end	

		Sunday Principal Service Weekday Eucharist	Third Service Morning Prayer	Second Service Evening Prayer
6 Wednesday				
W		Acts 12.24 – 13.5 Ps. 67 John 12. 44–end	Ps. 135 *alt.* Ps. 119. 57–80 Exod. ch. 33 Luke 3. 15–22	Ps. ***47***; 48 *alt.* Ps. ***59***; 60 (67) Deut. 10. 12–end Eph. 5. 1–14
7 Thursday				
W		Acts 13. 13–25 Ps. 89. 1–2, 20–26 John 13. 16–20	Ps. 118 *alt.* Ps. 56; ***57***; (63†) Exod. 34. 1–10, 27–end Luke 4. 1–13	Ps. 81; ***85*** *alt.* Ps. 61; ***62***; 64 Deut. 11. 8–end Eph. 5. 15–end
8 Friday	**Julian of Norwich, Spiritual Writer, c. 1417**			
W	Com. Religious *or* *also* 1 Cor. 13. 8–end Matt. 5. 13–16	Acts 13. 26–33 Ps. 2 John 14. 1–6	Ps. 33 *alt.* Ps. ***51***; 54 Exod. 35.20 – 36.7 Luke 4. 14–30	Ps. ***36***; 40 *alt.* Ps. 38 Deut. 12. 1–14 Eph. 6. 1–9
9 Saturday				
W		Acts 13. 44–end Ps. 98. 1–5 John 14. 7–14	Ps. 34 *alt.* Ps. 68 Exod. 40. 17–end Luke 4. 31–37	Ps. ***84***; 86 *alt.* Ps. 65; ***66*** Deut. 15. 1–18 Eph. 6. 10–end **ct**
10 Sunday	**THE FIFTH SUNDAY OF EASTER**			
W	*The reading from Acts must be used as either the first or second reading at the Principal Service.*	Acts 7. 55–end [*or* Gen. 8. 1–19] Ps. 31. 1–5, 15–16 (*or* 31. 1–5) 1 Pet. 2. 2–10 John 14. 1–14	Ps. 30 Ezek. 37. 1–12 John 5. 19–29	Ps. 147. 1–12 Zech. 4. 1–10 Rev. 21. 1–14 *Gospel*: Luke 2. 25–32 [33–38]
11 Monday				
W		Acts 14. 5–18 Ps. 118. 1–3, 14–15 John 14. 21–26	Ps. 145 *alt.* Ps. 71 Num. 9. 15–end; 10. 33–end Luke 4. 38–end	Ps. 105 *alt.* Ps. ***72***; 75 Deut. 16. 1–20 1 Pet. 1. 1–12
12 Tuesday	*Gregory Dix, Priest, Monk, Scholar, 1952*			
W		Acts 14. 19–end Ps. 145. 10–end John 14. 27–end	Ps. ***19***; 147. 1–12 *alt.* Ps. 73 Num. 11. 1–33 Luke 5. 1–11	Ps. 96; ***97*** *alt.* Ps. 74 Deut. 17. 8–end 1 Pet. 1. 13–end
13 Wednesday				
W		Acts 15. 1–6 Ps. 122. 1–5 John 15. 1–8	Ps. ***30***; 147. 13–end *alt.* Ps. 77 Num. ch. 12 Luke 5. 12–26	Ps. 98; ***99***; 100 *alt.* Ps. 119. 81–104 Deut. 18. 9–end 1 Pet. 2. 1–10 *or First EP of Matthias* Ps. 147 Isa. 22. 15–22 Phil. 3.13b – 4.1 **R ct**

	Calendar and Holy Communion	Morning Prayer	Evening Prayer	NOTES
	John the Evangelist, ante Portam Latinam			
W	CEG of 27 December	Exod. ch. 33 Luke 3. 15–22	Deut. 10. 12–end Eph. 5. 1–14	
W		Exod. 34. 1–10, 27–end Luke 4. 1–13	Deut. 11. 8–end Eph. 5. 15–end	
W		Exod. 35.20 – 36.7 Luke 4. 14–30	Deut. 12. 1–14 Eph. 6. 1–9	
W		Exod. 40. 17–end Luke 4. 31–37	Deut. 15. 1–18 Eph. 6. 10–end **ct**	
	THE FOURTH SUNDAY AFTER EASTER			
W	Job 19. 21–27a Ps. 66. 14–end Jas. 1. 17–21 John 16. 5–15	Ps. 30 Ezek. 37. 1–12 John 5. 19–29	Ps. 147. 1–12 Zech. 4. 1–10 Rev. 21. 1–14	
W		Num. 9. 15–end; 10. 33–end Luke 4. 38–end	Deut. 16. 1–20 1 Pet. 1. 1–12	
W		Num. 11. 1–33 Luke 5. 1–11	Deut. 17. 8–end 1 Pet. 1. 13–end	
W		Num. ch. 12 Luke 5. 12–26	Deut. 18. 9–end 1 Pet. 2. 1–10	

			Sunday Principal Service Weekday Eucharist	Third Service Morning Prayer	Second Service Evening Prayer
14 Thursday		**MATTHIAS THE APOSTLE***			
	R	*The reading from Acts must be used as either the first or second reading at the Eucharist.*	Isa. 22. 15–end *or* Acts 1. 15–end Ps. 15 Acts 1. 15–end *or* 1 Cor. 4. 1–7 John 15. 9–17	*MP*: Ps. 16; 147. 1–12 1 Sam. 2. 27–35 Acts 2. 37–end	*EP*: Ps. 80 1 Sam. 16. 1–13a Matt. 7. 15–27
		or, if Matthias is celebrated on 24 February:			
	W		Acts 15. 7–21 Ps. 96. 1–3, 7–10 John 15. 9–11	Ps. ***57***; 148 *alt.* Ps. 78. 1–39† Num. 13. 1–3, 17–end Luke 5. 27–end	Ps. 104 *alt.* Ps. 78. 40–end† Deut. ch. 19 1 Pet. 2. 11–end
15 Friday					
	W		Acts 15. 22–31 Ps. 57. 8–end John 15. 12–17	Ps. ***138***; 149 *alt.* Ps. 55 Num. 14. 1–25 Luke 6. 1–11	Ps. 66 *alt.* Ps. 69 Deut. 21.22 - 22.8 1 Pet. 3. 1–12
16 Saturday		*Caroline Chisholm, Social Reformer, 1877*			
	W		Acts 16. 1–10 Ps. 100 John 15. 18–21	Ps. ***146***; 150 *alt.* Ps. ***76***; 79 Num. 14. 26–end Luke 6. 12–26	Ps. 118 *alt.* Ps. 81; ***84*** Deut. 24. 5–end 1 Pet. 3. 13–end **ct**
17 Sunday		**THE SIXTH SUNDAY OF EASTER**			
	W	*The reading from Acts must be used as either the first or second reading at the Principal Service.*	Acts 17. 22–31 [*or* Gen. 8.20 - 9.17] Ps. 66. 7–end 1 Pet. 3. 13–end John 14. 15–21	Ps. 73. 21–28 Job 14. 1–2, 7–15; 19. 23–27a 1 Thess. 4. 13–end	Ps. 87; 36. 5–10 Zech. 8. 1–13 Rev. 21.22 - 22.5 *Gospel*: John 21. 1–14
18 Monday		Rogation Day**			
	W		Acts 16. 11–15 Ps. 149. 1–5 John 15.26 - 16.4	Ps. ***65***; 67 *alt.* Ps. ***80***; 82 Num. 16. 1–35 Luke 6. 27–38	Ps. ***121***; 122; 123 *alt.* Ps. ***85***; 86 Deut. ch. 26 1 Pet. 4. 1–11
19 Tuesday		**Dunstan, Archbishop of Canterbury, Restorer of Monastic Life, 988** Rogation Day**			
	W	Com. Bishop *or* *esp.* Matt. 24. 42–46 *also* Exod. 31. 1–5	Acts 16. 22–34 Ps. 138 John 16. 5–11	Ps. 124; 125; ***126***; 127 *alt.* Ps. 87; ***89. 1–18*** Num. 16. 36–end Luke 6. 39–end	Ps. ***128***; 129; 130; 131 *alt.* Ps. 89. 19–end Deut. 28. 1–14 1 Pet. 4. 12–end
20 Wednesday		**Alcuin of York, Deacon, Abbot of Tours, 804** Rogation Day**			
	W	Com. Religious *or* *also* Col. 3. 12–16 John 4. 19–24	Acts 17.15, 22 - 18.1 Ps. 148. 1–2, 11–end John 16. 12–15	Ps. ***132***; 133 *alt.* Ps. 119. 105–128 Num. 17. 1–11 Luke 7. 1–10	*First EP of Ascension Day* Ps. 15; 24 2 Sam. 23. 1–5 Col. 2.20 - 3.4 𝔚 **ct**

*Matthias may be celebrated on 24 February instead of 14 May.
**For Rogation Day provision, see p. 11.

	Calendar and Holy Communion	Morning Prayer	Evening Prayer	NOTES
W		Num. 13. 1–3, 17–end Luke 5. 27–end	Deut. ch. 19 1 Pet. 2. 11–end	
W		Num. 14. 1–25 Luke 6. 1–11	Deut. 21.22 - 22.8 1 Pet. 3. 1–12	
W		Num. 14. 26–end Luke 6. 12–26	Deut. 24. 5–end 1 Pet. 3. 13–end **ct**	
	THE FIFTH SUNDAY AFTER EASTER Rogation Sunday			
W	Joel 2. 21–26 Ps. 66. 1–8 Jas. 1. 22–end John 16. 23b–end	Ps. 73. 21–28 Job 14. 1–2, 7–15; 19. 23–27a 1 Thess. 4. 13–end	Ps. 87, 36. 5–10 Zech. 8. 1–13 Rev. 21.22 - 22.5	
	Rogation Day			
W	Job 28. 1–11 Ps. 107. 1–9 Jas. 5. 7–11 Luke 6. 36–42	Num. 16. 1–35 Luke 6. 27–38	Deut. ch. 26 1 Pet. 4. 1–11	
	Dunstan, Archbishop of Canterbury, Restorer of Monastic Life, 988 Rogation Day			
W	Com. Bishop *or* Deut. 8. 1–10 Ps. 121 Jas. 5. 16–end Luke 11. 5–13	Num. 16. 36–end Luke 6. 39–end	Deut. 28. 1–14 1 Pet. 4. 12–end	
	Rogation Day			
W	Deut. 34. 1–7 Ps. 108. 1–6 Eph. 4. 7–13 John 17. 1–11	Num. 17. 1–11 Luke 7. 1–10	*First EP of Ascension Day* Ps. 15; 24 2 Sam. 23. 1–5 Col. 2.20 - 3.4 **𝔚 ct**	

		Sunday Principal Service Weekday Eucharist	Third Service Morning Prayer	Second Service Evening Prayer
21 Thursday	**ASCENSION DAY**			
𝔚	*The reading from Acts must be used as either the first or second reading at the Eucharist.*	Acts 1. 1–11 *or* Dan. 7. 9–14 Ps. 47 *or* Ps. 93 Eph. 1. 15–end *or* Acts 1. 1–11 Luke 24. 44–end	*MP*: Ps. 110; 150 Isa. 52. 7–end Heb. 7. [11–25] 26–end	*EP*: Ps. 8 Song of the Three 29–37 *or* 2 Kings 2. 1–15 Rev. ch. 5 *Gospel*: Mark 16. 14–end
22 Friday				
W		Acts 18. 9–18 Ps. 47. 1–6 John 16. 20–23	Ps. 20; ***81*** *alt.* Ps. ***88***; (95) Num. 20. 1–13 Luke 7. 11–17 [Exod. 35.30 – 36.1 Gal. 5. 13–end]*	Ps. 145 *alt.* Ps. 102 Deut. 29. 2–15 1 John 1.1 – 2.6
23 Saturday				
W		Acts 18. 22–end Ps. 47. 1–2, 7–end John 16. 23–28	Ps. 21; ***47*** *alt.* Ps. 96; ***97***; 100 Num. 21. 4–9 Luke 7. 18–35 [Num. 11. 16–17, 24–29 1 Cor. ch. 2]*	Ps. 84; ***85*** *alt.* Ps. 104 Deut. ch. 30 1 John 2. 7–17 **ct**
24 Sunday	**THE SEVENTH SUNDAY OF EASTER (SUNDAY AFTER ASCENSION DAY)**			
W	*The reading from Acts must be used as either the first or second reading at the Principal Service.*	Acts 1. 6–14 [*or* Ezek. 36. 24–28] Ps. 68. 1–10, 32–end (*or* 68. 1–10) 1 Pet. 4. 12–14; 5. 6–11 John 17. 1–11	Ps. 104. 26–35 Isa. 65. 17–end Rev. 21. 1–8	Ps. 47 2 Sam. 23. 1–5 Eph. 1. 15–end *Gospel*: Mark 16. 14–end
25 Monday	**The Venerable Bede, Monk at Jarrow, Scholar, Historian, 735** *Aldhelm, Bishop of Sherborne, 709*			
W	Com. Religious *or* *also* Ecclus. 39. 1–10	Acts 19. 1–8 Ps. 68. 1–6 John 16. 29–end	Ps. ***93***; 96; 97 *alt.* Ps. ***98***; 99; 101 Num. 22. 1–35 Luke 7. 36–end [Num. 27. 15–end 1 Cor. ch. 3]*	Ps. 18 *alt.* Ps. ***105***† (*or* 103) Deut. 31. 1–13 1 John 2. 18–end
26 Tuesday	**Augustine, first Archbishop of Canterbury, 605** *John Calvin, Reformer, 1564; Philip Neri, Founder of the Oratorians, Spiritual Guide, 1595*			
W	Com. Bishop *or* *also* 1 Thess. 2. 2b–8 Matt. 13. 31–33	Acts 20. 17–27 Ps. 68. 9–10, 18–19 John 17. 1–11	Ps. 98; ***99***; 100 *alt.* Ps. ***106***† (*or* 103) Num. 22.36 – 23.12 Luke 8. 1–15 [1 Sam. 10. 1–10 1 Cor. 12. 1–13]*	Ps. 68 *alt.* Ps. 107† Deut. 31. 14–29 1 John 3. 1–10
27 Wednesday				
W		Acts 20. 28–end Ps. 68. 27–28, 32–end John 17. 11–19	Ps. 2; ***29*** *alt.* Ps. 110; ***111***; 112 Num. 23. 13–end Luke 8. 16–25 [1 Kings 19. 1–18 Matt. 3. 13–end]*	Ps. 36; ***46*** *alt.* Ps. 119. 129–152 Deut. 31.30 – 32.14 1 John 3. 11–end

* The alternative readings in square brackets may be used at one of the offices, in preparation for the Day of Pentecost.

	Calendar and Holy Communion	Morning Prayer	Evening Prayer	NOTES
	ASCENSION DAY			
𝔚	Dan. 7. 13–14 Ps. 68. 1–6 Acts 1. 1–11 Mark 16. 14–end *or* Luke 24. 44–end	Ps. 110; 150 Isa. 52. 7–end Heb. 7. [11–25] 26–end	Ps. 8 Song of the Three 29–37 *or* 2 Kings 2. 1–15 Rev. ch. 5	
W	Ascension CEG	Num. 20. 1–13 Luke 7. 11–17 [Exod. 35.30 – 36.1 Gal. 5. 13–end]*	Deut. 29. 2–15 1 John 1.1 – 2.6	
W	Ascension CEG	Num. 21. 4–9 Luke 7. 18–35 [Num. 11. 16–17, 24–29 1 Cor. ch. 2]*	Deut. ch. 30 1 John 2. 7–17 **ct**	
	THE SUNDAY AFTER ASCENSION DAY			
W	2 Kings 2. 9–15 Ps. 68. 32–end 1 Pet. 4. 7–11 John 15.26 – 16.4a	Ps. 104. 26–35 Isa. 65. 17–end Rev. 21. 1–8	Ps. 47 2 Sam. 23. 1–5 Eph. 1. 15–end	
W		Num. 22. 1–35 Luke 7. 36–end [Num. 27. 15–end 1 Cor. ch. 3]*	Deut. 31. 1–13 1 John 2. 18–end	
	Augustine, first Archbishop of Canterbury, 605			
W	Com. Bishop	Num. 22.36 – 23.12 Luke 8. 1–15 [1 Sam. 10. 1–10 1 Cor. 12. 1–13]*	Deut. 31. 14–29 1 John 3. 1–10	
	The Venerable Bede, Monk at Jarrow, Scholar, Historian, 735			
W	Com. Religious	Num. 23. 13–end Luke 8. 16–25 [1 Kings 19. 1–18 Matt. 3. 13–end]*	Deut. 31.30 – 32.14 1 John 3. 11–end	

		Sunday Principal Service Weekday Eucharist	Third Service Morning Prayer	Second Service Evening Prayer
28 Thursday	*Lanfranc, Prior of Le Bec, Archbishop of Canterbury, Scholar, 1089*			
W		Acts 22. 30; 23. 6–11 Ps. 16. 1, 5–end John 17. 20–end	Ps. ***24***; 72 *alt.* Ps. 113; ***115*** Num. ch. 24 Luke 8. 26–39 [Ezek. 11. 14–20 Matt. 9.35 - 10.20]*	Ps. 139 *alt.* Ps. 114; ***116***; 117 Deut. 32. 15–47 1 John 4. 1–6
29 Friday				
W		Acts 25. 13–21 Ps. 103. 1–2, 11–12, 19–20 John 21. 15–19	Ps. ***28***; 30 *alt.* Ps. 139 Num. 27. 12–end Luke 8. 40–end [Ezek. 36. 22–28 Matt. 12. 22–32]*	Ps. 147 *alt.* Ps. ***130***; 131; 137 Deut. ch. 33 1 John 4. 7–end
30 Saturday	**Josephine Butler, Social Reformer, 1906** *Joan of Arc, Visionary, 1431; Apolo Kivebulaya, Priest, Evangelist in Central Africa, 1933*			
W	Com. Saint *or* *esp.* Isa. 58. 6–11 *also* 1 John 3. 18–23 Matt. 9. 10–13	Acts 28. 16–20, 30–end Ps. 11. 4–end John 21. 20–end	Ps. 42; ***43*** *alt.* Ps. 120; ***121***; 122 Num. 32. 1–27 Luke 9. 1–17 [Mic. 3. 1–8 Eph. 6. 10–20]*	*First EP of Pentecost* Ps. 48 Deut. 16. 9–15 John 15.26 - 16.15 **R ct**
31 Sunday	**DAY OF PENTECOST (Whit Sunday)**			
R	*The reading from Acts must be used as either the first or second reading at the Principal Service.*	Acts 2. 1–21 *or* Num. 11. 24–30 Ps. 104. 26–36, 37b (*or* 104. 26–end) 1 Cor. 12. 3b–13 *or* Acts 2. 1–21 John 20. 19–23 *or* John 7. 37–39	*MP*: Ps. 87 Gen. 11. 1–9 Acts 10. 34–end	*EP*: Ps. 67; 133 Joel 2. 21–end Acts 2. 14–21 [22–38] *Gospel*: Luke 24. 44–end

June 2020

1 Monday	**THE VISIT OF THE BLESSED VIRGIN MARY TO ELIZABETH** (transferred from 31 May)** Ordinary Time resumes today			
W **DEL 9**		Zeph. 3. 14–18 Ps. 113 Rom. 12. 9–16 Luke 1. 39–49 [50–56]	*MP*: Ps. 85; 150 1 Sam. 2. 1–10 Mark 3. 31–end	*EP*: Ps. 122; 127; 128 Zech. 2. 10–end John 3. 25–30
	or, if The Visitation is celebrated on 2 July:			
Gr	**Justin, Martyr at Rome, c. 165** Com. Martyr *or* *esp.* John 15. 18–21 *also* 1 Macc. 2. 15–22 1 Cor. 1. 18–25	2 Pet. 1. 2–7 Ps. 91. 1–2, 14–end Mark 12. 1–12	Ps. 123; 124; 125; ***126*** Josh. ch. 1 Luke 9. 18–27	Ps. ***127***; 128; 129 Job ch. 1 Rom. 1. 1–17
2 Tuesday				
G		2 Pet. 3. 11–15a, 17–end Ps. 90. 1–4, 10, 14, 16 Mark 12. 13–17	Ps. ***132***; 133 Josh. ch. 2 Luke 9. 28–36	Ps. (134); ***135*** Job ch. 2 Rom. 1. 18–end

*The alternative readings in square brackets may be used at one of the offices, in preparation for the Day of Pentecost.
**The Visit of the Blessed Virgin Mary to Elizabeth may be celebrated on 2 July instead of 1 June this year.

	Calendar and Holy Communion	Morning Prayer	Evening Prayer	NOTES
W		Num. ch. 24 Luke 8. 26–39 [Ezek. 11. 14–20 Matt. 9.35 – 10.20]*	Deut. 32. 15–47 1 John 4. 1–6	
W		Num. 27. 12–end Luke 8. 40–end [Ezek. 36. 22–28 Matt. 12. 22–32]*	Deut. ch. 33 1 John 4. 7–end	
W		Num. 32. 1–27 Luke 9. 1–17 [Mic. 3. 1–8 Eph. 6. 10–20]*	*First EP of Whit Sunday* Ps. 48 Deut. 16. 9–15 John 15.26 – 16.15 **R ct**	
	WHIT SUNDAY			
R	Deut. 16. 9–12 Ps. 122 Acts 2. 1–11 John 14. 15–31a	Ps. 87 Gen. 11. 1–9 Acts 10. 34–end	Ps. 67; 133 Num. 11. 24–30 Acts 2. 14–21 [22–38]	
	Monday in Whitsun Week			
R	Acts 10. 34–end John 3. 16–21	Ezek. 11. 14–20 Acts 2. 12–36	Exod. 35.30 – 36.1 Acts 2. 37–end	
	Tuesday in Whitsun Week			
R	Acts 8. 14–17 John 10. 1–10	Ezek. 37. 1–14 1 Cor. 12. 1–13	2 Sam. 23. 1–5 1 Cor. 12.27 – 13.end	

		Sunday Principal Service Weekday Eucharist	Third Service Morning Prayer	Second Service Evening Prayer
3 Wednesday	*The Martyrs of Uganda, 1885–87 and 1977*			
G		2 Tim. 1. 1–3, 6–12 Ps. 123 Mark 12. 18–27	Ps. 119. 153–end Josh. ch. 3 Luke 9. 37–50	Ps. 136 Job ch. 3 Rom. 2. 1–16
4 Thursday	*Petroc, Abbot of Padstow, 6th century*			
G		2 Tim. 2. 8–15 Ps. 25. 4–12 Mark 12. 28–34	Ps. ***143***; 146 Josh. 4.1 - 5.1 Luke 9. 51–end	Ps. ***138***; 140; 141 Job ch. 4 Rom. 2. 17–end
5 Friday	**Boniface (Wynfrith) of Crediton, Bishop, Apostle of Germany, Martyr, 754**			
Gr	Com. Martyr *or* *also* Acts 20. 24–28	2 Tim. 3. 10–end Ps. 119. 161–168 Mark 12. 35–37	Ps. ***142***; 144 Josh. 5. 2–end Luke 10. 1–16	Ps. 145 Job ch. 5 Rom. 3. 1–20
6 Saturday	*Ini Kopuria, Founder of the Melanesian Brotherhood, 1945*			
G		2 Tim. 4. 1–8 Ps. 71. 7–16 Mark 12. 38–end	Ps. 147 Josh. 6. 1–20 Luke 10. 17–24	*First EP of Trinity Sunday* Ps. 97; 98 Exod. 34. 1–10 Mark 1. 1–13 **𝔚 ct**
7 Sunday	**TRINITY SUNDAY**			
𝔚		Isa. 40. 12–17, 27–end Ps. 8 2 Cor. 13. 11–end Matt. 28. 16–20	*MP*: Ps. 86. 8–13 Exod. 3. 1–6, 13–15 John 17. 1–11	*EP*: Ps. 93; 150 Isa. 6. 1–8 John 16. 5–15
8 Monday	**Thomas Ken, Bishop of Bath and Wells, Nonjuror, Hymn Writer, 1711**			
Gw **DEL 10**	Com. Bishop *or* *esp.* 2 Cor. 4. 1–10 Matt. 24. 42–46	1 Kings 17. 1–6 Ps. 121 Matt. 5. 1–12	Ps. ***1***: 2; 3 Josh. 7. 1–15 Luke 10. 25–37	Ps. ***4***; 7 Job ch. 7 Rom. 4. 1–12
9 Tuesday	**Columba, Abbot of Iona, Missionary, 597** *Ephrem of Syria, Deacon, Hymn Writer, Teacher, 373*			
Gw	Com. Missionary *or* *also* Titus 2. 11–end	1 Kings. 17. 7–16 Ps. 4 Matt. 5. 13–16	Ps. ***5***; 6; (8) Josh. 7. 16–end Luke 10. 38–end	Ps. ***9***; 10† Job ch. 8 Rom. 4. 13–end
10 Wednesday				
G		1 Kings 18. 20–39 Ps. 16. 1, 6–end Matt. 5. 17–19	Ps. 119. 1–32 Josh. 8. 1–29 Luke 11. 1–13	Ps. ***11***; 12; 13 Job ch. 9 Rom. 5. 1–11 *or First EP of Corpus Christi* Ps. 110; 111 Exod. 16. 2–15 John 6. 22–35 **W ct** *or First EP of Barnabas* Ps. 1; 15 Isa. 42. 5–12 Acts 14. 8–end **R ct**

	Calendar and Holy Communion	Morning Prayer	Evening Prayer	NOTES
	Ember Day			
R	Ember CEG *or* Acts 2. 14–21 John 6. 44–51	Josh. ch. 3 Luke 9. 37–50	Job ch. 3 Rom. 2. 1–16	
R	Acts 2. 22–28 Luke 9. 1–6	Josh. 4.1 – 5.1 Luke 9. 51–end	Job ch. 4 Rom. 2. 17–end	
	Boniface (Wynfrith) of Crediton, Bishop, Apostle of Germany, Martyr, 754 Ember Day			
R	Com. Martyr *or* Ember CEG *or* Acts 8. 5–8 Luke 5. 17–26	Josh. 5. 2–end Luke 10. 1–16	Job ch. 5 Rom. 3. 1–20	
	Ember Day			
R	Ember CEG *or* Acts 13. 44–end Matt. 20. 29–end	Josh. 6. 1–20 Luke 10. 17–24	*First EP of Trinity Sunday* Ps. 97; 98 Exod. 34. 1–10 Mark 1. 1–13 **𝔚 ct**	
	TRINITY SUNDAY			
𝔚	Isa. 6. 1–8 Ps. 8 Rev. 4. 1–11 John 3. 1–15	Ps. 86. 8–13 Exod. 3. 1–6, 13–15 John 17. 1–11	Ps. 93; 150 Isa. 40. 12–17, 27–end John 16. 5–15	
G		Josh. 7. 1–15 Luke 10. 25–37	Job ch. 7 Rom. 4. 1–12	
G		Josh. 7. 16–end Luke 10. 38–end	Job ch. 8 Rom. 4. 13–end	
G		Josh. 8. 1–29 Luke 11. 1–13	Job ch. 9 Rom. 5. 1–11 *or First EP of Barnabas* (Ps. 1; 15) Isa. 42. 5–12 Acts 14. 8–end **R ct**	

		Sunday Principal Service Weekday Eucharist	Third Service Morning Prayer	Second Service Evening Prayer
11 Thursday	**DAY OF THANKSGIVING FOR HOLY COMMUNION (CORPUS CHRISTI)** *(For Barnabas the Apostle, see provision on 12 June)*			
W		Gen. 14. 18–20 Ps. 116. 10–end 1 Cor. 11. 23–26 John 6. 51–58	*MP*: Ps. 147 Deut. 8. 2–16 1 Cor. 10. 1–17	*EP*: Ps. 23; 42; 43 Prov. 9. 1–5 Luke 9. 11–17
12 Friday	**BARNABAS THE APOSTLE**			
R	*The reading from Acts must be used as either the first or second reading at the Eucharist.*	Job 29. 11–16 *or* Acts 11. 19–end Ps. 112 Acts 11. 19–end *or* Gal. 2. 1–10 John 15. 12–17	*MP*: Ps. 100; 101; 117 Jer. 9. 23–24 Acts 4. 32–end	*EP*: Ps. 147 Eccles. 12. 9–end *or* Tobit 4. 5–11 Acts 9. 26–31
	or ferial provision if Barnabas was celebrated on 11 June:			
G		1 Kings 19. 9, 11–16 Ps. 27. 8–16 Matt. 5. 27–32	Ps. 17; ***19*** Josh. 9. 3–26 Luke 11. 29–36	Ps. 22 Job ch. 11 Rom. 6. 1–14
13 Saturday				
G		1 Kings 19. 19–end Ps. 16. 1–7 Matt. 5. 33–37	Ps. 20; 21; ***23*** Josh. 10. 1–15 Luke 11. 37–end	Ps. ***24***; 25 Job ch. 12 Rom. 6. 15–end **ct**
14 Sunday	**THE FIRST SUNDAY AFTER TRINITY (Proper 6)**			
G	*Track 1* Gen. 18. 1–15 [21. 1–7] Ps. 116. 1, 10–17 (*or* 116. 9–17) Rom. 5. 1–8 Matt. 9.35 - 10.8 [9–23]	*Track 2* Exod. 19. 2–8a Ps. 100 Rom. 5. 1–8 Matt. 9.35 - 10.8 [9–23]	Ps. 45 Deut. 10.12 - 11.1 Acts 23. 12–end	Ps. [42]; 43 1 Sam. 21. 1–15 Luke 11. 14–28
15 Monday	*Evelyn Underhill, Spiritual Writer, 1941*			
G **DEL 11**		1 Kings 21. 1–16 Ps. 5. 1–5 Matt. 5. 38–42	Ps. 27; ***30*** Josh. ch. 14 Luke 12. 1–12	Ps. 26; ***28***; 29 Job ch. 13 Rom. 7. 1–6
16 Tuesday	**Richard, Bishop of Chichester, 1253** *Joseph Butler, Bishop of Durham, Philosopher, 1752*			
Gw	Com. Bishop *or* *also* John 21. 15–19	1 Kings 21. 17–end Ps. 51. 1–9 Matt. 5. 43–end	Ps. 32; ***36*** Josh. 21.43 - 22.8 Luke 12. 13–21	Ps. 33 Job ch. 14 Rom. 7. 7–end
17 Wednesday	*Samuel and Henrietta Barnett, Social Reformers, 1913 and 1936*			
G		2 Kings 2. 1, 6–14 Ps. 31. 21–end Matt. 6. 1–6, 16–18	Ps. 34 Josh. 22. 9–end Luke 12. 22–31	Ps. 119. 33–56 Job ch. 15 Rom. 8. 1–11
18 Thursday	*Bernard Mizeki, Apostle of the MaShona, Martyr, 1896*			
G		Ecclus. 48. 1–14 *or* Isa. 63. 7–9 Ps. 97. 1–8 Matt. 6. 7–15	Ps. 37† Josh. ch. 23 Luke 12. 32–40	Ps. 39; ***40*** Job 16.1 - 17.2 Rom. 8. 12–17

	Calendar and Holy Communion	Morning Prayer	Evening Prayer	NOTES
	BARNABAS THE APOSTLE			
R	Job 29. 11–16 Ps. 112 Acts 11. 22–end John 15. 12–16	(Ps. 100; 101; 117) Jer. 9. 23–24 Acts 4. 32–end	(Ps. 147) Eccles. 12. 9–end *or* Tobit 4. 5–11 Acts 9. 26–31	
G		Josh. 9. 3–26 Luke 11. 29–36	Job ch. 11 Rom. 6. 1–14	
G		Josh. 10. 1–15 Luke 11. 37–end	Job ch. 12 Rom. 6. 15–end **ct**	
	THE FIRST SUNDAY AFTER TRINITY			
G	2 Sam. 9. 6–end Ps. 41. 1–4 1 John 4. 7–end Luke 16. 19–31	Ps. 45 Deut. 10.12 – 11.1 Acts 23. 12–end	Ps. [42]; 43 1 Sam. 21. 1–15 Luke 11. 14–28	
G		Josh. ch. 14 Luke 12. 1–12	Job ch. 13 Rom. 7. 1–6	
G		Josh. 21.43 – 22.8 Luke 12. 13–21	Job ch. 14 Rom. 7. 7–end	
	Alban, first Martyr of Britain, c. 250			
Gr	Com. Martyr	Josh. 22. 9–end Luke 12. 22–31	Job ch. 15 Rom. 8. 1–11	
G		Josh. ch. 23 Luke 12. 32–40	Job 16.1 – 17.2 Rom. 8. 12–17	

		Sunday Principal Service Weekday Eucharist	Third Service Morning Prayer	Second Service Evening Prayer
19 Friday	*Sundar Singh of India, Sadhu (holy man), Evangelist, Teacher, 1929*			
G		2 Kings 11. 1–4, 9–18, 20 Ps. 132. 1–5, 11–13 Matt. 6. 19–23	Ps. 31 Josh. 24. 1–28 Luke 12. 41–48	Ps. 35 Job 17. 3–end Rom. 8. 18–30
20 Saturday				
G		2 Chron. 24. 17–25 Ps. 89. 25–33 Matt. 6. 24–end	Ps. 41; ***42***; 43 Josh. 24. 29–end Luke 12. 49–end	Ps. 45; ***46*** Job ch. 18 Rom. 8. 31–end **ct**
21 Sunday	**THE SECOND SUNDAY AFTER TRINITY (Proper 7)**			
G	*Track 1* Gen. 21. 8–21 Ps. 86. 1–10, 16–end (*or* 86. 1–10) Rom. 6. 1b–11 Matt. 10. 24–39	*Track 2* Jer. 20. 7–13 Ps. 69. 8–11 [12–17] 18–20 (*or* 69. 14–20) Rom. 6. 1b–11 Matt. 10. 24–39	Ps. 49 Deut. 11. 1–15 Acts 27. 1–12	Ps. 46; [48] 1 Sam. 24. 1–17 Luke 14. 12–24
22 Monday	**Alban, first Martyr of Britain, c. 250**			
Gr **DEL 12**	Com. Martyr *or* *esp.* 2 Tim. 2. 3–13 John 12. 24–26	2 Kings 17. 5–8, 13–15, 18 Ps. 60. 1–5, 11–end Matt. 7. 1–5	Ps. 44 Judg. ch. 2 Luke 13. 1–9	Ps. ***47***; 49 Job ch. 19 Rom. 9. 1–18
23 Tuesday	**Etheldreda, Abbess of Ely, c. 678**			
Gw	Com. Religious *or* *also* Matt. 25. 1–13	2 Kings 19. 9b–11, 14–21, 31–36 Ps. 48. 1–2, 8–end Matt. 7. 6, 12–14	Ps. ***48***; 52 Judg. 4. 1–23 Luke 13. 10–21	Ps. 50 Job ch. 21 Rom. 9. 19–end *or First EP of The Birth of John the Baptist* Ps. 71 Judg. 13. 2–7, 24–end Luke 1. 5–25 **W ct**
24 Wednesday	**THE BIRTH OF JOHN THE BAPTIST** Ember Day*			
W		Isa. 40. 1–11 Ps. 85. 7–end Acts 13. 14b–26 *or* Gal. 3. 23–end Luke 1. 57–66, 80	*MP*: Ps. 50; 149 Ecclus. 48. 1–10 *or* Mal. 3. 1–6 Luke 3. 1–17	*EP*: Ps. 80; 82 Mal. ch. 4 Matt. 11. 2–19
25 Thursday				
G		2 Kings 24. 8–17 Ps. 79. 1–9, 12 Matt. 7. 21–end	Ps. 56; ***57***; (63†) Judg. 6. 1–24 Luke 14. 1–11	Ps. 61; ***62***; 64 Job ch. 23 Rom. 10. 11–end
26 Friday	Ember Day*			
G *or* **R**		2 Kings 25. 1–12 Ps. 137. 1–6 Matt. 8. 1–4	Ps. ***51***; 54 Judg. 6. 25–end Luke 14. 12–24	Ps. 38 Job ch. 24 Rom. 11. 1–12

*For Ember Day provision, see p. 11.

	Calendar and Holy Communion	Morning Prayer	Evening Prayer
G		Josh. 24. 1–28 Luke 12. 41–48	Job 17. 3–end Rom. 8. 18–30
	Translation of Edward, King of the West Saxons, 979		
Gr	Com. Martyr	Josh. 24. 29–end Luke 12. 49–end	Job ch. 18 Rom. 8. 31–end **ct**
	THE SECOND SUNDAY AFTER TRINITY		
G	Gen. 12. 1–4 Ps. 120 1 John 3. 13–end Luke 14. 16–24	Ps. 49 Deut. 11. 1–15 Acts 27. 1–12	Ps. 46; [48] 1 Sam. 24. 1–17 Luke 14. 1–14
G		Judg. ch. 2 Luke 13. 1–9	Job ch. 19 Rom. 9. 1–18
G		Judg. 4. 1–23 Luke 13. 10–21	Job ch. 21 Rom. 9. 19–end *or First EP of The Nativity of John the Baptist* (Ps. 71) Judg. 13. 2–7, 24–end Luke 1. 5–25 **W ct**
	THE NATIVITY OF JOHN THE BAPTIST		
W	Isa. 40. 1–11 Ps. 80. 1–7 Acts 13. 22–26 Luke 1. 57–80	(Ps. 50; 149) Ecclus. 48. 1–10 *or* Mal. 3. 1–6 Luke 3. 1–17	(Ps. 82) Mal. ch. 4 Matt. 11. 2–19
G		Judg. 6. 1–24 Luke 14. 1–11	Job ch. 23 Rom. 10. 11–end
G		Judg. 6. 25–end Luke 14. 12–24	Job ch. 24 Rom. 11. 1–12

NOTES

		Sunday Principal Service Weekday Eucharist	Third Service Morning Prayer	Second Service Evening Prayer
27 Saturday	Ember Day* *Cyril, Bishop of Alexandria, Teacher, 444*			
G *or* **R**		Lam. 2. 2, 10–14, 18–19 Ps. 74. 1–3, 21–end Matt. 8. 5–17	Ps. 68 Judg. ch. 7 Luke 14. 25–end	Ps. 65; **66** Job chs 25 & 26 Rom. 11. 13–24 **ct**
28 Sunday	**THE THIRD SUNDAY AFTER TRINITY (Proper 8)**			
Gw	*Track 1* Gen. 22. 1–14 Ps. 13 Rom. 6. 12–end Matt. 10. 40–end	*Track 2* Jer. 28. 5–9 Ps. 89. 1–4, 15–18 (*or* 89. 8–18) Rom. 6. 12–end Matt. 10. 40–end	Ps. 52; 53 Deut. 15. 1–11 Acts 27. [13–32] 33–end	Ps. 50 (*or* 50. 1–15) 1 Sam. 28. 3–19 Luke 17. 20–end *or First EP of Peter and Paul* Ps. 66; 67 Ezek. 3. 4–11 Gal. 1.13 - 2.8 *or, for Peter alone* Acts 9. 32–end **R ct**
29 Monday	**PETER AND PAUL, APOSTLES**			
R **DEL 13**	*The reading from Acts must be used as either the first or second reading at the Eucharist.*	Zech. 4. 1–6a, 10b–end *or* Acts 12. 1–11 Ps. 125 Acts 12. 1–11 *or* 2 Tim. 4. 6–8, 17–18 Matt. 16. 13–19	*MP*: Ps. 71; 113 Isa. 49. 1–6 Acts 11. 1–18	*EP*: Ps. 124; 138 Ezek. 34. 11–16 John 21. 15–22
	or, if Peter is commemorated alone:			
R	*The reading from Acts must be used as either the first or second reading at the Eucharist.*	Ezek. 3. 22–end *or* Acts 12. 1–11 Ps. 125 Acts 12. 1–11 *or* 1 Pet. 2. 19–end Matt. 16. 13–19	*MP*: Ps. 71; 113 Isa. 49. 1–6 Acts 11. 1–18	*EP*: Ps. 124; 138 Ezek. 34. 11–16 John 21. 15–22
30 Tuesday				
G		Amos 3. 1–8; 4. 11–12 Ps. 5. 8–end Matt. 8. 23–27	Ps. 73 Judg. 9. 1–21 Luke 15. 11–end	Ps. 74 Job ch. 28 Rom. 12. 1–8

July 2020

1 Wednesday	*Henry, John and Henry Venn the Younger, Priests, Evangelical Divines, 1797, 1813 and 1873*			
G		Amos 5. 14–15, 21–24 Ps. 50. 7–14 Matt. 8. 28–end	Ps. 77 Judg. 9. 22–end Luke 16. 1–18	Ps. 119. 81–104 Job ch. 29 Rom. 12. 9–end
2 Thursday				
G		Amos 7. 10–end Ps. 19. 7–10 Matt. 9. 1–8	Ps. 78. 1–39† Judg. 11. 1–11 Luke 16. 19–end	Ps. 78. 40–end† Job ch. 30 Rom. 13. 1–7 *or First EP of Thomas* Ps. 27 Isa. ch. 35 Heb. 10.35 - 11.1 **R ct**

*For Ember Day provision, see p. 11.
**Common Worship Morning and Evening Prayer provision for 31 May may be used.

	Calendar and Holy Communion	Morning Prayer	Evening Prayer	NOTES
G		Judg. ch. 7 Luke 14. 25–end	Job chs 25 & 26 Rom. 11. 13–24 **ct**	
	THE THIRD SUNDAY AFTER TRINITY			
G	2 Chron. 33. 9–13 Ps. 55. 17–23 1 Pet. 5. 5b–11 Luke 15. 1–10	Ps. 52; 53 Deut. 15. 1–11 Acts 27. [13–32] 33–end	Ps. 50 (*or* 50. 1–15) 1 Sam. 28. 3–19 Luke 17. 20–end *or First EP of Peter* (Ps. 66; 67) Ezek. 3. 4–11 Acts 9. 32–end **R ct**	
	PETER THE APOSTLE			
R	Ezek. 3. 4–11 Ps. 125 Acts 12. 1–11 Matt. 16. 13–19	(Ps. 71; 113) Isa. 49. 1–6 Acts 11. 1–18	(Ps. 124; 138) Ezek. 34. 11–16 John 21. 15–22	
G		Judg. 9. 1–21 Luke 15. 11–end	Job ch. 28 Rom. 12. 1–8	
G		Judg. 9. 22–end Luke 16. 1–18	Job ch. 29 Rom. 12. 9–end	
	The Visitation of the Blessed Virgin Mary**			
Gw	1 Sam. 2. 1–3 Ps. 113 Gal. 4. 1–5 Luke 1. 39–45	Judg. 11. 1–11 Luke 16. 19–end	Job ch. 30 Rom. 13. 1–7	

		Sunday Principal Service Weekday Eucharist	Third Service Morning Prayer	Second Service Evening Prayer
3 Friday	**THOMAS THE APOSTLE***			
R		Hab. 2. 1–4 Ps. 31. 1–6 Eph. 2. 19–end John 20. 24–29	*MP*: Ps. 92; 146 2 Sam. 15. 17–21 *or* Ecclus. ch. 2 John 11. 1–16	*EP*: Ps. 139 Job 42. 1–6 1 Pet. 1. 3–12
	or, if Thomas is not celebrated:			
G		Amos 8. 4–6, 9–12 Ps. 119. 1–8 Matt. 9. 9–13	Ps. 55 Judg. 11. 29–end Luke 17. 1–10	Ps. 69 Job ch. 31 Rom. 13. 8–end
4 Saturday				
G		Amos 9. 11–end Ps. 85. 8–end Matt. 9. 14–17	Ps. ***76***; 79 Judg. 12. 1–7 Luke 17. 11–19	Ps. 81; ***84*** Job ch. 32 Rom. 14. 1–12 **ct**
5 Sunday	**THE FOURTH SUNDAY AFTER TRINITY (Proper 9)**			
G	*Track 1* Gen. 24. 34–38, 42–49, 58–end Ps. 45. 10–end *or Canticle*: Song of Sol. 2. 8–13 Rom. 7. 15–25a Matt. 11. 16–19, 25–end	*Track 2* Zech. 9. 9–12 Ps. 145. 8–15 Rom. 7. 15–25a Matt. 11. 16–19, 25–end	Ps. 55. 1–15, 18–22 Deut. 24. 10–end Acts 28. 1–16	Ps. 56; [57] 2 Sam. 2. 1–11; 3. 1 Luke 18.31 – 19.10
6 Monday	*Thomas More, Scholar, and John Fisher, Bishop of Rochester, Reformation Martyrs, 1535*			
G **DEL 14**		Hos. 2. 14–16, 19–20 Ps. 145. 2–9 Matt. 9. 18–26	Ps. ***80***; 82 Judg. 13. 1–24 Luke 17. 20–end	Ps. ***85***; 86 Job ch. 33 Rom. 14. 13–end
7 Tuesday**				
G		Hos. 8. 4–7, 11–13 Ps. 103. 8–12 Matt. 9. 32–end	Ps. 87; ***89. 1–18*** Judg. ch. 14 Luke 18. 1–14	Ps. 89. 19–end Job ch. 38 Rom. 15. 1–13
8 Wednesday				
G		Hos. 10. 1–3, 7–8, 12 Ps. 115. 3–10 Matt. 10. 1–7	Ps. 119. 105–128 Judg. 15.1 – 16.3 Luke 18. 15–30	Ps. ***91***; 93 Job ch. 39 Rom. 15. 14–21
9 Thursday				
G		Hos. 11. 1, 3–4, 8–9 Ps. 105. 1–7 Matt. 10. 7–15	Ps. 90; ***92*** Judg. 16. 4–end Luke 18. 31–end	Ps. 94 Job ch. 40 Rom. 15. 22–end
10 Friday				
G		Hos. 14. 2–end Ps. 80. 1–7 Matt. 10. 16–23	Ps. ***88***; (95) Judg. ch. 17 Luke 19. 1–10	Ps. 102 Job ch. 41 Rom. 16. 1–16
11 Saturday	**Benedict of Nursia, Abbot of Monte Cassino, Father of Western Monasticism, c. 550**			
Gw	Com. Religious *or* *also* 1 Cor. 3. 10–11 Luke 18. 18–22	Isa. 6. 1–8 Ps. 51. 1–7 Matt. 10. 24–33	Ps. 96; ***97***; 100 Judg. 18. 1–20, 27–end Luke 19. 11–27	Ps. 104 Job ch. 42 Rom. 16. 17–end **ct**

*Thomas the Apostle may be celebrated on 21 December instead of 3 July.
**Thomas Becket may be celebrated on 7 July instead of 29 December.

	Calendar and Holy Communion	Morning Prayer	Evening Prayer
G		Judg. 11. 29–end Luke 17. 1–10	Job ch. 31 Rom. 13. 8–end
	Translation of Martin, Bishop of Tours, *c.* 397		
Gw	Com. Bishop	Judg. 12. 1–7 Luke 17. 11–19	Job ch. 32 Rom. 14. 1–12 **ct**
	THE FOURTH SUNDAY AFTER TRINITY		
G	Gen. 3. 17–19 Ps. 79. 8–10 Rom. 8. 18–23 Luke 6. 36–42	Ps. 55. 1–15, 18–22 Deut. 24. 10–end Acts 28. 1–16	Ps. 56; [57] 2 Sam. 2. 1–11; 3. 1 Luke 18.31 - 19.10
G		Judg. 13. 1–24 Luke 17. 20–end	Job ch. 33 Rom. 14. 13–end
G		Judg. ch. 14 Luke 18. 1–14	Job ch. 38 Rom. 15. 1–13
G		Judg. 15.1 - 16.3 Luke 18. 15–30	Job ch. 39 Rom. 15. 14–21
G		Judg. 16. 4–end Luke 18. 31–end	Job ch. 40 Rom. 15. 22–end
G		Judg. ch. 17 Luke 19. 1–10	Job ch. 41 Rom. 16. 1–16
G		Judg. 18. 1–20, 27–end Luke 19. 11–27	Job ch. 42 Rom. 16. 17–end **ct**

NOTES

			Sunday Principal Service Weekday Eucharist	Third Service Morning Prayer	Second Service Evening Prayer
12 Sunday		**THE FIFTH SUNDAY AFTER TRINITY (Proper 10)**			
	G	*Track 1* Gen. 25. 19–end Ps. 119. 105–112 Rom. 8. 1–11 Matt. 13. 1–9, 18–23	*Track 2* Isa. 55. 10–13 Ps. 65 (*or* 65. 8–end) Rom. 8. 1–11 Matt. 13. 1–9, 18–23	Ps. 64; 65 Deut. 28. 1–14 Acts 28. 17–end	Ps. 60; [63] 2 Sam. 7. 18–end Luke 19.41 - 20.8
13 Monday					
	G **DEL 15**		Isa. 1. 11–17 Ps. 50. 7–15 Matt. 10.34 - 11.1	Ps. ***98***; 99; 101 1 Sam. 1. 1–20 Luke 19. 28–40	Ps. ***105***† (*or* 103) Ezek. 1. 1–14 2 Cor. 1. 1–14
14 Tuesday		**John Keble, Priest, Tractarian, Poet, 1866**			
	Gw	Com. Pastor *or* *also* Lam. 3. 19–26 Matt. 5. 1–8	Isa. 7. 1–9 Ps. 48. 1–7 Matt. 11. 20–24	Ps. ***106***† (*or* 103) 1 Sam. 1.21 - 2.11 Luke 19. 41–end	Ps. 107† Ezek. 1.15 - 2.2 2 Cor. 1.15 - 2.4
15 Wednesday		**Swithun, Bishop of Winchester, c. 862** *Bonaventure, Friar, Bishop, Teacher, 1274*			
	Gw	Com. Bishop *or* *also* Jas. 5. 7–11, 13–18	Isa. 10. 5–7, 13–16 Ps. 94. 5–11 Matt. 11. 25–27	Ps. 110; ***111***; 112 1 Sam. 2. 12–26 Luke 20. 1–8	Ps. 119. 129–152 Ezek. 2.3 - 3.11 2 Cor. 2. 5–end
16 Thursday		*Osmund, Bishop of Salisbury, 1099*			
	G		Isa. 26. 7–9, 16–19 Ps. 102. 14–21 Matt. 11. 28–end	Ps. 113; ***115*** 1 Sam. 2. 27–end Luke 20. 9–19	Ps. 114; ***116***; 117 Ezek. 3. 12–end 2 Cor. ch. 3
17 Friday					
	G		Isa. 38. 1–6, 21–22, 7–8 *Canticle*: Isa. 38. 10–16 *or* Ps. 32. 1–8 Matt. 12. 1–8	Ps. 139 1 Sam. 3.1 - 4.1a Luke 20. 20–26	Ps. ***130***; 131; 137 Ezek. ch. 8 2 Cor. ch. 4
18 Saturday		*Elizabeth Ferard, first deaconess of the Church of England, Founder of the Community of St Andrew, 1883*			
	G		Mic. 2. 1–5 Ps. 10. 1–5a, 12 Matt. 12. 14–21	Ps. 120; ***121***; 122 1 Sam. 4. 1b–end Luke 20. 27–40	Ps. 118 Ezek. ch. 9 2 Cor. ch. 5 **ct**
19 Sunday		**THE SIXTH SUNDAY AFTER TRINITY (Proper 11)**			
	G	*Track 1* Gen. 28. 10–19a Ps. 139. 1–11, 23–24 (*or* 139. 1–11) Rom. 8. 12–25 Matt. 13. 24–30, 36–43	*Track 2* Wisd. 12. 13, 16–19 *or* Isa. 44. 6–8 Ps. 86. 11–end Rom. 8. 12–25 Matt. 13. 24–30, 36–43	Ps. 71 Deut. 30. 1–10 1 Pet. 3. 8–18	Ps. 67; [70] 1 Kings 2. 10–12; 3. 16–end Acts 4. 1–22 *Gospel*: Mark 6. 30–34, 53–end
20 Monday		*Margaret of Antioch, Martyr, 4th century; Bartolomé de las Casas, Apostle to the Indies, 1566*			
	G **DEL 16**		Mic. 6. 1–4, 6–8 Ps. 50. 3–7, 14 Matt. 12. 38–42	Ps. 123; 124; 125; ***126*** 1 Sam. ch. 5 Luke 20.41 - 21.4	Ps. ***127***; 128; 129 Ezek. 10. 1–19 2 Cor. 6.1 - 7.1

	Calendar and Holy Communion	Morning Prayer	Evening Prayer	NOTES
	THE FIFTH SUNDAY AFTER TRINITY			
G	1 Kings 19. 19–21 Ps. 84. 8–end 1 Pet. 3. 8–15a Luke 5. 1–11	Ps. 64; 65 Deut. 28. 1–14 Acts 28. 17–end	Ps. 60; [63] 2 Sam. 7. 18–end Luke 20. 1–8	
G		1 Sam. 1. 1–20 Luke 19. 28–40	Ezek. 1. 1–14 2 Cor. 1. 1–14	
G		1 Sam. 1.21 - 2.11 Luke 19. 41–end	Ezek. 1.15 - 2.2 2 Cor. 1.15 - 2.4	
	Swithun, Bishop of Winchester, c. 862			
Gw	Com. Bishop	1 Sam. 2. 12–26 Luke 20. 1–8	Ezek. 2.3 - 3.11 2 Cor. 2. 5–end	
G		1 Sam. 2. 27–end Luke 20. 9–19	Ezek. 3. 12–end 2 Cor. ch. 3	
G		1 Sam. 3.1 - 4.1a Luke 20. 20–26	Ezek. ch. 8 2 Cor. ch. 4	
G		1 Sam. 4. 1b–end Luke 20. 27–40	Ezek. ch. 9 2 Cor. ch. 5 **ct**	
	THE SIXTH SUNDAY AFTER TRINITY			
G	Gen. 4. 2b–15 Ps. 90. 12–end Rom. 6. 3–11 Matt. 5. 20–26	Ps. 71 Deut. 30. 1–10 1 Pet. 3. 13–22	Ps. 67; [70] 1 Kings 2. 10–12; 3. 16–end Acts 4. 1–22	
	Margaret of Antioch, Martyr, 4th century			
Gr	Com. Virgin Martyr	1 Sam. ch. 5 Luke 20.41 - 21.4	Ezek. 10. 1–19 2 Cor. 6.1 - 7.1	

		Sunday Principal Service Weekday Eucharist	Third Service Morning Prayer	Second Service Evening Prayer
21 Tuesday				
G		Mic. 7. 14–15, 18–20 Ps. 85. 1–7 Matt. 12. 46–end	Ps. ***132***; 133 1 Sam. 6. 1–16 Luke 21. 5–19	Ps. (134); ***135*** Ezek. 11. 14–end 2 Cor. 7. 2–end *or First EP of Mary Magdalene* Ps. 139 Isa. 25. 1–9 2 Cor. 1. 3–7 **W ct**
22 Wednesday	**MARY MAGDALENE**			
W		Song of Sol. 3. 1–4 Ps. 42. 1–10 2 Cor. 5. 14–17 John 20. 1–2, 11–18	*MP*: Ps. 30; 32; 150 1 Sam. 16. 14–end Luke 8. 1–3	*EP*: Ps. 63 Zeph. 3. 14–end Mark 15.40 - 16.7
23 Thursday	*Bridget of Sweden, Abbess of Vadstena, 1373*			
G		Jer. 2. 1–3, 7–8, 12–13 Ps. 36. 5–10 Matt. 13. 10–17	Ps. ***143***; 146 1 Sam. ch. 8 Luke 21. 29–end	Ps. ***138***; 140; 141 Ezek. 12. 17–end 2 Cor. 8.16 - 9.5
24 Friday				
G		Jer. 3. 14–17 Ps. 23 *or Canticle*: Jer. 31. 10–13 Matt. 13. 18–23	Ps. 142; ***144*** 1 Sam. 9. 1–14 Luke 22. 1–13	Ps. 145 Ezek. 13. 1–16 2 Cor. 9. 6–end *or First EP of James* Ps. 144 Deut. 30. 11–end Mark 5. 21–end **R ct**
25 Saturday	**JAMES THE APOSTLE**			
R	*The reading from Acts must be used as either the first or second reading at the Principal Service.*	Jer. 45. 1–5 *or* Acts 11.27 - 12.2 Ps. 126 Acts 11.27 - 12.2 *or* 2 Cor. 4. 7–15 Matt. 20. 20–28	*MP*: Ps. 7; 29; 117 2 Kings 1. 9–15 Luke 9. 46–56	*EP*: Ps. 94 Jer. 26. 1–15 Mark 1. 14–20
26 Sunday	**THE SEVENTH SUNDAY AFTER TRINITY (Proper 12)**			
G	*Track 1* Gen. 29. 15–28 Ps. 105. 1–11, 45b (*or* 105. 1–11) *or* Ps. 128 Rom. 8. 26–end Matt. 13. 31–33, 44–52	*Track 2* 1 Kings 3. 5–12 Ps. 119. 129–136 Rom. 8. 26–39 Matt. 13. 31–33, 44–52	Ps. 77 Song of Sol. ch. 2 *or* 1 Macc. 2. [1–14] 15–22 1 Pet. 4. 7–14	Ps. 75; [76] 1 Kings 6. 11–14, 23–end Acts 12. 1–17 *Gospel*: John 6. 1–21
27 Monday	*Brooke Foss Westcott, Bishop of Durham, Teacher, 1901*			
G **DEL 17**		Jer. 13. 1–11 Ps. 82 *or* Deut. 32. 18–21 Matt. 13. 31–35	Ps. ***1***; 2; 3 1 Sam. 10. 1–16 Luke 22. 24–30	Ps. ***4***; 7 Ezek. 14. 12–end 2 Cor. 11. 1–15
28 Tuesday				
G		Jer. 14. 17–end Ps. 79. 8–end Matt. 13. 36–43	Ps. ***5***; 6; (8) 1 Sam. 10. 17–end Luke 22. 31–38	Ps. ***9***; 10† Ezek. 18. 1–20 2 Cor. 11. 16–end

	Calendar and Holy Communion	Morning Prayer	Evening Prayer	NOTES
G		1 Sam. 6. 1–16 Luke 21. 5–19	Ezek. 11. 14–end 2 Cor. 7. 2–end *or First EP of Mary Magdalene* (Ps. 139) Isa. 25. 1–9 2 Cor. 1. 3–7 **W ct**	
	MARY MAGDALENE			
W	Zeph. 3. 14–end Ps. 30. 1–5 2 Cor. 5. 14–17 John 20. 11–18	(Ps. 30; 32; 150) 1 Sam. 16. 14–end Luke 8. 1–3	(Ps. 63) Song of Sol. 3. 1–4 Mark 15.40 - 16.7	
G		1 Sam. ch. 8 Luke 21. 29–end	Ezek. 12. 17–end 2 Cor. 8.16 - 9.5	
G		1 Sam. 9. 1–14 Luke 22. 1–13	Ezek. 13. 1–16 2 Cor. 9. 6–end *or First EP of James* (Ps. 144) Deut. 30. 11–end Mark 5. 21–end **R ct**	
	JAMES THE APOSTLE			
R	2 Kings 1. 9–15 Ps. 15 Acts 11.27 - 12.3a Matt. 20. 20–28	(Ps. 7; 29; 117) Jer. 45. 1–5 Luke 9. 46–56	(Ps. 94) Jer. 26. 1–15 Mark 1. 14–20	
	THE SEVENTH SUNDAY AFTER TRINITY			
G	1 Kings 17. 8–16 Ps. 34. 11–end Rom. 6. 19–end Mark 8. 1–10a	Ps. 77 Song of Sol. ch. 2 *or* 1 Macc. 2. [1–14] 15–22 1 Pet. 4. 7–14	Ps. 75; [76] 1 Kings 6. 11–14, 23–end Acts 12. 1–17	
G		1 Sam. 10. 1–16 Luke 22. 24–30	Ezek. 14. 12–end 2 Cor. 11. 1–15	
G		1 Sam. 10. 17–end Luke 22. 31–38	Ezek. 18. 1–20 2 Cor. 11. 16–end	

		Sunday Principal Service Weekday Eucharist	Third Service Morning Prayer	Second Service Evening Prayer
29 Wednesday	**Mary, Martha and Lazarus, Companions of Our Lord**			
Gw	Isa. 25. 6–9 *or* Ps. 49. 1–10, 16 Heb. 2. 10–15 John 12. 1–8	Jer. 15. 10, 16–end Ps. 59. 1–4, 18–end Matt. 13. 44–46	Ps. 119. 1–32 1 Sam. ch. 11 Luke 22. 39–46	Ps. ***11***; 12; 13 Ezek. 18. 21–32 2 Cor. ch. 12
30 Thursday	**William Wilberforce, Social Reformer, Olaudah Equiano and Thomas Clarkson, Anti-Slavery Campaigners, 1833, 1797 and 1846**			
Gw	Com. Saint *or* *also* Job 31. 16–23 Gal. 3. 26–29; 4. 6–7 Luke 4. 16–21	Jer. 18. 1–6 Ps. 146. 1–5 Matt. 13. 47–53	Ps. 14; ***15***; 16 1 Sam. ch. 12 Luke 22. 47–62	Ps. 18† Ezek. 20. 1–20 2 Cor. ch. 13
31 Friday	*Ignatius of Loyola, Founder of the Society of Jesus, 1556*			
G		Jer. 26. 1–9 Ps. 69. 4–10 Matt. 13. 54–end	Ps. 17; ***19*** 1 Sam. 13. 5–18 Luke 22. 63–end	Ps. 22 Ezek. 20. 21–38 Jas. 1. 1–11

August 2020

1 Saturday				
G		Jer. 26. 11–16, 24 Ps. 69. 14–20 Matt. 14. 1–12	Ps. 20; 21; ***23*** 1 Sam. 13.19 - 14.15 Luke 23. 1–12	Ps. ***24***; 25 Ezek. 24. 15–end Jas. 1. 12–end **ct**
2 Sunday	**THE EIGHTH SUNDAY AFTER TRINITY (Proper 13)**			
G	*Track 1* Gen. 32. 22–31 Ps. 17. 1–7, 16 (*or* 17. 1–7) Rom. 9. 1–5 Matt. 14. 13–21	*Track 2* Isa. 55. 1–5 Ps. 145. 8–9, 15–end (*or* 145. 15–end) Rom. 9. 1–5 Matt. 14. 13–21	Ps. 85 Song of Sol. 5. 2–end *or* 1 Macc. 3. 1–12 2 Pet. 1. 1–15	Ps. 80 (*or* 80. 1–8) 1 Kings 10. 1–13 Acts 13. 1–13 *Gospel*: John 6. 24–35
3 Monday				
G **DEL 18**		Jer. ch. 28 Ps. 119. 89–96 Matt. 14. 13–21 *or* 14. 22–end	Ps. 27; ***30*** 1 Sam. 14. 24–46 Luke 23. 13–25	Ps. 26; ***28***; 29 Ezek. 28. 1–19 Jas. 2. 1–13
4 Tuesday	*John-Baptiste Vianney, Curé d'Ars, Spiritual Guide, 1859*			
G		Jer. 30. 1–2, 12–15, 18–22 Ps. 102. 16–21 Matt. 14. 22–end *or* 15. 1–2, 10–14	Ps. 32; ***36*** 1 Sam. 15. 1–23 Luke 23. 26–43	Ps. 33 Ezek. 33. 1–20 Jas. 2. 14–end
5 Wednesday	**Oswald, King of Northumbria, Martyr, 642**			
Gr	Com. Martyr *or* *esp.* 1 Pet. 4. 12–end John 16. 29–end	Jer. 31. 1–7 Ps. 121 Matt. 15. 21–28	Ps. 34 1 Sam. ch. 16 Luke 23. 44–56a	Ps. 119. 33–56 Ezek. 33. 21–end Jas. ch. 3 *or First EP of The Transfiguration* Ps. 99; 110 Exod. 24. 12–end John 12. 27–36a **W ct**

	Calendar and Holy Communion	Morning Prayer	Evening Prayer	NOTES
G		1 Sam. ch. 11 Luke 22. 39–46	Ezek. 18. 21–32 2 Cor. ch. 12	
G		1 Sam. ch. 12 Luke 22. 47–62	Ezek. 20. 1–20 2 Cor. ch. 13	
G		1 Sam. 13. 5–18 Luke 22. 63–end	Ezek. 20. 21–38 Jas. 1. 1–11	
	Lammas Day			
G		1 Sam. 13.19 – 14.15 Luke 23. 1–12	Ezek. 24. 15–end Jas. 1. 12–end **ct**	
	THE EIGHTH SUNDAY AFTER TRINITY			
G	Jer. 23. 16–24 Ps. 31. 1–6 Rom. 8. 12–17 Matt. 7. 15–21	Ps. 85 Song of Sol. 5. 2–end *or* 1 Macc. 3. 1–12 2 Pet. 1. 1–15	Ps. 80 (*or* 80. 1–8) 1 Kings 10. 1–13 Acts 13. 1–13	
G		1 Sam. 14. 24–46 Luke 23. 13–25	Ezek. 28. 1–19 Jas. 2. 1–13	
G		1 Sam. 15. 1–23 Luke 23. 26–43	Ezek. 33. 1–20 Jas. 2. 14–end	
G		1 Sam. ch. 16 Luke 23. 44–56a	Ezek. 33. 21–end Jas. ch. 3 *or First EP of The Transfiguration* (Ps. 99; 110) Exod. 24. 12–end John 12. 27–36a **W ct**	

			Sunday Principal Service Weekday Eucharist	Third Service Morning Prayer	Second Service Evening Prayer
6 Thursday	**THE TRANSFIGURATION OF OUR LORD**				
𝔚			Dan. 7. 9–10, 13–14 Ps. 97 2 Pet. 1. 16–19 Luke 9. 28–36	*MP*: Ps. 27; 150 Ecclus. 48. 1–10 *or* 1 Kings 19. 1–16 1 John 3. 1–3	*EP*: Ps. 72 Exod. 34. 29–end 2 Cor. ch. 3
7 Friday	*John Mason Neale, Priest, Hymn Writer, 1866*				
G			Nahum 2. 1, 3; 3. 1–3, 6–7 Ps. 137. 1–6 *or* Deut. 32. 35–36, 39, 41 Matt. 16. 24–28	Ps. 31 1 Sam. 17. 31–54 Luke 24. 13–35	Ps. 35 Ezek. 34. 17–end Jas. 4.13 – 5.6
8 Saturday	**Dominic, Priest, Founder of the Order of Preachers, 1221**				
Gw	Com. Religious *also* Ecclus. 39. 1–10	*or*	Hab. 1.12 – 2.4 Ps. 9. 7–11 Matt. 17. 14–20	Ps. 41; ***42***; 43 1 Sam. 17.55 – 18.16 Luke 24. 36–end	Ps. 45; ***46*** Ezek. 36. 16–36 Jas. 5. 7–end **ct**
9 Sunday	**THE NINTH SUNDAY AFTER TRINITY (Proper 14)**				
G	*Track 1* Gen. 37. 1–4, 12–28 Ps. 105. 1–6, 16–22, 45b (*or* 105. 1–10) Rom. 10. 5–15 Matt. 14. 22–33		*Track 2* 1 Kings 19. 9–18 Ps. 85. 8–13 Rom. 10. 5–15 Matt. 14. 22–33	Ps. 88 Song of Sol. 8. 5–7 *or* 1 Macc. 14. 4–15 2 Pet. 3. 8–13	Ps. 86 1 Kings 11.41 – 12.20 Acts 14. 8–20 *Gospel*: John 6. 35, 41–51
10 Monday	**Laurence, Deacon at Rome, Martyr, 258**				
Gr **DEL 19**	Com. Martyr *also* 2 Cor. 9. 6–10	*or*	Ezek. 1. 2–5, 24–end Ps. 148. 1–4, 12–13 Matt. 17. 22–end	Ps. 44 1 Sam. 19. 1–18 Acts 1. 1–14	Ps. ***47***; 49 Ezek. 37. 1–14 Mark 1. 1–13
11 Tuesday	**Clare of Assisi, Founder of the Minoresses (Poor Clares), 1253** *John Henry Newman, Priest, Tractarian, 1890*				
Gw	Com. Religious *esp.* Song of Sol. 8. 6–7	*or*	Ezek. 2.8 – 3.4 Ps. 119. 65–72 Matt. 18. 1–5, 10, 12–14	Ps. ***48***; 52 1 Sam. 20. 1–17 Acts 1. 15–end	Ps. 50 Ezek. 37. 15–end Mark 1. 14–20
12 Wednesday					
G			Ezek. 9. 1–7; 10. 18–22 Ps. 113 Matt. 18. 15–20	Ps. 119. 57–80 1 Sam. 20. 18–end Acts 2. 1–21	Ps. ***59***; 60; (67) Ezek. 39. 21–end Mark 1. 21–28
13 Thursday	**Jeremy Taylor, Bishop of Down and Connor, Teacher, 1667** *Florence Nightingale, Nurse, Social Reformer, 1910; Octavia Hill, Social Reformer, 1912*				
Gw	Com. Teacher *also* Titus 2. 7–8, 11–14	*or*	Ezek. 12. 1–12 Ps. 78. 58–64 Matt. 18.21 – 19.1	Ps. 56; ***57***; (63†) 1 Sam. 21.1 – 22.5 Acts 2. 22–36	Ps. 61; ***62***; 64 Ezek. 43. 1–12 Mark 1. 29–end
14 Friday	*Maximilian Kolbe, Friar, Martyr, 1941*				
G			Ezek. 16. 1–15, 60–end Ps. 118. 14–18 *or Canticle*: Song of Deliverance Matt. 19. 3–12	Ps. ***51***; 54 1 Sam. 22. 6–end Acts 2. 37–end	Ps. 38 Ezek. 44. 4–16 Mark 2. 1–12 *or First EP of The Blessed Virgin Mary* Ps. 72 Prov. 8. 22–31 John 19. 23–27 **W ct**

	Calendar and Holy Communion	Morning Prayer	Evening Prayer	NOTES
	THE TRANSFIGURATION OF OUR LORD			
𝔚	Exod. 24. 12–end Ps. 84. 1–7 1 John 3. 1–3 Mark 9. 2–7	(Ps. 27; 150) Ecclus. 48. 1–10 *or* 1 Kings 19. 1–16 2 Pet. 1. 16–19	(Ps. 72) Exod. 34. 29–end 2 Cor. ch. 3	
	The Name of Jesus			
Gw	Jer. 14. 7–9 Ps. 8 Acts 4. 8–12 Matt. 1. 20–23	1 Sam. 17. 31–54 Luke 24. 13–35	Ezek. 34. 17–end Jas. 4.13 – 5.6	
G		1 Sam. 17.55 – 18.16 Luke 24. 36–end	Ezek. 36. 16–36 Jas. 5. 7–end **ct**	
	THE NINTH SUNDAY AFTER TRINITY			
G	Num. 10.35 – 11.3 Ps. 95 1 Cor. 10. 1–13 Luke 16. 1–9 *or* Luke 15. 11–end	Ps. 88 Song of Sol. 8. 5–7 *or* 1 Macc. 14. 4–15 2 Pet. 3. 8–13	Ps. 86 1 Kings 11.41 – 12.20 Acts 14. 8–20	
	Laurence, Deacon at Rome, Martyr, 258			
Gr	Com. Martyr	1 Sam. 19. 1–18 Acts 1. 1–14	Ezek. 37. 1–14 Mark 1. 1–13	
G		1 Sam. 20. 1–17 Acts 1. 15–end	Ezek. 37. 15–end Mark 1. 14–20	
G		1 Sam. 20. 18–end Acts 2. 1–21	Ezek. 39. 21–end Mark 1. 21–28	
G		1 Sam. 21.1 – 22.5 Acts 2. 22–36	Ezek. 43. 1–12 Mark 1. 29–end	
G		1 Sam. 22. 6–end Acts 2. 37–end	Ezek. 44. 4–16 Mark 2. 1–12	

		Sunday Principal Service Weekday Eucharist	Third Service Morning Prayer	Second Service Evening Prayer
15 Saturday	**THE BLESSED VIRGIN MARY***			
W		Isa. 61. 10–end *or* Rev. 11.19 – 12.6, 10 Ps. 45. 10–end Gal. 4. 4–7 Luke 1. 46–55	*MP*: Ps. 98; 138; 147. 1–12 Isa. 7. 10–15 Luke 11. 27–28	*EP*: Ps. 132 Song of Sol. 2. 1–7 Acts 1. 6–14
	or, if The Blessed Virgin Mary is celebrated on 8 September:			
G		Ezek. 18. 1–11a, 13b, 30, 32 Ps. 51. 1–3, 15–17 Matt. 19. 13–15	Ps. 68 1 Sam. ch. 23 Acts 3. 1–10	Ps. 65; ***66*** Ezek. 47. 1–12 Mark 2. 13–22 **ct**
16 Sunday	**THE TENTH SUNDAY AFTER TRINITY (Proper 15)**			
G	*Track 1* Gen. 45. 1–15 Ps. 133 Rom. 11. 1–2a, 29–32 Matt. 15. [10–20] 21–28	*Track 2* Isa. 56. 1, 6–8 Ps. 67 Rom. 11. 1–2a, 29–32 Matt. 15. [10–20] 21–28	Ps. 92 Jonah ch. 1 *or* Ecclus. 3. 1–15 2 Pet. 3. 14–end	Ps. 90 (*or* 90. 1–12) 2 Kings 4. 1–37 Acts 16. 1–15 *Gospel*: John 6. 51–58
17 Monday				
G **DEL 20**		Ezek. 24. 15–24 Ps. 78. 1–8 Matt. 19. 16–22	Ps. 71 1 Sam. ch. 24 Acts 3. 11–end	Ps. ***72***; 75 Prov. 1. 1–19 Mark 2.23 – 3.6
18 Tuesday				
G		Ezek. 28. 1–10 Ps. 107. 1–3, 40, 43 Matt. 19. 23–end	Ps. 73 1 Sam. ch. 26 Acts 4. 1–12	Ps. 74 Prov. 1. 20–end Mark 3. 7–19a
19 Wednesday				
G		Ezek. 34. 1–11 Ps. 23 Matt. 20. 1–16	Ps. 77 1 Sam. 28. 3–end Acts 4. 13–31	Ps. 119. 81–104 Prov. ch. 2 Mark 3. 19b–end
20 Thursday	**Bernard, Abbot of Clairvaux, Teacher, 1153** *William and Catherine Booth, Founders of the Salvation Army, 1912 and 1890*			
Gw	Com. Religious *or* *esp.* Rev. 19. 5–9	Ezek. 36. 23–28 Ps. 51. 7–12 Matt. 22. 1–14	Ps. 78. 1–39† 1 Sam. ch. 31 Acts 4.32 – 5.11	Ps. 78. 40–end† Prov. 3. 1–26 Mark 4. 1–20
21 Friday				
G		Ezek. 37. 1–14 Ps. 107. 1–8 Matt. 22. 34–40	Ps. 55 2 Sam. ch. 1 Acts 5. 12–26	Ps. 69 Prov. 3.27 – 4.19 Mark 4. 21–34
22 Saturday				
G		Ezek. 43. 1–7 Ps. 85. 7–end Matt. 23. 1–12	Ps. ***76***; 79 2 Sam. 2. 1–11 Acts 5. 27–end	Ps. 81; ***84*** Prov. 6. 1–9 Mark 4. 35–end **ct**

*The Blessed Virgin Mary may be celebrated on 8 September instead of 15 August.

	Calendar and Holy Communion	Morning Prayer	Evening Prayer	NOTES
	To celebrate The Blessed Virgin Mary, see *Common Worship* provision.			
G		1 Sam. ch. 23 Acts 3. 1–10	Ezek. 47. 1–12 Mark 2. 13–22 **ct**	
	THE TENTH SUNDAY AFTER TRINITY			
G	Jer. 7. 9–15 Ps. 17. 1–8 1 Cor. 12. 1–11 Luke 19. 41–47a	Ps. 92 Jonah ch. 1 *or* Ecclus. 3. 1–15 2 Pet. 3. 14–end	Ps. 90 (*or* 90. 1–12) 2 Kings 4. 1–37 Acts 16. 1–15	
G		1 Sam. ch. 24 Acts 3. 11–end	Prov. 1. 1–19 Mark 2.23 - 3.6	
G		1 Sam. ch. 26 Acts 4. 1–12	Prov. 1. 20–end Mark 3. 7–19a	
G		1 Sam. 28. 3–end Acts 4. 13–31	Prov. ch. 2 Mark 3. 19b–end	
G		1 Sam. ch. 31 Acts 4.32 - 5.11	Prov. 3. 1–26 Mark 4. 1–20	
G		2 Sam. ch. 1 Acts 5. 12–26	Prov. 3.27 - 4.19 Mark 4. 21–34	
G		2 Sam. 2. 1–11 Acts 5. 27–end	Prov. 6. 1–9 Mark 4. 35–end **ct**	

		Sunday Principal Service Weekday Eucharist	Third Service Morning Prayer	Second Service Evening Prayer
23 Sunday	**THE ELEVENTH SUNDAY AFTER TRINITY (Proper 16)**			
G	*Track 1* Exod. 1.8 – 2.10 Ps. 124 Rom. 12. 1–8 Matt. 16. 13–20	*Track 2* Isa. 51. 1–6 Ps. 138 Rom. 12. 1–8 Matt. 16. 13–20	Ps. 104. 1–25 Jonah ch. 2 *or* Ecclus. 3. 17–29 Rev. ch. 1	Ps. 95 2 Kings 6. 8–23 Acts 17. 15–end *Gospel*: John 6. 56–69 *or First EP of Bartholomew* Ps. 97 Isa. 61. 1–9 2 Cor. 6. 1–10 **R ct**
24 Monday	**BARTHOLOMEW THE APOSTLE**			
R **DEL 21**	*The reading from Acts must be used as either the first or second reading at the Eucharist.*	Isa. 43. 8–13 *or* Acts 5. 12–16 Ps. 145. 1–7 Acts 5. 12–16 *or* 1 Cor. 4. 9–15 Luke 22. 24–30	*MP*: Ps. 86; 117 Gen. 28. 10–17 John 1. 43–end	*EP*: Ps. 91; 116 Ecclus. 39. 1–10 *or* Deut. 18. 15–19 Matt. 10. 1–22
25 Tuesday				
G		2 Thess. 2. 1–3a, 14–end Ps. 98 Matt. 23. 23–26	Ps. 87; ***89. 1–18*** 2 Sam. 5. 1–12 Acts 7. 1–16	Ps. 89. 19–end Prov. 8. 22–end Mark 5. 21–34
26 Wednesday				
G		2 Thess. 3. 6–10, 16–end Ps. 128 Matt. 23. 27–32	Ps. 119. 105–128 2 Sam. 6. 1–19 Acts 7. 17–43	Ps. ***91***; 93 Prov. ch. 9 Mark 5. 35–end
27 Thursday	**Monica, Mother of Augustine of Hippo, 387**			
Gw	Com. Saint *or* *also* Ecclus. 26. 1–3, 13–16	1 Cor. 1. 1–9 Ps. 145. 1–7 Matt. 24. 42–end	Ps. 90; **92** 2 Sam. 7. 1–17 Acts 7. 44–53	Ps. 94 Prov. 10. 1–12 Mark 6. 1–13
28 Friday	**Augustine, Bishop of Hippo, Teacher, 430**			
Gw	Com. Teacher *or* *esp.* Ecclus. 39. 1–10 *also* Rom. 13. 11–13	1 Cor. 1. 17–25 Ps. 33. 6–12 Matt. 25. 1–13	Ps. ***88***; (95) 2 Sam. 7. 18–end Acts 7.54 – 8.3	Ps. 102 Prov. 11. 1–12 Mark 6. 14–29
29 Saturday	**The Beheading of John the Baptist**			
Gr	Jer. 1. 4–10 *or* Ps. 11 Heb. 11.32 – 12.2 Matt. 14. 1–12	1 Cor. 1. 26–end Ps. 33. 12–15, 20–end Matt. 25. 14–30	Ps. 96; ***97***; 100 2 Sam. ch. 9 Acts 8. 4–25	Ps. 104 Prov. 12. 10–end Mark 6. 30–44 **ct**
30 Sunday	**THE TWELFTH SUNDAY AFTER TRINITY (Proper 17)**			
G	*Track 1* Exod. 3. 1–15 Ps. 105. 1–6, 23–26, 45b *or* Ps. 115 Rom. 12. 9–end Matt. 16. 21–end	*Track 2* Jer. 15. 15–21 Ps. 26. 1–8 Rom. 12. 9–end Matt. 16. 21–end	Ps. 107. 1–32 Jonah 3. 1–9 *or* Ecclus. 11. 7–28 (*or* 19–28) Rev. 3. 14–end	Ps. 105. 1–15 2 Kings 6. 24–25; 7. 3–end Acts 18. 1–16 *Gospel*: Mark 7. 1–8, 14–15, 21–23

	Calendar and Holy Communion	Morning Prayer	Evening Prayer	NOTES
	THE ELEVENTH SUNDAY AFTER TRINITY			
G	1 Kings 3. 5–15 Ps. 28 1 Cor. 15. 1–11 Luke 18. 9–14	Ps. 104. 1–25 Jonah ch. 2 *or* Ecclus. 3. 17–29 Rev. ch. 1	Ps. 95 2 Kings 6. 8–23 Acts 17. 15–end *or First EP of Bartholomew* Ps. 97 Isa. 61. 1–9 2 Cor. 6. 1–10 **R ct**	
	BARTHOLOMEW THE APOSTLE			
R	Gen. 28. 10–17 Ps. 15 Acts 5. 12–16 Luke 22. 24–30	(Ps. 86; 117) Isa. 43. 8–13 John 1. 43–end	(Ps. 91; 116) Ecclus. 39. 1–10 *or* Deut. 18. 15–19 Matt. 10. 1–22	
G		2 Sam. 5. 1–12 Acts 7. 1–16	Prov. 8. 22–end Mark 5. 21–34	
G		2 Sam. 6. 1–19 Acts 7. 17–43	Prov. ch. 9 Mark 5. 35–end	
G		2 Sam. 7. 1–17 Acts 7. 44–53	Prov. 10. 1–12 Mark 6. 1–13	
	Augustine, Bishop of Hippo, 430			
Gw	Com. Doctor	2 Sam. 7. 18–end Acts 7.54 – 8.3	Prov. 11. 1–12 Mark 6. 14–29	
	The Beheading of John the Baptist			
Gr	2 Chron. 24. 17–21 Ps. 92. 11–end Heb. 11.32 – 12.2 Matt. 14. 1–12	2 Sam. ch. 9 Acts 8. 4–25	Prov. 12. 10–end Mark 6. 30–44 **ct**	
	THE TWELFTH SUNDAY AFTER TRINITY			
G	Exod. 34. 29–end Ps. 34. 1–10 2 Cor. 3. 4–9 Mark 7. 31–37	Ps. 107. 1–32 Jonah 3. 1–9 *or* Ecclus. 11. 7–28 (*or* 19–28) Rev. 3. 14–end	Ps. 105. 1–15 2 Kings 6. 24–25; 7. 3–end Acts 18. 1–16	

		Sunday Principal Service Weekday Eucharist	Third Service Morning Prayer	Second Service Evening Prayer
31 Monday	**Aidan, Bishop of Lindisfarne, Missionary, 651**			
Gw **DEL 22**	Com. Missionary *or* *also* 1 Cor. 9. 16–19	1 Cor. 2. 1–5 Ps. 33. 12–21 Luke 4. 16–30	Ps. ***98***; 99; 101 2 Sam. ch. 11 Acts 8. 26–end	Ps. ***105***† (*or* 103) Prov. 14.31 – 15.17 Mark 6. 45–end

September 2020

		Sunday Principal Service Weekday Eucharist	Third Service Morning Prayer	Second Service Evening Prayer
1 Tuesday	*Giles of Provence, Hermit, c. 710*			
G		1 Cor. 2. 10b–end Ps. 145. 10–17 Luke 4. 31–37	Ps. ***106***† (*or* 103) 2 Sam. 12. 1–25 Acts 9. 1–19a	Ps. 107† Prov. 15. 18–end Mark 7. 1–13
2 Wednesday	*The Martyrs of Papua New Guinea, 1901 and 1942*			
G		1 Cor. 3. 1–9 Ps. 62 Luke 4. 38–end	Ps. 110; ***111***; 112 2 Sam. 15. 1–12 Acts 9. 19b–31	Ps. 119. 129–152 Prov. 18. 10–end Mark 7. 14–23
3 Thursday	**Gregory the Great, Bishop of Rome, Teacher, 604**			
Gw	Com. Teacher *or* *also* 1 Thess. 2. 3–8	1 Cor. 3. 18–end Ps. 24. 1–6 Luke 5. 1–11	Ps. 113; ***115*** 2 Sam. 15. 13–end Acts 9. 32–end	Ps. 114; ***116***; 117 Prov. 20. 1–22 Mark 7. 24–30
4 Friday	*Birinus, Bishop of Dorchester (Oxon), Apostle of Wessex, 650**			
G		1 Cor. 4. 1–5 Ps. 37. 3–8 Luke 5. 33–end	Ps. 139 2 Sam. 16. 1–14 Acts 10. 1–16	Ps. ***130***; 131; 137 Prov. 22. 1–16 Mark 7. 31–end
5 Saturday				
G		1 Cor. 4. 6–15 Ps. 145. 18–end Luke 6. 1–5	Ps. 120; ***121***; 122 2 Sam. 17. 1–23 Acts 10. 17–33	Ps. 118 Prov. 24. 23–end Mark 8. 1–10 **ct**
6 Sunday	**THE THIRTEENTH SUNDAY AFTER TRINITY (Proper 18)**			
G	*Track 1* Exod. 12. 1–14 Ps. 149 Rom. 13. 8–end Matt. 18. 15–20	*Track 2* Ezek. 33. 7–11 Ps. 119. 33–40 Rom. 13. 8–end Matt. 18. 15–20	Ps. 119. 17–32 Jonah 3.10 – 4.11 *or* Ecclus. 27.30 – 28.9 Rev. 8. 1–5	Ps. 108; [115] Ezek. 12.21 – 13.16 Acts 19. 1–20 *Gospel*: Mark 7. 24–end
7 Monday				
G **DEL 23**		1 Cor. 5. 1–8 Ps. 5. 5–9a Luke 6. 6–11	Ps. 123; 124; 125; ***126*** 2 Sam. 18. 1–18 Acts 10. 34–end	Ps. ***127***; 128; 129 Prov. 25. 1–14 Mark 8. 11–21
8 Tuesday	**The Birth of the Blessed Virgin Mary****			
Gw	Com. BVM *or*	1 Cor. 6. 1–11 Ps. 149. 1–5 Luke 6. 12–19	Ps. ***132***; 133 2 Sam. 18.19 – 19.8a Acts 11. 1–18	Ps. (134); ***135*** Prov. 25. 15–end Mark 8. 22–26
9 Wednesday	*Charles Fuge Lowder, Priest, 1880*			
G		1 Cor. 7. 25–31 Ps. 45. 11–end Luke 6. 20–26	Ps. 119. 153–end 2 Sam. 19. 8b–23 Acts 11. 19–end	Ps. 136 Prov. 26. 12–end Mark 8.27 – 9.1

*Cuthbert may be celebrated on 4 September instead of 20 March.
**The Blessed Virgin Mary may be celebrated on 8 September instead of 15 August.

	Calendar and Holy Communion	Morning Prayer	Evening Prayer
G		2 Sam. ch. 11 Acts 8. 26–end	Prov. 14.31 – 15.17 Mark 6. 45–end
	Giles of Provence, Hermit, c. 710		
Gw	Com. Abbot	2 Sam. 12. 1–25 Acts 9. 1–19a	Prov. 15. 18–end Mark 7. 1–13
G		2 Sam. 15. 1–12 Acts 9. 19b–31	Prov. 18. 10–end Mark 7. 14–23
G		2 Sam. 15. 13–end Acts 9. 32–end	Prov. 20. 1–22 Mark 7. 24–30
G		2 Sam. 16. 1–14 Acts 10. 1–16	Prov. 22. 1–16 Mark 7. 31–end
G		2 Sam. 17. 1–23 Acts 10. 17–33	Prov. 24. 23–end Mark 8. 1–10 **ct**
	THE THIRTEENTH SUNDAY AFTER TRINITY		
G	Lev. 19. 13–18 Ps. 74. 20–end Gal. 3. 16–22 *or* Heb. 13. 1–6 Luke 10. 23b–37	Ps. 119. 17–32 Jonah 3.10 – 4.11 *or* Ecclus. 27.30 – 28.9 Rev. 8. 1–5	Ps. 108; [115] Ezek. 12.21 – 13.16 Mark 7. 24–30
	Evurtius, Bishop of Orleans, 4th century		
Gw	Com. Bishop	2 Sam. 18. 1–18 Acts 10. 34–end	Prov. 25. 1–14 Mark 8. 11–21
	The Nativity of the Blessed Virgin Mary		
Gw	Gen. 3. 9–15 Ps. 45. 11–18 Rom. 5. 12–17 Luke 11. 27–28	2 Sam. 18.19 – 19.8a Acts 11. 1–18	Prov. 25. 15–end Mark 8. 22–26
G		2 Sam. 19. 8b–23 Acts 11. 19–end	Prov. 26. 12–end Mark 8.27 – 9.1

NOTES

		Sunday Principal Service Weekday Eucharist	Third Service Morning Prayer	Second Service Evening Prayer
10 Thursday				
G		1 Cor. 8. 1–7, 11–end Ps. 139. 1–9 Luke 6. 27–38	Ps. ***143***; 146 2 Sam. 19. 24–end Acts 12. 1–17	Ps. ***138***; 140; 141 Prov. 27. 1–22 Mark 9. 2–13
11 Friday				
G		1 Cor. 9. 16–19, 22–end Ps. 84. 1–6 Luke 6. 39–42	Ps. 142; ***144*** 2 Sam. 23. 1–7 Acts 12. 18–end	Ps. 145 Prov. 30. 1–9, 24–31 Mark 9. 14–29
12 Saturday				
G		1 Cor. 10. 14–22 Ps. 116. 10–end Luke 6. 43–end	Ps. 147 2 Sam. ch. 24 Acts 13. 1–12	Ps. ***148***; 149; 150 Prov. 31. 10–end Mark 9. 30–37 **ct**
13 Sunday	**THE FOURTEENTH SUNDAY AFTER TRINITY (Proper 19)**			
G	*Track 1* Exod. 14. 19–end Ps. 114 *or Canticle*: Exod. 15. 1b–11, 20–21 Rom. 14. 1–12 Matt. 18. 21–35	*Track 2* Gen. 50. 15–21 Ps. 103. 1–13 (*or* 103. 8–13) Rom. 14. 1–12 Matt. 18. 21–35	Ps. 119. 65–88 Isa. 44.24 – 45.8 Rev. 12. 1–12	Ps. 119. 41–48 [49–64] Ezek. 20. 1–8, 33–44 Acts 20. 17–end *Gospel*: Mark 8. 27–end *or First EP of Holy Cross Day* Ps. 66 Isa. 52.13 – 53.end Eph. 2. 11–end **R ct**
14 Monday	**HOLY CROSS DAY**			
R **DEL 24**		Num. 21. 4–9 Ps. 22. 23–28 Phil. 2. 6–11 John 3. 13–17	*MP*: Ps. 2; 8; 146 Gen. 3. 1–15 John 12. 27–36a	*EP*: Ps. 110; 150 Isa. 63. 1–16 1 Cor. 1. 18–25
15 Tuesday	**Cyprian, Bishop of Carthage, Martyr, 258**			
Gr	Com. Martyr *or* *esp.* 1 Pet. 4. 12–end *also* Matt. 18. 18–22	1 Cor. 12. 12–14, 27–end Ps. 100 Luke 7. 11–17	Ps. ***5***; 6; (8) 1 Kings 1.32 – 2.4, 10–12 Acts 13.44 – 14.7	Ps. ***9***; 10† Wisd. ch. 2 *or* 1 Chron. ch. 13 Mark 10. 1–16
16 Wednesday	**Ninian, Bishop of Galloway, Apostle of the Picts, c. 432** *Edward Bouverie Pusey, Priest, Tractarian, 1882*			
Gw	Com. Missionary *or* *esp.* Acts 13. 46–49 Mark 16. 15–end	1 Cor. 12.13b – 13.end Ps. 33. 1–12 Luke 7. 31–35	Ps. 119. 1–32 1 Kings ch. 3 Acts 14. 8–end	Ps. ***11***; 12; 13 Wisd. 3. 1–9 *or* 1 Chron. 15.1 – 16.3 Mark 10. 17–31
17 Thursday	**Hildegard, Abbess of Bingen, Visionary, 1179**			
Gw	Com. Religious *or* *also* 1 Cor. 2. 9–13 Luke 10. 21–24	1 Cor. 15. 1–11 Ps. 118. 1–2, 17–20 Luke 7. 36–end	Ps. 14; ***15***; 16 1 Kings 4.29 – 5.12 Acts 15. 1–21	Ps. 18† Wisd. 4. 7–end *or* 1 Chron. ch. 17 Mark 10. 32–34
18 Friday				
G		1 Cor. 15. 12–20 Ps. 17. 1–8 Luke 8. 1–3	Ps. 17; ***19*** 1 Kings 6. 1, 11–28 Acts 15. 22–35	Ps. 22 Wisd. 5. 1–16 *or* 1 Chron. 21.1 – 22.1 Mark 10. 35–45

	Calendar and Holy Communion	Morning Prayer	Evening Prayer
G		2 Sam. 19. 24–end Acts 12. 1–17	Prov. 27. 1–22 Mark 9. 2–13
G		2 Sam. 23. 1–7 Acts 12. 18–end	Prov. 30. 1–9, 24–31 Mark 9. 14–29
G		2 Sam. ch. 24 Acts 13. 1–12	Prov. 31. 10–end Mark 9. 30–37 ct
	THE FOURTEENTH SUNDAY AFTER TRINITY		
G	2 Kings 5. 9–16 Ps. 118. 1–9 Gal. 5. 16–24 Luke 17. 11–19	Ps. 119. 65–88 Isa. 44.24 – 45.8 Rev. 12. 1–12	Ps. 119. 41–48 [49–64] Ezek. 20. 1–8, 33–44 Acts 20. 17–end
	HOLY CROSS DAY To celebrate Holy Cross as a festival, see *Common Worship* provision.		
Gr	Num. 21. 4–9 Ps. 67 1 Cor. 1. 17–25 John 12. 27–33	1 Kings 1. 5–31 Acts 13. 13–43	Wisd. ch. 1 *or* 1 Chron. 10.1 – 11.9 Mark 9. 38–end
G		1 Kings 1.32 – 2.4, 10–12 Acts 13.44 – 14.7	Wisd. ch. 2 *or* 1 Chron. ch. 13 Mark 10. 1–16
	Ember Day		
G	Ember CEG	1 Kings ch. 3 Acts 14. 8–end	Wisd. 3. 1–9 *or* 1 Chron. 15.1 – 16.3 Mark 10. 17–31
	Lambert, Bishop of Maastricht, Martyr, 709		
Gr	Com. Martyr	1 Kings 4.29 – 5.12 Acts 15. 1–21	Wisd. 4. 7–end *or* 1 Chron. ch. 17 Mark 10. 32–34
	Ember Day		
G	Ember CEG	1 Kings 6. 1, 11–28 Acts 15. 22–35	Wisd. 5. 1–16 *or* 1 Chron. 21.1 – 22.1 Mark 10. 35–45

NOTES

		Sunday Principal Service Weekday Eucharist	Third Service Morning Prayer	Second Service Evening Prayer
19 Saturday	*Theodore of Tarsus, Archbishop of Canterbury, 690*			
G		1 Cor. 15. 35–37, 42–49 Ps. 30. 1–5 Luke 8. 4–15	Ps. 20; 21; ***23*** 1 Kings 8. 1–30 Acts 15.36 – 16.5	Ps. ***24***; 25 Wisd. 5.17 – 6.11 *or* 1 Chron. 22. 2–end Mark 10. 46–end **ct**
20 Sunday	**THE FIFTEENTH SUNDAY AFTER TRINITY (Proper 20)**			
G	*Track 1* Exod. 16. 2–15 Ps. 105. 1–6, 37–end (*or* 105. 37–end) Phil. 1. 21–end Matt. 20. 1–16	*Track 2* Jonah 3.10 – 4.end Ps. 145. 1–8 Phil. 1. 21–end Matt. 20. 1–16	Ps. 119. 153–end Isa. 45. 9–22 Rev. 14. 1–5	Ps. 119. 113–136 (*or* 119. 121–128) Ezek. 33.23, 30 – 34.10 Acts 26. 1, 9–25 *Gospel*: Mark 9. 30–37 *or First EP of Matthew* Ps. 34 Isa. 33. 13–17 Matt. 6. 19–end **R ct**
21 Monday	**MATTHEW, APOSTLE AND EVANGELIST**			
R **DEL 25**		Prov. 3. 13–18 Ps. 119. 65–72 2 Cor. 4. 1–6 Matt. 9. 9–13	*MP*: Ps. 49; 117 1 Kings 19. 15–end 2 Tim. 3. 14–end	*EP*: Ps. 119. 33–40, 89–96 Eccles. 5. 4–12 Matt. 19. 16–end
22 Tuesday				
G		Prov. 21. 1–6, 10–13 Ps. 119. 1–8 Luke 8. 19–21	Ps. 32; ***36*** 1 Kings 8.63 – 9.9 Acts 16. 25–end	Ps. 33 Wisd. 7. 1–14 *or* 1 Chron. 28. 11–end Mark 11. 12–26
23 Wednesday	Ember Day*			
G *or* **R**		Prov. 30. 5–9 Ps. 119. 105–112 Luke 9. 1–6	Ps. 34 1 Kings 10. 1–25 Acts 17. 1–15	Ps. 119. 33–56 Wisd. 7.15 – 8.4 *or* 1 Chron. 29. 1–9 Mark 11. 27–end
24 Thursday				
G		Eccles. 1. 2–11 Ps. 90. 1–6 Luke 9. 7–9	Ps. 37† 1 Kings 11. 1–13 Acts 17. 16–end	Ps. 39; ***40*** Wisd. 8. 5–18 *or* 1 Chron. 29. 10–20 Mark 12. 1–12
25 Friday	**Lancelot Andrewes, Bishop of Winchester, Spiritual Writer, 1626** *Sergei of Radonezh, Russian Monastic Reformer, Teacher, 1392* Ember Day*			
Gw *or* **Rw**	Com. Bishop *or* *esp.* Isa. 6. 1–8	Eccles. 3. 1–11 Ps. 144. 1–4 Luke 9. 18–22	Ps. 31 1 Kings 11. 26–end Acts 18. 1–21	Ps. 35 Wisd. 8.21 – 9.end *or* 1 Chron. 29. 21–end Mark 12. 13–17
26 Saturday	*Wilson Carlile, Founder of the Church Army, 1942* Ember Day*			
G *or* **R**		Eccles. 11.9 – 12.8 Ps. 90. 1–2, 12–end Luke 9. 43b–45	Ps. 41; ***42***; 43 1 Kings 12. 1–24 Acts 18.22 – 19.7	Ps. 45; ***46*** Wisd. 10.15 – 11.10 *or* 2 Chron. 1. 1–13 Mark 12. 18–27 **ct**

*For Ember Day provision, see p. 11.

	Calendar and Holy Communion	Morning Prayer	Evening Prayer	NOTES
	Ember Day			
G	Ember CEG	1 Kings 8. 1-30 Acts 15.36 - 16.5	Wisd. 5.17 - 6.11 *or* 1 Chron. 22. 2-end Mark 10. 46-end **ct**	
	THE FIFTEENTH SUNDAY AFTER TRINITY			
G	Josh. 24. 14-25 Ps. 92. 1-6 Gal. 6. 11-end Matt. 6. 24-end	Ps. 119. 153-end Isa. 45. 9-22 Rev. 14. 1-5	Ps. 119. 113-136 (*or* 119. 121-128) Ezek. 33.23, 30 - 34.10 Acts 26. 1, 9-25 *or First EP of Matthew* Ps. 34 Prov. 3. 3-18 Matt. 6. 19-end **R ct**	
	MATTHEW, APOSTLE AND EVANGELIST			
R	Isa. 33. 13-17 Ps. 119. 65-72 2 Cor. 4. 1-6 Matt. 9. 9-13	(Ps. 49; 117) 1 Kings 19. 15-end 2 Tim. 3. 14-end	(Ps. 119. 33-40, 89-96) Eccles. 5. 4-12 Matt. 19. 16-end	
G		1 Kings 8.63 - 9.9 Acts 16. 25-end	Wisd. 7. 1-14 *or* 1 Chron. 28. 11-end Mark 11. 12-26	
G		1 Kings 10. 1-25 Acts 17. 1-15	Wisd. 7.15 - 8.4 *or* 1 Chron. 29. 1-9 Mark 11. 27-end	
G		1 Kings 11. 1-13 Acts 17. 16-end	Wisd. 8. 5-18 *or* 1 Chron. 29. 10-20 Mark 12. 1-12	
G		1 Kings 11. 26-end Acts 18. 1-21	Wisd. 8.21 - 9.end *or* 1 Chron. 29. 21-end Mark 12. 13-17	
	Cyprian, Bishop of Carthage, Martyr, 258			
Gr	Com. Martyr	1 Kings 12. 1-24 Acts 18.22 - 19.7	Wisd. 10.15 - 11.10 *or* 2 Chron. 1. 1-13 Mark 12. 18-27 **ct**	

		Sunday Principal Service Weekday Eucharist	Third Service Morning Prayer	Second Service Evening Prayer
27 Sunday	**THE SIXTEENTH SUNDAY AFTER TRINITY (Proper 21)**			
G	*Track 1* Exod. 17. 1–7 Ps. 78. 1–4, 12–16 (*or* 78. 1–7) Phil. 2. 1–13 Matt. 21. 23–32	*Track 2* Ezek. 18. 1–4, 25–end Ps. 25. 1–8 Phil. 2. 1–13 Matt. 21. 23–32	Ps. 125; 126; 127 Isa. 48. 12–21 Luke 11. 37–54	Ps. [120; 123]; 124 Ezek. 37. 15–end 1 John 2. 22–end *Gospel*: Mark 9. 38–end
28 Monday				
G **DEL 26**		Job 1. 6–end Ps. 17. 1–11 Luke 9. 46–50	Ps. 44 1 Kings 12.25 – 13.10 Acts 19. 8–20	Ps. ***47***; 49 Wisd. 11.21 – 12.2 *or* 2 Chron. 2. 1–16 Mark 12. 28–34 *or First EP of Michael and All Angels* Ps. 91 2 Kings 6. 8–17 Matt. 18. 1–6, 10 **W ct**
29 Tuesday	**MICHAEL AND ALL ANGELS**			
W	*The reading from Revelation must be used as either the first or second reading at the Eucharist.*	Gen. 28. 10–17 *or* Rev. 12. 7–12 Ps. 103. 19–end Rev. 12. 7–12 *or* Heb. 1. 5–end John 1. 47–end	*MP*: Ps. 34; 150 Tobit 12. 6–end *or* Dan. 12. 1–4 Acts 12. 1–11	*EP*: Ps. 138; 148 Dan. 10. 4–end Rev. ch. 5
30 Wednesday	*Jerome, Translator of the Scriptures, Teacher, 420*			
G		Job 9. 1–12, 14–16 Ps. 88. 1–6, 11 Luke 9. 57–end	Ps. 119. 57–80 1 Kings ch. 17 Acts 20. 1–16	Ps. ***59***; 60; (67) Wisd. 13. 1–9 *or* 2 Chron. ch. 5 Mark 13. 1–13

October 2020

1 Thursday	*Remigius, Bishop of Rheims, Apostle of the Franks, 533; Anthony Ashley Cooper, Earl of Shaftesbury, Social Reformer, 1885*			
G		Job 19. 21–27a Ps. 27. 13–16 Luke 10. 1–12	Ps. 56; ***57***; (63†) 1 Kings 18. 1–20 Acts 20. 17–end	Ps. 61; ***62***; 64 Wisd. 16.15 – 17.1 *or* 2 Chron. 6. 1–21 Mark 13. 14–23
2 Friday				
G		Job 38. 1, 12–21; 40. 3–5 Ps. 139. 6–11 Luke 10. 13–16	Ps. ***51***; 54 1 Kings 18. 21–end Acts 21. 1–16	Ps. 38 Wisd. 18. 6–19 *or* 2 Chron. 6. 22–end Mark 13. 24–31
3 Saturday	*George Bell, Bishop of Chichester, Ecumenist, Peacemaker, 1958*			
G		Job 42. 1–3, 6, 12–end Ps. 119. 169–end Luke 10. 17–24	Ps. 68 1 Kings ch. 19 Acts 21. 17–36	Ps. 65; **66** Wisd. ch. 19 *or* 2 Chron. ch. 7 Mark 13. 32–end **ct** *or First EP of Dedication Festival* Ps. 24 2 Chron. 7. 11–16 John 4. 19–29 **𝔚 ct**

	Calendar and Holy Communion	Morning Prayer	Evening Prayer	NOTES
	THE SIXTEENTH SUNDAY AFTER TRINITY			
G	1 Kings 17. 17–end Ps. 102. 12–17 Eph. 3. 13–end Luke 7. 11–17	Ps. 125; 126; 127 Isa. 48. 12–21 Luke 11. 37–54	Ps. [120; 123]; 124 Ezek. 37. 15–end 1 John 2. 22–end	
G		1 Kings 12.25 – 13.10 Acts 19. 8–20	Wisd. 11.21 – 12.2 *or* 2 Chron. 2. 1–16 Mark 12. 28–34 *or First EP of Michael and All Angels* (Ps. 91) 2 Kings 6. 8–17 John 1. 47–51 **W ct**	
	MICHAEL AND ALL ANGELS			
W	Dan. 10. 10–19a Ps. 103. 17–22 Rev. 12. 7–12 Matt. 18. 1–10	(Ps. 34; 150) Tobit 12. 6–end *or* Dan. 12. 1–4 Acts 12. 1–11	(Ps. 138; 148) Gen. 28. 10–17 Rev. ch. 5	
	Jerome, Translator of the Scriptures, Teacher, 420			
Gw	Com. Doctor	1 Kings ch. 17 Acts 20. 1–16	Wisd. 13. 1–9 *or* 2 Chron. ch. 5 Mark 13. 1–13	
	Remigius, Bishop of Rheims, Apostle of the Franks, 533			
Gw	Com. Bishop	1 Kings 18. 1–20 Acts 20. 17–end	Wisd. 16.15 – 17.1 *or* 2 Chron. 6. 1–21 Mark 13. 14–23	
G		1 Kings 18. 21–end Acts 21. 1–16	Wisd. 18. 6–19 *or* 2 Chron. 6. 22–end Mark 13. 24–31	
G		1 Kings ch. 19 Acts 21. 17–36	Wisd. ch. 19 *or* 2 Chron. ch. 7 Mark 13. 32–end **ct** *or First EP of Dedication Festival* Ps. 24 2 Chron. 7. 11–16 John 4. 19–29 **𝔚 ct**	

		Sunday Principal Service Weekday Eucharist	Third Service Morning Prayer	Second Service Evening Prayer
4 Sunday	**THE SEVENTEENTH SUNDAY AFTER TRINITY (Proper 22)**			
G	*Track 1* Exod. 20. 1–4, 7–9, 12–20 Ps. 19 (*or* 19. 7–end) Phil. 3. 4b–14 Matt. 21. 33–end	*Track 2* Isa. 5. 1–7 Ps. 80. 9–17 Phil. 3. 4b–14 Matt. 21. 33–end	Ps. 128; 129; 134 Isa. 49. 13–23 Luke 12. 1–12	Ps. 136 (*or* 136. 1–9) Prov. 2. 1–11 1 John 2. 1–17 *Gospel*: Mark 10. 2–16
	or, if observed as Dedication Festival:			
𝔴		1 Kings 8. 22–30 *or* Rev. 21. 9–14 Ps. 122 Heb. 12. 18–24 Matt. 21. 12–16	*MP*: Ps. 48; 150 Hag. 2. 6–9 Heb. 10. 19–25	*EP*: Ps. 132 Jer. 7. 1–11 1 Cor. 3. 9–17 *Gospel*: Luke 19. 1–10
5 Monday				
G **DEL 27**		Gal. 1. 6–12 Ps. 111. 1–6 Luke 10. 25–37	Ps. 71 1 Kings ch. 21 Acts 21.37 - 22.21	Ps. ***72***; 75 1 Macc. 1. 1–19 *or* 2 Chron. 9. 1–12 Mark 14. 1–11
6 Tuesday	**William Tyndale, Translator of the Scriptures, Reformation Martyr, 1536**			
Gr	Com. Martyr *or* *also* Prov. 8. 4–11 2 Tim. 3. 12–end	Gal. 1. 13–end Ps. 139. 1–9 Luke 10. 38–end	Ps. 73 1 Kings 22. 1–28 Acts 22.22 - 23.11	Ps. 74 1 Macc. 1. 20–40 *or* 2 Chron. 10.1 - 11.4 Mark 14. 12–25
7 Wednesday				
G		Gal. 2. 1–2, 7–14 Ps. 117 Luke 11. 1–4	Ps. 77 1 Kings 22. 29–45 Acts 23. 12–end	Ps. 119. 81–104 1 Macc. 1. 41–end *or* 2 Chron. ch. 12 Mark 14. 26–42
8 Thursday				
G		Gal. 3. 1–5 *Canticle*: Benedictus Luke 11. 5–13	Ps. 78. 1–39† 2 Kings 1. 2–17 Acts 24. 1–23	Ps. 78. 40–end† 1 Macc. 2. 1–28 *or* 2 Chron. 13.1 - 14.1 Mark 14. 43–52
9 Friday	*Denys, Bishop of Paris, and his Companions, Martyrs, c. 250; Robert Grosseteste, Bishop of Lincoln, Philosopher, Scientist, 1253*			
G		Gal. 3. 7–14 Ps. 111. 4–end Luke 11. 15–26	Ps. 55 2 Kings 2. 1–18 Acts 24.24 - 25.12	Ps. 69 1 Macc. 2. 29–48 *or* 2 Chron. 14. 2–end Mark 14. 53–65
10 Saturday	**Paulinus, Bishop of York, Missionary, 644** *Thomas Traherne, Poet, Spiritual Writer, 1674*			
Gw	Com. Missionary *or* *esp.* Matt. 28. 16–end	Gal. 3. 22–end Ps. 105. 1–7 Luke 11. 27–28	Ps. ***76***; 79 2 Kings 4. 1–37 Acts 25. 13–end	Ps. 81; ***84*** 1 Macc. 2. 49–end *or* 2 Chron. 15. 1–15 Mark 14. 66–end **ct**

	Calendar and Holy Communion	Morning Prayer	Evening Prayer	NOTES
	THE SEVENTEENTH SUNDAY AFTER TRINITY			
G	Prov. 25. 6–14 Ps. 33. 6–12 Eph. 4. 1–6 Luke 14. 1–11	Ps. 128; 129; 134 Isa. 49. 13–23 Luke 12. 1–12	Ps. 136 (*or* 136. 1–9) Prov. 2. 1–11 1 John 2. 1–17	
	or, if observed as Dedication Festival:			
𝔚	2 Chron. 7. 11–16 Ps. 122 1 Cor. 3. 9–17 *or* 1 Pet. 2. 1–5 Matt. 21. 12–16 *or* John 10. 22–29	Ps. 48; 150 Hag. 2. 6–9 Heb. 10. 19–25	Ps. 132 Jer. 7. 1–11 Luke 19. 1–10	
G		1 Kings ch. 21 Acts 21.37 – 22.21	1 Macc. 1. 1–19 *or* 2 Chron. 9. 1–12 Mark 14. 1–11	
	Faith of Aquitaine, Martyr, *c.* 304			
Gr	Com. Virgin Martyr	1 Kings 22. 1–28 Acts 22.22 – 23.11	1 Macc. 1. 20–40 *or* 2 Chron. 10.1 – 11.4 Mark 14. 12–25	
G		1 Kings 22. 29–45 Acts 23. 12–end	1 Macc. 1. 41–end *or* 2 Chron. ch. 12 Mark 14. 26–42	
G		2 Kings 1. 2–17 Acts 24. 1–23	1 Macc. 2. 1–28 *or* 2 Chron. 13.1 – 14.1 Mark 14. 43–52	
	Denys, Bishop of Paris, Martyr, *c.* 250			
Gr	Com. Martyr	2 Kings 2. 1–18 Acts 24.24 – 25.12	1 Macc. 2. 29–48 *or* 2 Chron. 14. 2–end Mark 14. 53–65	
G		2 Kings 4. 1–37 Acts 25. 13–end	1 Macc. 2. 49–end *or* 2 Chron. 15. 1–15 Mark 14. 66–end **ct**	

		Sunday Principal Service Weekday Eucharist	Third Service Morning Prayer	Second Service Evening Prayer
11 Sunday	**THE EIGHTEENTH SUNDAY AFTER TRINITY (Proper 23)**			
G	*Track 1* Exod. 32. 1–14 Ps. 106. 1–6, 19–23 (*or* 106. 1–6) Phil. 4. 1–9 Matt. 22. 1–14	*Track 2* Isa. 25. 1–9 Ps. 23 Phil. 4. 1–9 Matt. 22. 1–14	Ps. 138; 141 Isa. 50. 4–10 Luke 13. 22–30	Ps. 139. 1–18 (*or* 139. 1–11) Prov. 3. 1–18 1 John 3. 1–15 *Gospel*: Mark 10. 17–31
12 Monday	**Wilfrid of Ripon, Bishop, Missionary, 709** *Elizabeth Fry, Prison Reformer, 1845; Edith Cavell, Nurse, 1915*			
Gw **DEL 28**	Com. Missionary *or* *esp.* Luke 5. 1–11 *also* 1 Cor. 1. 18–25	Gal. 4. 21–24, 26–27, 31; 5. 1 Ps. 113 Luke 11. 29–32	Ps. ***80***; 82 2 Kings ch. 5 Acts 26. 1–23	Ps. ***85***; 86 1 Macc. 3. 1–26 *or* 2 Chron. 17. 1–12 Mark 15. 1–15
13 Tuesday	**Edward the Confessor, King of England, 1066**			
Gw	Com. Saint *or* *also* 2 Sam. 23. 1–5 1 John 4. 13–16	Gal. 5. 1–6 Ps. 119. 41–48 Luke 11. 37–41	Ps. 87; ***89. 1–18*** 2 Kings 6. 1–23 Acts 26. 24–end	Ps. 89. 19–end 1 Macc. 3. 27–41 *or* 2 Chron. 18. 1–27 Mark 15. 16–32
14 Wednesday				
G		Gal. 5. 18–end Ps. 1 Luke 11. 42–46	Ps. 119. 105–128 2 Kings 9. 1–16 Acts 27. 1–26	Ps. ***91***; 93 1 Macc. 3. 42–end *or* 2 Chron. 18.28 – 19.end Mark 15. 33–41
15 Thursday	**Teresa of Avila, Teacher, 1582**			
Gw	Com. Teacher *or* *also* Rom. 8. 22–27	Eph. 1. 1–10 Ps. 98. 1–4 Luke 11. 47–end	Ps. 90; **92** 2 Kings 9. 17–end Acts 27. 27–end	Ps. 94 1 Macc. 4. 1–25 *or* 2 Chron. 20. 1–23 Mark 15. 42–end
16 Friday	*Nicholas Ridley, Bishop of London, and Hugh Latimer, Bishop of Worcester, Reformation Martyrs, 1555*			
G		Eph. 1. 11–14 Ps. 33. 1–6, 12 Luke 12. 1–7	Ps. ***88***; (95) 2 Kings 12. 1–19 Acts 28. 1–16	Ps. 102 1 Macc. 4. 26–35 *or* 2 Chron. 22.10 – 23.end Mark 16. 1–8
17 Saturday	**Ignatius, Bishop of Antioch, Martyr, c. 107**			
Gr	Com. Martyr *or* *also* Phil. 3. 7–12 John 6. 52–58	Eph. 1. 15–end Ps. 8 Luke 12. 8–12	Ps. 96; **97**; 100 2 Kings 17. 1–23 Acts 28. 17–end	Ps. 104 1 Macc. 4. 36–end *or* 2 Chron. 24. 1–22 Mark 16. 9–end **ct** *or First EP of Luke* Ps. 33 Hos. 6. 1–3 2 Tim. 3. 10–end **R ct**
18 Sunday	**LUKE THE EVANGELIST** (or transferred to 19 October)			
R		Isa. 35. 3–6 *or* Acts 16. 6–12a Ps. 147. 1–7 2 Tim. 4. 5–17 Luke 10. 1–9	*MP*: Ps. 145; 146 Isa. ch. 55 Luke 1. 1–4	*EP*: Ps. 103 Ecclus. 38. 1–14 *or* Isa. 61. 1–6 Col. 4. 7–end

(*continued overleaf*)

	Calendar and Holy Communion	Morning Prayer	Evening Prayer	NOTES
	THE EIGHTEENTH SUNDAY AFTER TRINITY			
G	Deut. 6. 4–9 Ps. 122 1 Cor. 1. 4–8 Matt. 22. 34–end	Ps. 138; 141 Isa. 50. 4–10 Luke 13. 22–30	Ps. 139. 1–18 (*or* 139. 1–11) Prov. 3. 1–18 1 John 3. 1–15	
G		2 Kings ch. 5 Acts 26. 1–23	1 Macc. 3. 1–26 *or* 2 Chron. 17. 1–12 Mark 15. 1–15	
	Edward the Confessor, King of England, 1066, translated 1163			
Gw	Com. Saint	2 Kings 6. 1–23 Acts 26. 24–end	1 Macc. 3. 27–41 *or* 2 Chron. 18. 1–27 Mark 15. 16–32	
G		2 Kings 9. 1–16 Acts 27. 1–26	1 Macc. 3. 42–end *or* 2 Chron. 18.28 – 19.end Mark 15. 33–41	
G		2 Kings 9. 17–end Acts 27. 27–end	1 Macc. 4. 1–25 *or* 2 Chron. 20. 1–23 Mark 15. 42–end	
G		2 Kings 12. 1–19 Acts 28. 1–16	1 Macc. 4. 26–35 *or* 2 Chron. 22.10 – 23.end Mark 16. 1–8	
	Etheldreda, Abbess of Ely, 679			
Gw	Com. Abbess	2 Kings 17. 1–23 Acts 28. 17–end	1 Macc. 4. 36–end *or* 2 Chron. 24. 1–22 Mark 16. 9–end **ct** *or First EP of Luke* (Ps. 33) Hos. 6. 1–3 2 Tim. 3. 10–end **R ct**	
	LUKE THE EVANGELIST (or transferred to 19 October)			
R	Isa. 35. 3–6 Ps. 147. 1–6 2 Tim. 4. 5–15 Luke 10. 1–9 *or* Luke 7. 36–end	Ps. 145; 146 Isa. ch. 55 Luke 1. 1–4	Ps. 103 Ecclus. 38. 1–14 *or* Isa. 61. 1–6 Col. 4. 7–end	

		Sunday Principal Service Weekday Eucharist	Third Service Morning Prayer	Second Service Evening Prayer
18 Sunday	**LUKE THE EVANGELIST** *(continued)*			
	or, for The Nineteenth Sunday after Trinity (Proper 24):			
G	*Track 1* Exod. 33. 12–end Ps. 99 1 Thess. 1. 1–10 Matt. 22. 15–22	*Track 2* Isa. 45. 1–7 Ps. 96. 1–9 [10–13] 1 Thess. 1. 1–10 Matt. 22. 15–22	Ps. 145; 149 Isa. 54. 1–14 Luke 13. 31–end	Ps. 142 [143. 1–11] Prov. 4. 1–18 1 John 3.16 - 4.6 *Gospel*: Mark 10. 35–45
19 Monday	**Henry Martyn, Translator of the Scriptures, Missionary in India and Persia, 1812**			
Gw **DEL 29**	Com. Missionary *or* *esp.* Mark 16. 15–end *also* Isa. 55. 6–11	Eph. 2. 1–10 Ps. 100 Luke 12. 13–21	Ps. ***98***; 99; 101 2 Kings 17. 24–end Phil. 1. 1–11	Ps. ***105***† (*or* 103) 1 Macc. 6. 1–17 *or* 2 Chron. 26. 1–21 John 13. 1–11
20 Tuesday				
G		Eph. 2. 12–end Ps. 85. 7–end Luke 12. 35–38	Ps. ***106***† (*or* 103) 2 Kings 18. 1–12 Phil. 1. 12–end	Ps. 107† 1 Macc. 6. 18–47 *or* 2 Chron. ch. 28 John 13. 12–20
21 Wednesday				
G		Eph. 3. 2–12 Ps. 98 Luke 12. 39–48	Ps. 110; ***111***; 112 2 Kings 18. 13–end Phil. 2. 1–13	Ps. 119. 129–152 1 Macc. 7. 1–20 *or* 2 Chron. 29. 1–19 John 13. 21–30
22 Thursday				
G		Eph. 3. 14–end Ps. 33. 1–6 Luke 12. 49–53	Ps. 113; ***115*** 2 Kings 19. 1–19 Phil. 2. 14–end	Ps. 114; ***116***; 117 1 Macc. 7. 21–end *or* 2 Chron. 29. 20–end John 13. 31–end
23 Friday				
G		Eph. 4. 1–6 Ps. 24. 1–6 Luke 12. 54–end	Ps. 139 2 Kings 19. 20–36 Phil. 3.1 - 4.1	Ps. ***130***; 131; 137 1 Macc. 9. 1–22 *or* 2 Chron. ch. 30 John 14. 1–14
24 Saturday				
G		Eph. 4. 7–16 Ps. 122 Luke 13. 1–9	Ps. 120; ***121***; 122 2 Kings ch. 20 Phil. 4. 2–end	Ps. 118 1 Macc. 13. 41–end; 14. 4–15 *or* 2 Chron. 32. 1–22 John 14. 15–end **ct**
25 Sunday	**THE LAST SUNDAY AFTER TRINITY (Proper 25)***			
G	*Track 1* Deut. 34. 1–12 Ps. 90. 1–6, 13–end (*or* 90. 1–6) 1 Thess. 2. 1–8 Matt. 22. 34–end	*Track 2* Lev. 19. 1–2, 15–18 Ps. 1 1 Thess. 2. 1–8 Matt. 22. 34–end	Ps. 119. 137–152 Isa. 59. 9–20 Luke 14. 1–14	Ps. 119. 89–104 Eccles. chs 11 and 12 2 Tim. 2. 1–7 *Gospel*: Mark 12. 28–34
	or, if being observed as Bible Sunday:			
G		Neh. 8. 1–4a [5–6] 8–12 Ps. 119. 9–16 Col. 3. 12–17 Matt. 24. 30–35	Ps. 119. 137–152 Deut. 17. 14–15, 18–end John 5. 36b–end	Ps. 119. 89–104 Isa. 55. 1–11 Luke 4. 14–30

*If the Dedication Festival is kept on this Sunday, use the provision given on 3 and 4 October.

	Calendar and Holy Communion	Morning Prayer	Evening Prayer	NOTES
	LUKE THE EVANGELIST			
	or, for The Nineteenth Sunday after Trinity:			
G	Gen. 18. 23–32 Ps. 141. 1–9 Eph. 4. 17–end Matt. 9. 1–8	Ps. 138 Isa. 54. 1–14 Luke 13. 31–end	Ps. 142 [143. 1–11] Prov. 4. 1–18 1 John 3.16 - 4.6	
G		2 Kings 17. 24–end Phil. 1. 1–11	1 Macc. 6. 1–17 *or* 2 Chron. 26. 1–21 John 13. 1–11	
G		2 Kings 18. 1–12 Phil. 1. 12–end	1 Macc. 6. 18–47 *or* 2 Chron. ch. 28 John 13. 12–20	
G		2 Kings 18. 13–end Phil. 2. 1–13	1 Macc. 7. 1–20 *or* 2 Chron. 29. 1–19 John 13. 21–30	
G		2 Kings 19. 1–19 Phil. 2. 14–end	1 Macc. 7. 21–end *or* 2 Chron. 29. 20–end John 13. 31–end	
G		2 Kings 19. 20–36 Phil. 3.1 - 4.1	1 Macc. 9. 1–22 *or* 2 Chron. ch. 30 John 14. 1–14	
G		2 Kings ch. 20 Phil. 4. 2–end	1 Macc. 13. 41–end; 14. 4–15 *or* 2 Chron. 32. 1–22 John 14. 15–end **ct**	
	THE TWENTIETH SUNDAY AFTER TRINITY			
G	Prov. 9. 1–6 Ps. 145. 15–end Eph. 5. 15–21 Matt. 22. 1–14	Ps. 119. 137–152 Isa. 59. 9–20 Luke 14. 11–24	Ps. 119. 89–104 Eccles. chs 11 and 12 2 Tim. 2. 1–7	

		Sunday Principal Service Weekday Eucharist	Third Service Morning Prayer	Second Service Evening Prayer
26 Monday	**Alfred the Great, King of the West Saxons, Scholar, 899** *Cedd, Abbot of Lastingham, Bishop of the East Saxons, 664**			
Gw **DEL 30**	Com. Saint *or* *also* 2 Sam. 23. 1–5 John 18. 33–37	Eph. 4.32 – 5.8 Ps. 1 Luke 13. 10–17	Ps. 123; 124; 125; ***126*** 2 Kings 21. 1–18 1 Tim. 1. 1–17	Ps. ***127***; 128; 129 2 Macc. 4. 7–17 *or* 2 Chron. 33. 1–13 John 15. 1–11
27 Tuesday				
G		Eph. 5. 21–end Ps. 128 Luke 13. 18–21	Ps. ***132***; 133 2 Kings 22.1 – 23.3 1 Tim. 1.18 – 2.end	Ps. (134); ***135*** 2 Macc. 6. 12–end *or* 2 Chron. 34. 1–18 John 15. 12–17 *or First EP of Simon and Jude* Ps. 124; 125; 126 Deut. 32. 1–4 John 14. 15–26 **R ct**
28 Wednesday	**SIMON AND JUDE, APOSTLES**			
R		Isa. 28. 14–16 Ps. 119. 89–96 Eph. 2. 19–end John 15. 17–end	*MP*: Ps. 116; 117 Wisd. 5. 1–16 *or* Isa. 45. 18–end Luke 6. 12–16	*EP*: Ps. 119. 1–16 1 Macc. 2. 42–66 *or* Jer. 3. 11–18 Jude 1–4, 17–end
29 Thursday	**James Hannington, Bishop of Eastern Equatorial Africa, Martyr in Uganda, 1885**			
Gr	Com. Martyr *or* *esp.* Matt. 10. 28–39	Eph. 6. 10–20 Ps. 144. 1–2, 9–11 Luke 13. 31–end	Ps. ***143***; 146 2 Kings. 23.36 – 24.17 1 Tim. ch. 4	Ps. ***138***; 140; 141 2 Macc. 7. 20–41 *or* 2 Chron. 35. 1–19 John 16. 1–15
30 Friday				
G		Phil. 1. 1–11 Ps. 111 Luke 14. 1–6	Ps. 142; ***144*** 2 Kings 24.18 – 25.12 1 Tim. 5. 1–16	Ps. 145 Tobit ch. 1 *or* 2 Chron. 35.20 – 36.10 John 16. 16–22
31 Saturday	*Martin Luther, Reformer, 1546*			
G		Phil. 1. 18–26 Ps. 42. 1–7 Luke 14. 1, 7–11	Ps. 147 2 Kings 25. 22–end 1 Tim. 5. 17–end	*First EP of All Saints* Ps. 1; 5 Ecclus. 44. 1–15 *or* Isa. 40. 27–end Rev. 19. 6–10 **𝔚 ct**

November 2020

1 Sunday	**ALL SAINTS' DAY**			
𝔚		Rev. 7. 9–end Ps. 34. 1–10 1 John 3. 1–3 Matt. 5. 1–12	*MP*: Ps. 15; 84; 149 Isa. ch. 35 Luke 9. 18–27	*EP*: Ps. 148; 150 Isa. 65. 17–end Heb. 11.32 – 12.2

*Chad may be celebrated with Cedd on 26 October instead of 2 March.

	Calendar and Holy Communion	Morning Prayer	Evening Prayer	NOTES
G		2 Kings 21. 1–18 1 Tim. 1. 1–17	2 Macc. 4. 7–17 *or* 2 Chron. 33. 1–13 John 15. 1–11	
G		2 Kings 22.1 – 23.3 1 Tim. 1.18 – 2.end	2 Macc. 6. 12–end *or* 2 Chron. 34. 1–18 John 15. 12–17 *or First EP of Simon and Jude* (Ps. 124; 125; 126) Deut. 32. 1–4 John 14. 15–26 **R ct**	
	SIMON AND JUDE, APOSTLES			
R	Isa. 28. 9–16 Ps. 116. 11–end Jude 1–8 *or* Rev. 21. 9–14 John 15. 17–end	(Ps. 119. 89–96) Wisd. 5. 1–16 *or* Isa. 45. 18–end Luke 6. 12–16	(Ps. 119. 1–16) 1 Macc. 2. 42–66 *or* Jer. 3. 11–18 Eph. 2. 19–end	
G		2 Kings. 23.36 – 24.17 1 Tim. ch. 4	2 Macc. 7. 20–41 *or* 2 Chron. 35. 1–19 John 16. 1–15	
G		2 Kings 24.18 – 25.12 1 Tim. 5. 1–16	Tobit ch. 1 *or* 2 Chron. 35.20 – 36.10 John 16. 16–22	
G		2 Kings 25. 22–end 1 Tim. 5. 17–end	*First EP of All Saints* Ps. 1; 5 Ecclus. 44. 1–15 *or* Isa. 40. 27–end Rev. 19. 6–10 **𝔚 ct**	
	ALL SAINTS' DAY			
𝔚	Isa. 66. 20–23 Ps. 33. 1–5 Rev. 7. 2–4 [5–8] 9–12 Matt. 5. 1–12	Ps. 15; 84; 149 Isa. ch. 35 Luke 9. 18–27	Ps. 148; 150 Isa. 65. 17–end Heb. 11.32 – 12.2	

		Sunday Principal Service Weekday Eucharist	Third Service Morning Prayer	Second Service Evening Prayer
2 Monday	**Commemoration of the Faithful Departed (All Souls' Day)**			
Rp *or* **Gp** **DEL 31**	Lam. 3. 17–26, 31–33 *or* *or* Wisd. 3. 1–9 Ps. 23 *or* Ps. 27. 1–6, 16–end Rom. 5. 5–11 *or* 1 Pet. 1. 3–9 John 5. 19–25 *or* John 6. 37–40	Phil. 2. 1–4 Ps. 131 Luke 14. 12–14	Ps. **2**; 146 *alt.* Ps. ***1***; 2; 3 Dan. ch. 1 Rev. ch. 1	Ps. **92**; 96; 97 *alt.* Ps. ***4***; 7 Isa. 1. 1–20 Matt. 1. 18–end
3 Tuesday	**Richard Hooker, Priest, Anglican Apologist, Teacher, 1600** *Martin of Porres, Friar, 1639*			
Rw *or* **Gw**	Com. Teacher *or* *esp.* John 16. 12–15 *also* Ecclus. 44. 10–15	Phil. 2. 5–11 Ps. 22. 22–27 Luke 14. 15–24	Ps. ***5***; 147. 1–12 *alt.* Ps. ***5***; 6; (8) Dan. 2. 1–24 Rev. 2. 1–11	Ps. 98; 99; ***100*** *alt.* Ps. ***9***; 10† Isa. 1. 21–end Matt. 2. 1–15
4 Wednesday				
R *or* **G**		Phil. 2. 12–18 Ps. 27. 1–5 Luke 14. 25–33	Ps. ***9***; 147. 13–end *alt.* Ps. 119. 1–32 Dan. 2. 25–end Rev. 2. 12–end	Ps. 111; ***112***; 116 *alt.* Ps. ***11***; 12; 13 Isa. 2. 1–11 Matt. 2. 16–end
5 Thursday				
R *or* **G**		Phil. 3. 3–8a Ps. 105. 1–7 Luke 15. 1–10	Ps. 11; ***15***; 148 *alt.* Ps. 14; ***15***; 16 Dan. 3. 1–18 Rev. 3. 1–13	Ps. 118 *alt.* Ps. 18† Isa. 2. 12–end Matt. ch. 3
6 Friday	*Leonard, Hermit, 6th century; William Temple, Archbishop of Canterbury, Teacher, 1944*			
R *or* **G**		Phil. 3.17 - 4.1 Ps. 122 Luke 16. 1–8	Ps. ***16***; 149 *alt.* Ps. 17; ***19*** Dan. 3. 19–end Rev. 3. 14–end	Ps. 137; 138; ***143*** *alt.* Ps. 22 Isa. 3. 1–15 Matt. 4. 1–11
7 Saturday	**Willibrord of York, Bishop, Apostle of Frisia, 739**			
Rw *or* **Gw**	Com. Missionary *or* *esp.* Isa. 52. 7–10 Matt. 28. 16–end	Phil. 4. 10–19 Ps. 112 Luke 16. 9–15	Ps. ***18. 31–end***; 150 *alt.* Ps. 20; 21; ***23*** Dan. 4. 1–18 Rev. ch. 4	Ps. 145 *alt.* Ps. ***24***; 25 Isa. 4.2 - 5.7 Matt. 4. 12–22 **ct**
8 Sunday	**THE THIRD SUNDAY BEFORE ADVENT** (Remembrance Sunday)			
R *or* **G**	Wisd. 6. 12–16 *or* *Canticle*: Wisd. 6. 17–20 1 Thess. 4. 13–end Matt. 25. 1–13	Amos 5. 18–24 Ps. 70 1 Thess. 4. 13–end Matt. 25. 1–13	Ps. 91 Deut. 17. 14–end 1 Tim. 2. 1–7	Ps. [20]; 82 Judg. 7. 2–22 John 15. 9–17
9 Monday	*Margery Kempe, Mystic, c. 1440*			
R *or* **G** **DEL 32**		Titus 1. 1–9 Ps. 24. 1–6 Luke 17. 1–6	Ps. 19; ***20*** *alt.* Ps. 27; ***30*** Dan. 4. 19–end Rev. ch. 5	Ps. 34 *alt.* Ps. 26; ***28***; 29 Isa. 5. 8–24 Matt. 4.23 - 5.12

	Calendar and Holy Communion	Morning Prayer	Evening Prayer	NOTES
	To celebrate All Souls' Day, see *Common Worship* provision.			
G		Dan. ch. 1 Rev. ch. 1	Isa. 1. 1–20 Matt. 1. 18–end	
G		Dan. 2. 1–24 Rev. 2. 1–11	Isa. 1. 21–end Matt. 2. 1–15	
G		Dan. 2. 25–end Rev. 2. 12–end	Isa. 2. 1–11 Matt. 2. 16–end	
G		Dan. 3. 1–18 Rev. 3. 1–13	Isa. 2. 12–end Matt. ch. 3	
	Leonard, Hermit, 6th century			
Gw	Com. Abbot	Dan. 3. 19–end Rev. 3. 14–end	Isa. 3. 1–15 Matt. 4. 1–11	
G		Dan. 4. 1–18 Rev. ch. 4	Isa. 4.2 – 5.7 Matt. 4. 12–22 **ct**	
	THE TWENTY-SECOND SUNDAY AFTER TRINITY			
G	Gen. 45. 1–7, 15 Ps. 133 Phil. 1. 3–11 Matt. 18. 21–end	Ps. 91 Deut. 17. 14–end 1 Tim. 2. 1–7	Ps. [20]; 82 Judg. 7. 2–22 John 15. 9–17	
G		Dan. 4. 19–end Rev. ch. 5	Isa. 5. 8–24 Matt. 4.23 – 5.12	

		Sunday Principal Service Weekday Eucharist	Third Service Morning Prayer	Second Service Evening Prayer
10 Tuesday	**Leo the Great, Bishop of Rome, Teacher, 461**			
Rw *or* **Gw**	Com. Teacher *or* *also* 1 Pet. 5. 1–11	Titus 2. 1–8, 11–14 Ps. 37. 3–5, 30–32 Luke 17. 7–10	Ps. ***21***; 24 *alt.* Ps. 32; ***36*** Dan. 5. 1–12 Rev. ch. 6	Ps. 36; ***40*** *alt.* Ps. 33 Isa. 5. 25–end Matt. 5. 13–20
11 Wednesday	**Martin, Bishop of Tours, *c.* 397**			
Rw *or* **Gw**	Com. Bishop *or* *also* 1 Thess. 5. 1–11 Matt. 25. 34–40	Titus 3. 1–7 Ps. 23 Luke 17. 11–19	Ps. ***23***; 25 *alt.* Ps. 34 Dan. 5. 13–end Rev. 7. 1–4, 9–end	Ps. 37 *alt.* Ps. 119. 33–56 Isa. ch. 6 Matt. 5. 21–37
12 Thursday				
R *or* **G**		Philem. 7–20 Ps. 146. 4–end Luke 17. 20–25	Ps. ***26***; 27 *alt.* Ps. 37† Dan. ch. 6 Rev. ch. 8	Ps. 42; ***43*** *alt.* Ps. 39; ***40*** Isa. 7. 1–17 Matt. 5. 38–end
13 Friday	**Charles Simeon, Priest, Evangelical Divine, 1836**			
Rw *or* **Gw**	Com. Pastor *or* *esp.* Mal. 2. 5–7 *also* Col. 1. 3–8 Luke 8. 4–8	2 John 4–9 Ps. 119. 1–8 Luke 17. 26–end	Ps. 28; ***32*** *alt.* Ps. 31 Dan. 7. 1–14 Rev. 9. 1–12	Ps. 31 *alt.* Ps. 35 Isa. 8. 1–15 Matt. 6. 1–18
14 Saturday	*Samuel Seabury, first Anglican Bishop in North America, 1796*			
R *or* **G**		3 John 5–8 Ps. 112 Luke 18. 1–8	Ps. 33 *alt.* Ps. 41; ***42***; 43 Dan. 7. 15–end Rev. 9. 13–end	Ps. 84; ***86*** *alt.* Ps. 45; ***46*** Isa. 8.16 – 9.7 Matt. 6. 19–end **ct**
15 Sunday	**THE SECOND SUNDAY BEFORE ADVENT**			
R *or* **G**		Zeph. 1. 7, 12–end Ps. 90. 1–8 [9–11] 12 (*or* 90. 1–8) 1 Thess. 5. 1–11 Matt. 25. 14–30	Ps. 98 Dan. 10. 19–end Rev. ch. 4	Ps. 89. 19–37 (*or* 89. 19–29) 1 Kings 1. 15–40 (*or* 1–40) Rev. 1. 4–18 *Gospel*: Luke 9. 1–6
16 Monday	**Margaret, Queen of Scotland, Philanthropist, Reformer of the Church, 1093** *Edmund Rich of Abingdon, Archbishop of Canterbury, 1240*			
Rw *or* **Gw** **DEL 33**	Com. Saint *or* *also* Prov. 31. 10–12, 20, 26–end 1 Cor. 12.13 – 13.3 Matt. 25. 34–end	Rev. 1. 1–4; 2. 1–5 Ps. 1 Luke 18. 35–end	Ps. 46; ***47*** *alt.* Ps. 44 Dan. 8. 1–14 Rev. ch. 10	Ps. 70; ***71*** *alt.* Ps. ***47***; 49 Isa. 9.8 – 10.4 Matt. 7. 1–12
17 Tuesday	**Hugh, Bishop of Lincoln, 1200**			
Rw *or* **Gw**	Com. Bishop *or* *also* 1 Tim. 6. 11–16	Rev. 3. 1–6, 14–end Ps. 15 Luke 19. 1–10	Ps. 48; ***52*** *alt.* Ps. ***48***; 52 Dan. 8. 15–end Rev. 11. 1–14	Ps. ***67***; 72 *alt.* Ps. 50 Isa. 10. 5–19 Matt. 7. 13–end
18 Wednesday	**Elizabeth of Hungary, Princess of Thuringia, Philanthropist, 1231**			
Rw *or* **Gw**	Com. Saint *or* *esp.* Matt. 25. 31–end *also* Prov. 31. 10–end	Rev. ch. 4 Ps. 150 Luke 19. 11–28	Ps. ***56***; 57 *alt.* Ps. 119. 57–80 Dan. 9. 1–19 Rev. 11. 15–end	Ps. 73 *alt.* Ps. ***59***; 60; (67) Isa. 10. 20–32 Matt. 8. 1–13

	Calendar and Holy Communion	Morning Prayer	Evening Prayer	NOTES
G		Dan. 5. 1–12 Rev. ch. 6	Isa. 5. 25–end Matt. 5. 13–20	
	Martin, Bishop of Tours, c. 397			
Gw	Com. Bishop	Dan. 5. 13–end Rev. 7. 1–4, 9–end	Isa. ch. 6 Matt. 5. 21–37	
G		Dan. ch. 6 Rev. ch. 8	Isa. 7. 1–17 Matt. 5. 38–end	
	Britius, Bishop of Tours, 444			
Gw	Com. Bishop	Dan. 7. 1–14 Rev. 9. 1–12	Isa. 8. 1–15 Matt. 6. 1–18	
G		Dan. 7. 15–end Rev. 9. 13–end	Isa. 8.16 - 9.7 Matt. 6. 19–end **ct**	
	THE TWENTY-THIRD SUNDAY AFTER TRINITY			
G	Isa. 11. 1–10 Ps. 44. 1–9 Phil. 3. 17–end Matt. 22. 15–22	Ps. 98 Dan. 10. 19–end Rev. ch. 4	Ps. 89. 19–37 (*or* 89. 19–29) 1 Kings 1. 15–40 (*or* 1–40) Rev. 1. 4–18	
G		Dan. 8. 1–14 Rev. ch. 10	Isa. 9.8 - 10.4 Matt. 7. 1–12	
	Hugh, Bishop of Lincoln, 1200			
Gw	Com. Bishop	Dan. 8. 15–end Rev. 11. 1–14	Isa. 10. 5–19 Matt. 7. 13–end	
G		Dan. 9. 1–19 Rev. 11. 15–end	Isa. 10. 20–32 Matt. 8. 1–13	

		Sunday Principal Service Weekday Eucharist	Third Service Morning Prayer	Second Service Evening Prayer
19 Thursday	**Hilda, Abbess of Whitby, 680** *Mechtild, Béguine of Magdeburg, Mystic, 1280*			
Rw *or* **Gw**	Com. Religious *or* *esp.* Isa. 61.10 - 62.5	Rev. 5. 1–10 Ps. 149. 1–5 Luke 19. 41–44	Ps. 61; ***62*** *alt.* Ps. 56; ***57***; (63†) Dan. 9. 20–end Rev. ch. 12	Ps. 74; ***76*** *alt.* Ps. 61; ***62***; 64 Isa. 10.33 - 11.9 Matt. 8. 14–22
20 Friday	**Edmund, King of the East Angles, Martyr, 870** *Priscilla Lydia Sellon, a Restorer of the Religious Life in the Church of England, 1876*			
R *or* **Gr**	Com. Martyr *or* *also* Prov. 20. 28; 21. 1–4, 7	Rev. 10. 8–end Ps. 119. 65–72 Luke 19. 45–end	Ps. ***63***; 65 *alt.* Ps. ***51***; 54 Dan. 10.1 - 11.1 Rev. 13. 1–10	Ps. 77 *alt.* Ps. 38 Isa. 11.10 - 12.end Matt. 8. 23–end
21 Saturday				
R *or* **G**		Rev. 11. 4–12 Ps. 144. 1–9 Luke 20. 27–40	Ps. 78. 1–39 *alt.* Ps. 68 Dan. ch. 12 Rev. 13. 11–end	Ps. 78. 40–end *alt.* Ps. 65; ***66*** Isa. 13. 1–13 Matt. 9. 1–17 **ct** *or First EP of Christ the King* Ps. 99; 100 Isa. 10.33 - 11.9 1 Tim. 6. 11–16 **R** *or* **W ct**
22 Sunday	**CHRIST THE KING** The Sunday Next Before Advent			
R *or* **W**		Ezek. 34. 11–16, 20–24 Ps. 95. 1–7 Eph. 1. 15–end Matt. 25. 31–end	*MP*: Ps. 29; 110 Isa. 4.2 - 5.7 Luke 19. 29–38	*EP*: Ps. 93; [97] 2 Sam. 23. 1–7 *or* 1 Macc. 2. 15–29 Matt. 28. 16–end
23 Monday	**Clement, Bishop of Rome, Martyr, c. 100**			
R *or* **Gr** **DEL 34**	Com. Martyr *or* *also* Phil. 3.17 - 4.3 Matt. 16. 13–19	Rev. 14. 1–5 Ps. 24. 1–6 Luke 21. 1–4	Ps. 92; ***96*** *alt.* Ps. 71 Isa. 40. 1–11 Rev. 14. 1–13	Ps. ***80***; 81 *alt.* Ps. ***72***; 75 Isa. 14. 3–20 Matt. 9. 18–34
24 Tuesday				
R *or* **G**		Rev. 14. 14–19 Ps. 96 Luke 21. 5–11	Ps. ***97***; 98; 100 *alt.* Ps. 73 Isa. 40. 12–26 Rev. 14.14 - 15.end	Ps. 99; ***101*** *alt.* Ps. 74 Isa. ch. 17 Matt. 9.35 - 10.15
25 Wednesday	*Catherine of Alexandria, Martyr, 4th century; Isaac Watts, Hymn Writer, 1748*			
R *or* **G**		Rev. 15. 1–4 Ps. 98 Luke 21. 12–19	Ps. 110; 111; ***112*** *alt.* Ps. 77 Isa. 40.27 - 41.7 Rev. 16. 1–11	Ps. 121; ***122***; 123; 124 *alt.* Ps. 119. 81–104 Isa. ch. 19 Matt. 10. 16–33
26 Thursday				
R *or* **G**		Rev. 18. 1–2, 21–23; 19. 1–3, 9 Ps. 100 Luke 21. 20–28	Ps. ***125***; 126; 127; 128 *alt.* Ps. 78. 1–39† Isa. 41. 8–20 Rev. 16. 12–end	Ps. 131; 132; ***133*** *alt.* Ps. 78. 40–end† Isa. 21. 1–12 Matt. 10.34 - 11.1

	Calendar and Holy Communion	Morning Prayer	Evening Prayer	NOTES
G		Dan. 9. 20–end Rev. ch. 12	Isa. 10.33 – 11.9 Matt. 8. 14–22	
	Edmund, King of the East Angles, Martyr, 870			
Gr	Com. Martyr	Dan. 10.1 – 11.1 Rev. 13. 1–10	Isa. 11.10 – 12.end Matt. 8. 23–end	
G		Dan. ch. 12 Rev. 13. 11–end	Isa. 13. 1–13 Matt. 9. 1–17 **ct**	
	THE SUNDAY NEXT BEFORE ADVENT To celebrate Christ the King, see *Common Worship* provision.			
G	Jer. 23. 5–8 Ps. 85. 8–end Col. 1. 13–20 John 6. 5–14	Ps. 29; 110 Isa. 4.2 – 5.7 Luke 19. 29–38	Ps. 93; [97] 2 Sam. 23. 1–7 *or* 1 Macc. 2. 15–29 Matt. 28. 16–end	
	Clement, Bishop of Rome, Martyr, c. 100			
Gr	Com. Martyr	Isa. 40. 1–11 Rev. 14. 1–13	Isa. 14. 3–20 Matt. 9. 18–34	
G		Isa. 40. 12–26 Rev. 14.14 – 15.end	Isa. ch. 17 Matt. 9.35 – 10.15	
	Catherine of Alexandria, Martyr, 4th century			
Gr	Com. Virgin Martyr	Isa. 40.27 – 41.7 Rev. 16. 1–11	Isa. ch. 19 Matt. 10. 16–33	
G		Isa. 41. 8–20 Rev. 16. 12–end	Isa. 21. 1–12 Matt. 10.34 – 11.1	

		Sunday Principal Service Weekday Eucharist	Third Service Morning Prayer	Second Service Evening Prayer
27 Friday				
R *or* **G**		Rev. 20.1–4, 11 – 21.2 Ps. 84. 1–6 Luke 21. 29–33	Ps. 139 *alt.* Ps. 55 Isa. 41.21 – 42.9 Rev. ch. 17	Ps. ***146***; 147 *alt.* Ps. 69 Isa. 22. 1–14 Matt. 11. 2–19
28 Saturday				
R *or* **G**		Rev. 22. 1–7 Ps. 95. 1–7 Luke 21. 34–36	Ps. 145 *alt.* Ps. ***76***; 79 Isa. 42. 10–17 Rev. ch. 18	Ps. 148; 149; ***150*** *alt.* Ps. 81; ***84*** Isa. ch. 24 Matt. 11. 20–end **ct**
29 Sunday	**THE FIRST SUNDAY OF ADVENT** *Common Worship* Year B begins			
R *or* **G**		Isa. 64. 1–9 Ps. 80. 1–8, 18–20 (*or* 80. 1–8) 1 Cor. 1. 3–9 Mark 13. 24–end	Ps. 44 Isa. 2. 1–5 Luke 12. 35–48	Ps. 25 (*or* 25. 1–9) Isa. 1. 1–20 Matt. 21. 1–13 *or First EP of Andrew the Apostle* Ps. 48 Isa. 49. 1–9a 1 Cor. 4. 9–16 **R ct**
30 Monday	**ANDREW THE APOSTLE**			
R		Isa. 52. 7–10 Ps. 19. 1–6 Rom. 10. 12–18 Matt. 4. 18–22	*MP*: Ps. 47; 147. 1–12 Ezek. 47. 1–12 *or* Ecclus. 14. 20–end John 12. 20–32	*EP*: Ps. 87; 96 Zech. 8. 20–end John 1. 35–42

December 2020

1 Tuesday	*Charles de Foucauld, Hermit in the Sahara, 1916* Daily Eucharistic Lectionary Year 1 begins			
P		Isa. 11. 1–10 Ps. 72. 1–4, 18–19 Luke 10. 21–24	Ps. ***80***; 82 *alt.* Ps. ***5***; 6; (8) Isa. 43. 1–13 Rev. ch. 20	Ps. ***74***; 75 *alt.* ***9***; 10† Isa. 26. 1–13 Matt. 12. 22–37
2 Wednesday				
P		Isa. 25. 6–10a Ps. 23 Matt. 15. 29–37	Ps. 5; ***7*** *alt.* Ps. 119. 1–32 Isa. 43. 14–end Rev. 21. 1–8	Ps. 76; ***77*** *alt.* Ps. ***11***; 12; 13 Isa. 28. 1–13 Matt. 12. 38–end
3 Thursday	*Francis Xavier, Missionary, Apostle of the Indies, 1552*			
P		Isa. 26. 1–6 Ps. 118. 18–27a Matt. 7. 21, 24–27	Ps. ***42***; 43 *alt.* Ps. 14; ***15***; 16 Isa. 44. 1–8 Rev. 21. 9–21	Ps. ***40***; 46 *alt.* Ps. 18† Isa. 28. 14–end Matt. 13. 1–23
4 Friday	*John of Damascus, Monk, Teacher, c. 749; Nicholas Ferrar, Deacon, Founder of the Little Gidding Community, 1637*			
P		Isa. 29. 17–end Ps. 27. 1–4, 16–17 Matt. 9. 27–31	Ps. ***25***; 26 *alt.* Ps. 17; ***19*** Isa. 44. 9–23 Rev. 21.22 – 22.5	Ps. 16; ***17*** *alt.* Ps. 22 Isa. 29. 1–14 Matt. 13. 24–43

	Calendar and Holy Communion	Morning Prayer	Evening Prayer	NOTES
G		Isa. 41.21 - 42.9 Rev. ch. 17	Isa. 22. 1-14 Matt. 11. 2-19	
G		Isa. 42. 10-17 Rev. ch. 18	Isa. ch. 24 Matt. 11. 20-end **ct**	
	THE FIRST SUNDAY IN ADVENT Advent 1 Collect until Christmas Eve			
P	Mic. 4. 1-4, 6-7 Ps. 25. 1-9 Rom. 13. 8-14 Matt. 21. 1-13	Ps. 44 Isa. 2. 1-5 Luke 12. 35-48	Ps. 9 Isa. 1. 1-20 Mark 13. 24-end *or First EP of Andrew the Apostle* Ps. 48 Isa. 49. 1-9a 1 Cor. 4. 9-16 **R ct**	
	ANDREW THE APOSTLE			
R	Zech. 8. 20-end Ps. 92. 1-5 Rom. 10. 9-end Matt. 4. 18-22	(Ps. 47; 147. 1-12) Ezek. 47. 1-12 *or* Ecclus. 14. 20-end John 12. 20-32	(Ps. 87; 96) Isa. 52. 7-10 John 1. 35-42	
P		Isa. 43. 1-13 Rev. ch. 20	Isa. 26. 1-13 Matt. 12. 22-37	
P		Isa. 43. 14-end Rev. 21. 1-8	Isa. 28. 1-13 Matt. 12. 38-end	
P		Isa. 44. 1-8 Rev. 21. 9-21	Isa. 28. 14-end Matt. 13. 1-23	
P		Isa. 44. 9-23 Rev. 21.22 - 22.5	Isa. 29. 1-14 Matt. 13. 24-43	

		Sunday Principal Service Weekday Eucharist	Third Service Morning Prayer	Second Service Evening Prayer
5 Saturday				
P		Isa. 30. 19–21, 23–26 Ps. 146. 4–9 Matt. 9.35 – 10.1, 6–8	Ps. ***9***; (10) *alt*. Ps. 20; 21; ***23*** Isa. 44.24 – 45.13 Rev. 22. 6–end	Ps. ***27***; 28 *alt*. Ps. ***24***; 25 Isa. 29. 15–end Matt. 13. 44–end **ct**
6 Sunday	**THE SECOND SUNDAY OF ADVENT**			
P		Isa. 40. 1–11 Ps. 85. 1–2, 8–end (*or* 85. 8–end) 2 Pet. 3. 8–15a Mark 1. 1–8	Ps. 80 Baruch 5. 1–9 *or* Zeph. 3. 14–end Luke 1. 5–20	Ps. 40 (*or* 40. 12–end) 1 Kings 22. 1–28 Rom. 15. 4–13 *Gospel*: Matt. 11. 2–11
7 Monday	**Ambrose, Bishop of Milan, Teacher, 397**			
Pw	Com. Teacher *or* *also* Isa. 41. 9b–13 Luke 22. 24–30	Isa. ch. 35 Ps. 85. 7–end Luke 5. 17–26	Ps. 44 *alt*. Ps. 27; ***30*** Isa. 45. 14–end 1 Thess. ch. 1	Ps. ***144***; 146 *alt*. Ps. 26; ***28***; 29 Isa. 30. 1–18 Matt. 14. 1–12
8 Tuesday	**The Conception of the Blessed Virgin Mary**			
Pw	Com. BVM *or*	Isa. 40. 1–11 Ps. 96. 1, 10–end Matt. 18. 12–14	Ps. ***56***; 57 *alt*. Ps. 32; ***36*** Isa. ch. 46 1 Thess. 2. 1–12	Ps. ***11***; 12; 13 *alt*. Ps. 33 Isa. 30. 19–end Matt. 14. 13–end
9 Wednesday	Ember Day*			
P		Isa. 40. 25–end Ps. 103. 8–13 Matt. 11. 28–end	Ps. ***62***; 63 *alt*. Ps. 34 Isa. ch. 47 1 Thess. 2. 13–end	Ps. ***10***; 14 *alt*. Ps. 119. 33–56 Isa. ch. 31 Matt. 15. 1–20
10 Thursday				
P		Isa. 41. 13–20 Ps. 145. 1, 8–13 Matt. 11. 11–15	Ps. 53; ***54***; 60 *alt*. Ps. 37† Isa. 48. 1–11 1 Thess. ch. 3	Ps. 73 *alt*. Ps. 39; ***40*** Isa. ch. 32 Matt. 15. 21–28
11 Friday	Ember Day*			
P		Isa. 48. 17–19 Ps. 1 Matt. 11. 16–19	Ps. 85; ***86*** *alt*. Ps. 31 Isa. 48. 12–end 1 Thess. 4. 1–12	Ps. 82; ***90*** *alt*. Ps. 35 Isa. 33. 1–22 Matt. 15. 29–end
12 Saturday	Ember Day*			
P		Ecclus. 48. 1–4, 9–11 *or* 2 Kings 2. 9–12 Ps. 80. 1–4, 18–19 Matt. 17. 10–13	Ps. 145 *alt*. Ps. 41; ***42***; 43 Isa. 49. 1–13 1 Thess. 4. 13–end	Ps. 93; ***94*** *alt*. Ps. 45; ***46*** Isa. ch. 35 Matt. 16. 1–12 **ct**
13 Sunday	**THE THIRD SUNDAY OF ADVENT**			
P		Isa. 61. 1–4, 8–end Ps. 126 *or Canticle*: Magnificat 1 Thess. 5. 16–24 John 1. 6–8, 19–28	Ps. 50. 1–6; 62 Isa. ch. 12 Luke 1. 57–66	Ps. 68. 1–19 (*or* 68. 1–8) Mal. 3. 1–4; ch. 4 Phil. 4. 4–7 *Gospel*: Matt. 14. 1–12

*For Ember Day provision, see p. 11.

	Calendar and Holy Communion	Morning Prayer	Evening Prayer	NOTES
P		Isa. 44.24 – 45.13 Rev. 22. 6–end	Isa. 29. 15–end Matt. 13. 44–end **ct**	
	THE SECOND SUNDAY IN ADVENT			
P	2 Kings 22. 8–10; 23. 1–3 Ps. 50. 1–6 Rom. 15. 4–13 Luke 21. 25–33	Ps. 80 Baruch 5. 1–9 *or* Zeph. 3. 14–end Luke 1. 5–20	Ps. 40 (*or* 40. 12–end) 1 Kings 22. 1–28 2 Pet. 3. 8–15a	
P		Isa. 45. 14–end 1 Thess. ch. 1	Isa. 30. 1–18 Matt. 14. 1–12	
	The Conception of the Blessed Virgin Mary			
Pw		Isa. ch. 46 1 Thess. 2. 1–12	Isa. 30. 19–end Matt. 14. 13–end	
P		Isa. ch. 47 1 Thess. 2. 13–end	Isa. ch. 31 Matt. 15. 1–20	
P		Isa. 48. 1–11 1 Thess. ch. 3	Isa. ch. 32 Matt. 15. 21–28	
P		Isa. 48. 12–end 1 Thess. 4. 1–12	Isa. 33. 1–22 Matt. 15. 29–end	
P		Isa. 49. 1–13 1 Thess. 4. 13–end	Isa. ch. 35 Matt. 16. 1–12 **ct**	
	THE THIRD SUNDAY IN ADVENT			
P	Isa. ch. 35 Ps. 80. 1–7 1 Cor. 4. 1–5 Matt. 11. 2–10	Ps. 62 Isa. ch. 12 Luke 1. 57–66	Ps. 68. 1–19 (*or* 68. 1–8) Mal. 3. 1–4; ch. 4 Matt. 14. 1–12	

		Sunday Principal Service Weekday Eucharist	Third Service Morning Prayer	Second Service Evening Prayer
14 Monday	**John of the Cross, Poet, Teacher, 1591**			
Pw	Com. Teacher *or* *esp.* 1 Cor. 2. 1–10 *also* John 14. 18–23	Num. 24. 2–7, 15–17 Ps. 25. 3–8 Matt. 21. 23–27	Ps. 40 *alt.* Ps. 44 Isa. 49. 14–25 1 Thess. 5. 1–11	Ps. 25; ***26*** *alt.* Ps. ***47***; 49 Isa. 38. 1–8, 21–22 Matt. 16. 13–end
15 Tuesday				
P		Zeph. 3. 1–2, 9–13 Ps. 34. 1–6, 21–22 Matt. 21. 28–32	Ps. ***70***; 74 *alt.* Ps. ***48***; 52 Isa. ch. 50 1 Thess. 5. 12–end	Ps. ***50***; 54 *alt.* Ps. 50 Isa. 38. 9–20 Matt. 17. 1–13
16 Wednesday				
P		Isa. 45. 6b–8, 18, 21b–end Ps. 85. 7–end Luke 7. 18b–23	Ps. ***75***; 96 *alt.* Ps. 119. 57–80 Isa. 51. 1–8 2 Thess. ch. 1	Ps. 25; ***82*** *alt.* Ps. ***59***; 60; (67) Isa. ch. 39 Matt. 17. 14–21
17 Thursday	O Sapientia* *Eglantyne Jebb, Social Reformer, Founder of 'Save the Children', 1928*			
P		Gen. 49. 2, 8–10 Ps. 72. 1–5, 18–19 Matt. 1. 1–17	Ps. ***76***; 97 *alt.* Ps. 56; ***57***; (63†) Isa. 51. 9–16 2 Thess. ch. 2	Ps. 44 *alt.* Ps. 61; ***62***; 64 Zeph. 1.1 – 2.3 Matt. 17. 22–end
18 Friday				
P		Jer. 23. 5–8 Ps. 72. 1–2, 12–13, 18–end Matt. 1. 18–24	Ps. 77; ***98*** *alt.* Ps. ***51***; 54 Isa. 51. 17–end 2 Thess. ch. 3	Ps. 49 *alt.* Ps. 38 Zeph. 3. 1–13 Matt. 18. 1–20
19 Saturday				
P		Judg. 13. 2–7, 24–end Ps. 71. 3–8 Luke 1. 5–25	Ps. 144; ***146*** Isa. 52. 1–12 Jude	Ps. 10; ***57*** Zeph. 3. 14–end Matt. 18. 21–end **ct**
20 Sunday	**THE FOURTH SUNDAY OF ADVENT**			
P		2 Sam. 7. 1–11, 16 *Canticle*: Magnificat *or* Ps. 89. 1–4, 19–26 (*or* 1–8) Rom. 16. 25–end Luke 1. 26–38	Ps. 144 Isa. 7. 10–16 Rom. 1. 1–7	Ps. 113 [131] Zech. 2. 10–end Luke 1. 39–55
21 Monday**				
P		Zeph. 3. 14–18 Ps. 33. 1–4, 11–12, 20–end Luke 1. 39–45	Ps. ***121***; 122; 123 Isa. 52.13 – 53.end 2 Pet. 1. 1–15	Ps. 80; ***84*** Mal. 1. 1, 6–end Matt. 19. 1–12

*Evening Prayer readings from the Additional Weekday Lectionary (see p. 119) may be used from 17 to 23 December.
**Thomas the Apostle may be celebrated on 21 December instead of 3 July.

	Calendar and Holy Communion	Morning Prayer	Evening Prayer	NOTES
P		Isa. 49. 14–25 1 Thess. 5. 1–11	Isa. 38. 1–8, 21–22 Matt. 16. 13–end	
P		Isa. ch. 50 1 Thess. 5. 12–end	Isa. 38. 9–20 Matt. 17. 1–13	
	O Sapientia Ember Day			
P	Ember CEG	Isa. 51. 1–8 2 Thess. ch. 1	Isa. ch. 39 Matt. 17. 14–21	
P		Isa. 51. 9–16 2 Thess. ch. 2	Zeph. 1.1 – 2.3 Matt. 17. 22–end	
	Ember Day			
P	Ember CEG	Isa. 51. 17–end 2 Thess. ch. 3	Zeph. 3. 1–13 Matt. 18. 1–20	
	Ember Day			
P	Ember CEG	Isa. 52. 1–12 Jude	Zeph. 3. 14–end Matt. 18. 21–end **ct**	
	THE FOURTH SUNDAY IN ADVENT			
P	Isa. 40. 1–9 Ps. 145. 17–end Phil. 4. 4–7 John 1. 19–28	Ps. 144 Isa. 7. 10–16 Rom. 1. 1–7	Ps. 113 [131] Zech. 2. 10–end Luke 1. 39–55 *or First EP of Thomas* Ps. 27 Isa. ch. 35 Heb. 10.35 – 11.1 **R ct**	
	THOMAS THE APOSTLE			
R	Job 42. 1–6 Ps. 139. 1–11 Eph. 2. 19–end John 20. 24–end	(Ps. 92; 146) 2 Sam. 15. 17–21 *or* Ecclus. ch. 2 John 11. 1–16	(Ps. 139) Hab. 2. 1–4 1 Pet. 1. 3–12	

		Sunday Principal Service Weekday Eucharist	Third Service Morning Prayer	Second Service Evening Prayer
22 Tuesday				
P		1 Sam. 1. 24–end Ps. 113 Luke 1. 46–56	Ps. ***124***; 125; 126; 127 Isa. ch. 54 2 Pet. 1.16 – 2.3	Ps. 24; ***48*** Mal. 2. 1–16 Matt. 19. 13–15
23 Wednesday				
P		Mal. 3. 1–4; 4. 5–end Ps. 25. 3–9 Luke 1. 57–66	Ps. 128; 129; ***130***; 131 Isa. ch. 55 2 Pet. 2. 4–end	Ps. 89. 1–37 Mal. 2.17 – 3.12 Matt. 19. 16–end
24 Thursday	**CHRISTMAS EVE**			
P		*Morning Eucharist* 2 Sam. 7. 1–5, 8–11, 16 Ps. 89. 2, 19–27 Acts 13. 16–26 Luke 1. 67–79	Ps. ***45***; 113 Isa. 56. 1–8 2 Pet. ch. 3	Ps. 85 Zech. ch. 2 Rev. 1. 1–8
25 Friday	**CHRISTMAS DAY**			
𝔚	*Any of the following sets of readings may be used on the evening of Christmas Eve and on Christmas Day. Set III should be used at some service during the celebration.*	*I* Isa. 9. 2–7 Ps. 96 Titus 2. 11–14 Luke 2. 1–14 [15–20] *II* Isa. 62. 6–end Ps. 97 Titus 3. 4–7 Luke 2. [1–7] 8–20 *III* Isa. 52. 7–10 Ps. 98 Heb. 1. 1–4 [5–12] John 1. 1–14	*MP*: Ps. ***110***; 117 Isa. 62. 1–5 Matt. 1. 18–end	*EP*: Ps. 8 Isa. 65. 17–25 Phil. 2. 5–11 *or* Luke 2. 1–20 *if it has not been used at the principal service of the day*
26 Saturday	**STEPHEN, DEACON, FIRST MARTYR**			
R	*The reading from Acts must be used as either the first or second reading at the Eucharist.*	2 Chron. 24. 20–22 *or* Acts 7. 51–end Ps. 119. 161–168 Acts 7. 51–end *or* Gal. 2. 16b–20 Matt. 10. 17–22	*MP*: Ps. ***13***; 31. 1–8; 150 Jer. 26. 12–15 Acts ch. 6	*EP*: Ps. 57; ***86*** Gen. 4. 1–10 Matt. 23. 34–end **ct**
27 Sunday	**JOHN, APOSTLE AND EVANGELIST** (or transferred to 29 December)			
W		Exod. 33. 7–11a Ps. 117 1 John ch. 1 John 21. 19b–end	*MP*: Ps. ***21***; 147. 13–end Exod. 33. 12–end 1 John 2. 1–11	*EP*: Ps. 97 Isa. 6. 1–8 1 John 5. 1–12
	or, for The First Sunday of Christmas:			
W		Isa. 61.10 – 62.3 Ps. 148 (*or* 148. 7–end) Gal. 4. 4–7 Luke 2. 15–21	Ps. 105. 1–11 Isa. 63. 7–9 Eph. 3. 5–12	Ps. 132 Isa. ch. 35 Col. 1. 9–20 *or* Luke 2. 41–end

	Calendar and Holy Communion	Morning Prayer	Evening Prayer	NOTES
P		Isa. ch. 54 2 Pet. 1.16 – 2.3	Mal. 2. 1–16 Matt. 19. 13–15	
P		Isa. ch. 55 2 Pet. 2. 4–end	Mal. 2.17 – 3.12 Matt. 19. 16–end	
	CHRISTMAS EVE			
P	Collect (1) Christmas Eve (2) Advent 1 Mic. 5. 2–5a Ps. 24 Titus 3. 3–7 Luke 2. 1–14	Isa. 56. 1–8 2 Pet. ch. 3	Zech. ch. 2 Rev. 1. 1–8	
	CHRISTMAS DAY			
𝔚	Isa. 9. 2–7 Ps. 98 Heb. 1. 1–12 John 1. 1–14	Ps. 110; 117 Isa. 62. 1–5 Matt. 1. 18–end	Ps. 8 Isa. 65. 17–25 Phil. 2. 5–11 *or* Luke 2. 1–20	
	STEPHEN, DEACON, FIRST MARTYR			
R	Collect (1) Stephen (2) Christmas 2 Chron. 24. 20–22 Ps. 119. 161–168 Acts 7. 55–end Matt. 23. 34–end	(Ps. 13; 31. 1–8; 150) Jer. 26. 12–15 Acts ch. 6	(Ps. 57; 86) Gen. 4. 1–10 Matt. 10. 17–22 **ct**	
	JOHN, APOSTLE AND EVANGELIST (or transferred to 29 December)			
W	Collect (1) John (2) Christmas Exod. 33. 18–end Ps. 92. 11–end 1 John ch. 1 John 21. 19b–end *or, for The Sunday after Christmas Day:*	Ps. 21; 147. 13–end Exod. 33. 7–11a 1 John 2. 1–11	Ps. 97 Isa. 6. 1–8 1 John 5. 1–12	
W	Isa. 62. 10–12 Ps. 45. 1–7 Gal. 4. 1–7 Matt. 1. 18–end	Ps. 105. 1–11 Isa. 63. 7–9 Eph. 3. 5–12	Ps. 132 Isa. ch. 35 1 John 1. 1–7	

		Sunday Principal Service Weekday Eucharist	Third Service Morning Prayer	Second Service Evening Prayer
28 Monday	**THE HOLY INNOCENTS**			
R		Jer. 31. 15–17 Ps. 124 1 Cor. 1. 26–29 Matt. 2. 13–18	*MP*: Ps. ***36***; 146 Baruch 4. 21–27 *or* Gen. 37. 13–20 Matt. 18. 1–10	*EP*: Ps. 123; ***128*** Isa. 49. 14–25 Mark 10. 13–16
29 Tuesday	**Thomas Becket, Archbishop of Canterbury, Martyr, 1170*** (For John, Apostle and Evangelist, see provision on 27 December)			
Wr	Com. Martyr *or* *esp.* Matt. 10. 28–33 *also* Ecclus. 51. 1–8	1 John 2. 3–11 Ps. 96. 1–4 Luke 2. 22–35	Ps. ***19***; 20 Isa. 57. 15–end John 1. 1–18	Ps. 131; ***132*** Jonah ch. 1 Col. 1. 1–14
30 Wednesday				
W		1 John 2. 12–17 Ps. 96. 7–10 Luke 2. 36–40	Ps. 111; 112; ***113*** Isa. 59. 1–15a John 1. 19–28	Ps. ***65***; 84 Jonah ch. 2 Col. 1. 15–23
31 Thursday	*John Wyclif, 1384*			
W		1 John 2. 18–21 Ps. 96. 1, 11–end John 1. 1–18	Ps. 102 Isa. 59. 15b–end John 1. 29–34	Ps. ***90***; 148 Jonah chs 3 & 4 Col. 1.24 - 2.7 *or First EP of The Naming of Jesus* Ps. 148 Jer. 23. 1–6 Col. 2. 8–15 **ct**

*Thomas Becket may be celebrated on 7 July instead of 29 December.

	Calendar and Holy Communion	Morning Prayer	Evening Prayer	NOTES
	THE HOLY INNOCENTS			
R	Collect (1) Innocents (2) Christmas Jer. 31. 10–17 Ps. 123 Rev. 14. 1–5 Matt. 2. 13–18	(Ps. 36; 146) Baruch 4. 21–27 *or* Gen. 37. 13–20 Matt. 18. 1–10	(Ps. 124; 128) Isa. 49. 14–25 Mark 10. 13–16	
	CEG of Christmas			
W		Isa. 57. 15–end John 1. 1–18	Jonah ch. 1 Col. 1. 1–14	
W		Isa. 59. 1–15a John 1. 19–28	Jonah ch. 2 Col. 1. 15–23	
	Silvester, Bishop of Rome, 335			
W	Com. Bishop	Isa. 59. 15b–end John 1. 29–34	Jonah chs 3 & 4 Col. 1.24 - 2.7 *or First EP of The Circumcision of Christ* (Ps. 148) Jer. 23. 1–6 Col. 2. 8–15 **ct**	

The *Common Worship* Additional Weekday Lectionary

The Additional Weekday Lectionary provides two readings on a one-year cycle for each day (except for Sundays, Principal Feasts and Holy Days, Festivals and Holy Week). They 'stand alone' and are intended particularly for use in those churches and cathedrals that attract occasional rather than regular congregations. The Additional Weekday Lectionary has been designed to complement rather than replace the existing Weekday Lectionary. Thus a church with a regular congregation in the morning and a congregation made up mainly of visitors in the evening would continue to use the Weekday Lectionary in the morning but might choose to use this Additional Weekday Lectionary for Evening Prayer.

Psalms are not provided, since the Weekday Lectionary already offers a variety of approaches with regard to psalmody. This Lectionary is not intended for use at the Eucharist; the Daily Eucharistic Lectionary is already authorized for that purpose.

On Sundays, Principal Feasts, other Principal Holy Days, Festivals, and in Holy Week, where no readings are provided in this table, the lectionary provision in the main part of this volume should be used.

Date		Old Testament	New Testament
December 2019			
1	S	THE FIRST SUNDAY OF ADVENT	
2	M	Mal. 3. 1–6	Matt. 3. 1–6
3	Tu	Zeph. 3. 14–end	1 Thess. 4. 13–end
4	W	Isa. 65.17 – 66.2	Matt. 24. 1–14
5	Th	Mic. 5. 2–5a	John 3. 16–21
6	F	Isa. 66. 18–end	Luke 13. 22–30
7	Sa	Mic. 7. 8–15	Rom. 15.30 – 16.7, 25–end
8	S	THE SECOND SUNDAY OF ADVENT	
9	M	Jer. 7. 1–11	Phil. 4. 4–9
10	Tu	Dan. 7. 9–14	Matt. 24. 15–28
11	W	Amos 9. 11–end	Rom. 13. 8–end
12	Th	Jer. 23. 5–8	Mark 11. 1–11
13	F	Jer. 33. 14–22	Luke 21. 25–36
14	Sa	Zech. 14. 4–11	Rev. 22. 1–7
15	S	THE THIRD SUNDAY OF ADVENT	
16	M	Isa. 40. 1–11	Matt. 3. 1–12
17	Tu	Ecclus. 24. 1–9 *or* Prov. 8. 22–31	1 Cor. 2. 1–13
18	W	Exod. 3. 1–6	Acts 7. 20–36
19	Th	Isa. 11. 1–9	Rom. 15. 7–13
20	F	Isa. 22. 21–23	Rev. 3. 7–13
21	Sa	Num. 24. 15b–19	Rev. 22. 10–21
22	S	THE FOURTH SUNDAY OF ADVENT	
23	M	Isa. 7. 10–15	Matt. 1. 18–23
24	Tu	*At Evening Prayer, the readings for Christmas Eve are used. At other services, the following readings are used:* Isa. 29. 13–18	1 John 4. 7–16
25	W	**CHRISTMAS DAY**	
26	Th	STEPHEN	
27	F	JOHN THE EVANGELIST	
28	Sa	THE HOLY INNOCENTS	
29	S	THE FIRST SUNDAY OF CHRISTMAS	
30	M	Isa. 9. 2–7	John 8. 12–20
31	Tu	Eccles. 3. 1–13	Rev. 21. 1–8
January 2020			
1	W	**NAMING AND CIRCUMCISION OF JESUS**	
2	Th	Isa. 66. 6–14	Matt. 12. 46–50
3	F	Deut. 6. 4–15	John 10. 31–end
4	Sa	*Where The Epiphany is celebrated on Sunday 5 January, the readings for the Eve of the Epiphany are used at Evening Prayer. At other services, the following readings are used:* Isa. 63. 7–16	Gal. 3.23 – 4.7
5	S	THE SECOND SUNDAY OF CHRISTMAS *At Evening Prayer the readings for the Eve of The Epiphany are used.*	
6	M	**THE EPIPHANY** *Where The Epiphany is celebrated on Sunday 5 January, the following readings are used:* Isa. ch. 12	2 Cor. 2. 12–end
7	Tu	Gen. 25. 19–end	Eph. 1. 1–6
8	W	Joel 2. 28–end	Eph. 1. 7–14
9	Th	Prov. 8. 12–21	Eph. 1. 15–end
10	F	Gen. 19. 15–29	Eph. 2. 1–10
11	Sa	*At Evening Prayer, the readings for the Eve of the Baptism of Christ are used. At other services, the following readings are used:* Gen. 17. 1–14	Eph. 2. 11–end
12	S	THE BAPTISM OF CHRIST (The First Sunday of Epiphany)	
13	M	Isa. 41. 14–20	John 1. 29–34
14	Tu	Exod. 17. 1–7	Acts 8. 26–end
15	W	Exod. 15. 1–19	Col. 2. 8–15
16	Th	Zech. 6. 9–15	1 Pet. 2. 4–10
17	F	Isa. 51. 7–16	Gal. 6. 14–18
18	Sa	Lev. 16. 11–22	Heb. 10. 19–25
19	S	THE SECOND SUNDAY OF EPIPHANY	
20	M	1 Kings. 17. 8–16	Mark 8. 1–10
21	Tu	1 Kings 19. 1–9a	Mark 1. 9–15
22	W	1 Kings 19. 9b–18	Mark 9. 2–13
23	Th	Lev. 11. 1–8, 13–19, 41–45	Acts 10. 9–16
24	F	Isa. 49. 8–13	Acts 10. 34–43
25	Sa	THE CONVERSION OF PAUL	
26	S	THE THIRD SUNDAY OF EPIPHANY	
27	M	Ezek. 37. 15–end	John 17. 1–19
28	Tu	Ezek. 20. 39–44	John 17. 20–end
29	W	Neh. 2. 1–10	Rom. 12. 1–8
30	Th	Deut. 26. 16–end	Rom. 14. 1–9
31	F	Lev. 19. 9–28	Rom. 15. 1–7
February 2020			
1	Sa	*At Evening Prayer, the readings for the Eve of the Presentation are used. At other services, the following readings are used:* Jer. 33. 1–11	1 Pet. 5.5b–end
2	S	**THE PRESENTATION**	
3	M	Gen. 1. 26–end	Mark 10. 1–16
4	Tu	Ruth 1. 1–18	1 John 3. 14–end
5	W	1 Sam. 1. 19b–end	Luke 2. 41–end
6	Th	Gen. 47. 1–12	Eph. 3. 14–end
7	F	2 Sam. 1. 17–end	Rom. 8. 28–end
8	Sa	Song of Sol. 2. 8–end	1 Cor. ch. 13
9	S	THE THIRD SUNDAY BEFORE LENT	
10	M	Exod. 23. 1–13	Jas. 2. 1–13
11	Tu	Deut. 10. 12–end	Heb. 13. 1–16
12	W	Isa. 58. 6–end	Matt. 25. 31–end
13	Th	Isa. 42. 1–9	Luke 4. 14–21
14	F	Amos 5. 6–15	Eph. 4. 25–end
15	Sa	Amos 5. 18–24	John 2. 13–22
16	S	THE SECOND SUNDAY BEFORE LENT	
17	M	Isa. 61. 1–9	Mark 6. 1–13
18	Tu	Isa. 52. 1–10	Rom. 10. 5–21
19	W	Isa. 52.13 – 53.6	Rom. 15. 14–21
20	Th	Isa. 53. 4–12	2 Cor. 4. 1–10
21	F	Zech. 8. 16–end	Matt. 10. 1–15
22	Sa	Jer. 1. 4–10	Matt. 10. 16–22
23	S	THE SUNDAY NEXT BEFORE LENT	
24	M	2 Kings 2. 13–22	3 John
25	Tu	Judges 14. 5–17	Rev. 10. 4–11
26	W	**ASH WEDNESDAY**	

27	Th	Gen. 2. 7–end	Heb. 2. 5–end
28	F	Gen. 4. 1–12	Heb. 4. 12–end
29	Sa	2 Kings 22. 11–end	Heb. 5. 1–10

March 2020

1	S	THE FIRST SUNDAY OF LENT	
2	M	Gen. 6. 11–end; 7. 11–16	Luke 4. 14–21
3	Tu	Deut. 31. 7–13	1 John 3. 1–10
4	W	Gen. 11. 1–9	Matt. 24. 15–28
5	Th	Gen. 13. 1–13	1 Pet. 2. 13–end
6	F	Gen. 21. 1–8	Luke 9. 18–27
7	Sa	Gen. 32. 22–32	2 Pet. 1. 10–end
8	S	THE SECOND SUNDAY OF LENT	
9	M	1 Chron. 21. 1–17	1 John 2. 1–8
10	Tu	Zech. ch. 3	2 Pet. 2. 1–10a
11	W	Job 1. 1–22	Luke 21.34 – 22.6
12	Th	2 Chron. 29. 1–11	Mark 11. 15–19
13	F	Exod. 19. 1–9a	1 Pet. 1. 1–9
14	Sa	Exod. 19. 9b–19	Acts 7. 44–50
15	S	THE THIRD SUNDAY OF LENT	
16	M	Josh. 4. 1–13	Luke 9. 1–11
17	Tu	Exod. 15. 22–27	Heb. 10. 32–end
18	W	Gen. 9. 8–17	1 Pet. 3. 18–end
19	Th	JOSEPH OF NAZARETH	
20	F	Num. 20. 1–13	1 Cor. 10. 23–end
21	Sa	Isa. 43. 14–end	Heb. 3. 1–15
22	S	THE FOURTH SUNDAY OF LENT **(Mothering Sunday)**	
23	M	2 Kings 24.18 – 25.7	1 Cor. 15. 20–34
24	Tu	*At Evening Prayer, the readings for the Eve of the Annunciation are used. At other services, the following readings are used:*	
		Jer. 13. 12–19	Acts 13. 26–35
25	W	**THE ANNUNCIATION**	
26	Th	Jer. 22. 11–19	Luke 11. 37–52
27	F	Jer. 17. 1–14	Luke 6. 17–26
28	Sa	Ezra ch. 1	2 Cor. 1. 12–19
29	S	THE FIFTH SUNDAY OF LENT **(Passiontide begins)**	
30	M	Joel 2. 12–17	2 John
31	Tu	Isa. 58. 1–14	Mark 10. 32–45

April 2020

1	W	Joel 36. 1–12	John 14. 1–14
2	Th	Jer. 9. 17–22	Luke 13. 31–35
3	F	Lam. 5. 1–3, 19–22	John 12. 20–26
4	Sa	Job 17. 6–end	John 12. 27–36
5	S	PALM SUNDAY	
		HOLY WEEK	
12	S	**EASTER DAY**	
13	M	Isa. 54. 1–14	Rom. 1. 1–7
14	Tu	Isa. 51. 1–11	John 5. 19–29
15	W	Isa. 26. 1–19	John 20. 1–10
16	Th	Isa. 43. 14–21	Rev. 1. 4–end
17	F	Isa. 42. 10–17	1 Thess. 5. 1–11
18	Sa	Job 14. 1–14	John 21. 1–14
19	S	THE SECOND SUNDAY OF EASTER	
20	M	Ezek. 1. 22–end	Rev. ch. 4
21	Tu	Prov. 8. 1–11	Acts 16. 6–15
22	W	Hos. 5.15 – 6.6	1 Cor. 15. 1–11
23	Th	GEORGE	
24	F	Gen. 6. 9–end	1 Pet. 3. 8–end
25	Sa	MARK	
26	S	THE THIRD SUNDAY OF EASTER	
27	M	Exod. 24. 1–11	Rev. ch. 5
28	Tu	Lev. 19. 9–18, 32–end	Matt. 5. 38–end
29	W	Gen. 3. 8–21	1 Cor. 15. 12–28
30	Th	Isa. 33. 13–22	Mark 6. 47–end

May 2020

1	F	PHILIP AND JAMES	
2	Sa	Isa. 61.10 – 62.5	Luke 24. 1–12
3	S	THE FOURTH SUNDAY OF EASTER	
4	M	Jer. 31. 10–17	Rev. 7. 9–end
5	Tu	Job 31. 13–23	Matt. 7. 1–12
6	W	Gen. 2. 4b–9	1 Cor. 15. 35–49
7	Th	Prov. 28. 3–end	Mark 10. 17–31
8	F	Eccles. 12. 1–8	Rom. 6. 1–11
9	Sa	1 Chron. 29. 10–13	Luke 24. 13–35
10	S	THE FIFTH SUNDAY OF EASTER	
11	M	Gen. 15. 1–18	Rom. 4. 13–end
12	Tu	Deut. 8. 1–10	Matt. 6. 19–end
13	W	Hos. 13. 4–14	1 Cor. 15. 50–end
14	Th	MATTHIAS	
		Where Matthias is celebrated on 24 February:	
		Exod. 3. 1–15	Mark 12. 18–27
15	F	Ezek. 36. 33–end	Rom. 8. 1–11
16	Sa	Isa. 38. 9–20	Luke 24. 33–end
17	S	THE SIXTH SUNDAY OF EASTER	
18	M	Prov. 4. 1–13	Phil. 2. 1–11
19	Tu	Isa. 32. 12–end	Rom. 5. 1–11
20	W	*At Evening Prayer, the readings for the Eve of Ascension Day are used. At other services, the following readings are used:*	
		Isa. 43. 1–13	Titus 2.11 – 3.8
21	Th	**ASCENSION DAY**	
22	F	Exod. 35.30 – 36.1	Gal. 5. 13–end
23	Sa	Num. 11. 16–17, 24–29	1 Cor. ch. 2
24	S	THE SEVENTH SUNDAY OF EASTER (Sunday after Ascension Day)	
25	M	Num. 27. 15–end	1 Cor. ch. 3
26	Tu	1 Sam. 10. 1–10	1 Cor. 12. 1–13
27	W	1 Kings 19. 1–18	Matt. 3. 13–end
28	Th	Ezek. 11. 14–20	Matt. 9.35 – 10.20
29	F	Ezek. 36. 22–28	Matt. 12. 22–32
30	Sa	*At Evening Prayer, the readings for the Eve of Pentecost are used. At other services, the following readings are used:*	
		Mic. 3. 1–8	Eph. 6. 10–20
31	S	**PENTECOST** (Whit Sunday)	

June 2020

1	M	THE VISITATION	
		Where The Visitation is celebrated on 2 July:	
		Gen. 12. 1–9	Rom. 4. 13–end
2	Tu	Gen. 13. 1–12	Rom. 12. 9–end
3	W	Gen. ch. 15	Rom. 4. 1–8
4	Th	Gen. 22. 1–18	Heb. 11. 8–19
5	F	Isa. 51. 1–8	John 8. 48–end
6	Sa	*At Evening Prayer, the readings for the Eve of Trinity Sunday are used. At other services, the following readings are used:*	
		Ecclus. 44. 19–23 *or* Josh. 2. 1–15	Jas. 2. 14–26
7	S	**TRINITY SUNDAY**	
8	M	Exod. 2. 1–10	Heb. 11. 23–31
9	Tu	Exod. 2. 11–end	Acts 7. 17–29
10	W	Exod. 3. 1–12	Acts 7. 30–38
11	Th	BARNABAS (or transferred to 12 June) *or Day of Thanksgiving for the Institution of the Holy Communion*	
12	F	Exod. 34. 1–10	Mark 7. 1–13
13	Sa	Exod. 34. 27–end	2 Cor. 3. 7–end
14	S	THE FIRST SUNDAY AFTER TRINITY	
15	M	Gen. 37. 1–11	Rom. 12. 9–21
16	Tu	Gen. 41. 15–40	Mark 13. 1–13
17	W	Gen. 42. 17–end	Matt. 18. 1–14
18	Th	Gen. 45. 1–15	Acts 7. 9–16
19	F	Gen. 47. 1–12	1 Thess. 5. 12–end
20	Sa	Gen. 50. 4–21	Luke 15. 11–end
21	S	THE SECOND SUNDAY AFTER TRINITY	
22	M	Isa. ch. 32	Jas. 3. 13–end
23	Tu	Prov. 3. 1–18	Matt. 5. 1–12
24	W	THE BIRTH OF JOHN THE BAPTIST	
25	Th	Jer. 6. 9–15	1 Tim. 2. 1–6
26	F	1 Sam. 16. 14–end	John 14. 15–end
27	Sa	Isa. 6. 1–9	Rev. 19. 9–end

28	S	**THE THIRD SUNDAY AFTER TRINITY**	
29	M	**PETER AND PAUL**	
30	Tu	Prov. 1. 20–end	Jas. 5. 13–end

July 2020

1	W	Isa. 5. 8–24	Jas. 1. 17–25
2	Th	Isa. 57. 14–end	John 13. 1–17
3	F	**THOMAS**	
		Where Thomas is celebrated on 21 December:	
		Jer. 15. 15–end	Luke 16. 19–31
4	Sa	Isa. 25. 1–9	Acts 2. 22–33
5	S	**THE FOURTH SUNDAY AFTER TRINITY**	
6	M	Exod. 20. 1–17	Matt. 6. 1–15
7	Tu	Prov. 6. 6–19	Luke 4. 1–14
8	W	Isa. 24. 1–15	1 Cor. 6. 1–11
9	Th	Job ch. 7	Matt. 7. 21–29
10	F	Jer. 20. 7–end	Matt. 27. 27–44
11	Sa	Job ch. 28	Heb. 11.32 – 12.2
12	S	**THE FIFTH SUNDAY AFTER TRINITY**	
13	M	Exod. 32. 1–14	Col. 3. 1–11
14	Tu	Prov. 9. 1–12	2 Thess. 2.13 – 3.5
15	W	Isa. 26. 1–9	Rom. 8. 12–27
16	Th	Jer. 8.18 – 9.6	John 13. 21–35
17	F	2 Sam. 5. 1–12	Matt. 27. 45–56
18	Sa	Hos. 11. 1–11	Matt. 28. 1–7
19	S	**THE SIXTH SUNDAY AFTER TRINITY**	
20	M	Exod. 40. 1–16	Luke 14. 15–24
21	Tu	Prov. 11. 1–12	Mark 12. 38–44
22	W	**MARY MAGDALENE**	
23	Th	Job ch. 38	Luke 18. 1–14
24	F	Job 42. 1–6	John 3. 1–15
25	Sa	**JAMES**	
26	S	**THE SEVENTH SUNDAY AFTER TRINITY**	
27	M	Num. 23. 1–12	1 Cor. 1. 10–17
28	Tu	Prov. 12. 1–12	Gal. 3. 1–14
29	W	Isa. 49. 8–13	2 Cor. 8. 1–11
30	Th	Hos. ch. 14	John 15. 1–17
31	F	2 Sam. 18. 18–end	Matt. 27. 57–66

August 2020

1	Sa	Isa. 55. 1–7	Mark 16. 1–8
2	S	**THE EIGHTH SUNDAY AFTER TRINITY**	
3	M	Joel 3. 16–21	Mark 4. 21–34
4	Tu	Prov. 12. 13–end	John 1. 43–51
5	W	Isa. 55. 8–end	2 Tim. 2. 8–19
6	Th	**THE TRANSFIGURATION**	
7	F	Jer. 14. 1–9	Luke 8. 4–15
8	Sa	Eccles. 5. 10–19	1 Tim. 6. 6–16
9	S	**THE NINTH SUNDAY AFTER TRINITY**	
10	M	Josh. 1. 1–9	1 Cor. 9. 19–end
11	Tu	Prov. 15. 1–11	Gal. 2. 15–end
12	W	Isa. 49. 1–7	1 John 1
13	Th	Prov. 27. 1–12	John 15. 12–27
14	F	Isa. 59. 8–end	Mark 15. 6–20
15	Sa	**THE BLESSED VIRGIN MARY**	
		Where the Blessed Virgin Mary is celebrated on 8 September:	
		Zech. 7.8 – 8.8	Luke 20. 27–40
16	S	**THE TENTH SUNDAY AFTER TRINITY**	
17	M	Judg. 13. 1–23	Luke 10. 38–42
18	Tu	Prov. 15. 15–end	Matt. 15. 21–28
19	W	Isa. 45. 1–7	Eph. 4. 1–16
20	Th	Jer. 16. 1–15	Luke 12. 35–48
21	F	Jer. 18. 1–11	Heb. 1. 1–9
22	Sa	Jer. 26. 1–19	Eph. 3. 1–13
23	S	**THE ELEVENTH SUNDAY AFTER TRINITY**	
24	M	**BARTHOLOMEW**	
25	Tu	Prov. 16. 1–11	Phil. 3. 4b–end
26	W	Deut. 11. 1–21	2 Cor. 9. 6–end
27	Th	Ecclus. ch. 2 *or* Eccles. 2. 12–25	John 16. 1–15
28	F	Obad. 1–10	John 19. 1–16
29	Sa	2 Kings 2. 11–14	Luke 24. 36–end
30	S	**THE TWELFTH SUNDAY AFTER TRINITY**	
31	M	1 Sam. 17. 32–50	Matt. 8. 14–22

September 2020

1	Tu	Prov. 17. 1–15	Luke 7. 1–17
2	W	Jer. 5. 20–end	2 Pet. 3. 8–end
3	Th	Dan. 2. 1–23	Luke 10. 1–20
4	F	Dan. 3. 1–28	Rev. ch. 15
5	Sa	Dan. ch. 6	Phil. 2. 14–24
6	S	**THE THIRTEENTH SUNDAY AFTER TRINITY**	
7	M	2 Sam. 7. 4–17	2 Cor. 5. 1–10
8	Tu	Prov. 18. 10–21	Rom. 14. 10–end
9	W	Judg. 4. 1–10	Rom. 1. 8–17
10	Th	Isa. 49. 14–end	John 16. 16–24
11	F	Job 9. 1–24	Mark 15. 21–32
12	Sa	Exod. 19. 1–9	John 20. 11–18
13	S	**THE FOURTEENTH SUNDAY AFTER TRINITY**	
14	M	**HOLY CROSS DAY**	
15	Tu	Prov. 21. 1–18	Mark 6. 30–44
16	W	Hos. 11. 1–11	1 John 4. 9–end
17	Th	Lam. 3. 34–48	Rom. 7. 14–end
18	F	1 Kings 19. 4–18	1 Thess. ch. 3
19	Sa	Ecclus. 4. 11–28 *or* Deut. 29. 2–15	2 Tim. 3. 10–end
20	S	**THE FIFTEENTH SUNDAY AFTER TRINITY**	
21	M	**MATTHEW**	
22	Tu	Prov. 8. 1–11	Luke 6. 39–end
23	W	Prov. 2. 1–15	Col. 1. 9–20
24	Th	Baruch 3. 14–end *or* Gen. 1. 1–13	John 1. 1–18
25	F	Ecclus. 1. 1–20 *or* Deut. 7. 7–16	1 Cor. 1. 18–end
26	Sa	Wisd. 9. 1–12 *or* Jer. 1. 4–10	Luke 2. 41–end
27	S	**THE SIXTEENTH SUNDAY AFTER TRINITY**	
28	M	Gen. 21. 1–13	Luke 1. 26–38
29	Tu	**MICHAEL AND ALL ANGELS**	
30	W	2 Kings 4. 1–7	John 2. 1–11

October 2020

1	Th	2 Kings 4. 25b–37	Mark 3. 19b–35
2	F	Judith 8. 9–17, 28–36 *or* Ruth 1. 1–18	John 19. 25b–30
3	Sa	Exod. 15. 19–27	Acts 1. 6–14
4	S	**THE SEVENTEENTH SUNDAY AFTER TRINITY**	
5	M	Exod. 19. 16–end	Heb. 12. 18–end
6	Tu	1 Chron. 16. 1–13	Rev. 11. 15–end
7	W	1 Chron. 29. 10–19	Col. 3. 12–17
8	Th	Neh. 8. 1–12	1 Cor. 14. 1–12
9	F	Isa. 1. 10–17	Mark 12. 28–34
10	Sa	Dan. 6. 6–23	Rev. 12. 7–12
11	S	**THE EIGHTEENTH SUNDAY AFTER TRINITY**	
12	M	2 Sam. 22. 4–7, 17–20	Heb. 7.26 – 8.6
13	Tu	Prov. 22. 17–end	2 Cor. 12. 1–10
14	W	Hos. ch. 14	Jas. 2. 14–26
15	Th	Isa. 24. 1–15	John 16. 25–33
16	F	Jer. 14. 1–9	Luke 23. 44–56
17	Sa	Zech. 8. 14–end	John 20. 19–end
18	S	**LUKE (THE NINETEENTH SUNDAY AFTER TRINITY)**	
19	M	1 Kings 3. 3–14	1 Tim. 3.14 – 4.8
20	Tu	Prov. 27. 11–end	Gal. 6. 1–10
21	W	Isa. 51. 1–6	2 Cor. 1. 1–11
22	Th	Ecclus. 18. 1–14 *or* Job ch. 26	1 Cor. 11. 17–end
23	F	Ecclus. 28. 2–12 *or* Job 19. 21–end	Mark 15. 33–47
24	Sa	Isa. 44. 21–end	John 21. 15–end
25	S	**THE LAST SUNDAY AFTER TRINITY**	
26	M	Isa. 42. 14–21	Luke 1. 5–25
27	Tu	1 Sam. 4. 12–end	Luke 1. 57–80
28	W	**SIMON AND JUDE**	
29	Th	Isa. ch. 35	Matt. 11. 2–19
30	F	2 Sam. 11. 1–17	Matt. 14. 1–12
31	Sa	*At Evening Prayer, the readings for the Eve of All*	

		Saints are used. At other services, the following readings are used:	
		Isa. 43. 15–21	Acts 19. 1–10

November 2020

1	S	**ALL SAINTS' DAY**	
2	M	Esther 3. 1–11; 4. 7–17	Matt. 18. 1–10
3	Tu	Ezek. 18. 21–end	Matt. 18. 12–20
4	W	Prov. 3. 27–end	Matt. 18. 21–end
5	Th	Exod. 23. 1–9	Matt. 19. 1–15
6	F	Prov. 3. 13–18	Matt. 19. 16–end
7	Sa	Deut. 28. 1–6	Matt. 20. 1–16
8	S	**THE THIRD SUNDAY BEFORE ADVENT**	
9	M	Isa. 40. 21–end	Rom. 11. 25–end
10	Tu	Ezek. 34. 20–end	John 10. 1–18
11	W	Lev. 26. 3–13	Titus 2. 1–10
12	Th	Hos. 6. 1–6	Matt. 9. 9–13
13	F	Mal. ch. 4	John 4. 5–26
14	Sa	Mic. 6. 6–8	Col. 3. 12–17
15	S	**THE SECOND SUNDAY BEFORE ADVENT**	
16	M	Mic. 7. 1–7	Matt. 10. 24–39
17	Tu	Hab. 3. 1–19a	1 Cor. 4. 9–16
18	W	Zech. 8. 1–13	Mark 13. 3–8
19	Th	Zech. 10. 6–end	1 Pet. 5. 1–11
20	F	Mic. 4. 1–5	Luke 9. 28–36
21	Sa	*At Evening Prayer, the readings for the Eve of Christ the King are used. At other services, the following readings are used:*	
		Exod. 16. 1–21	John 6. 3–15
22	S	**CHRIST THE KING** (The Sunday next before Advent)	
23	M	Jer. 30. 1–3, 10–17	Rom. 12. 9–21
24	Tu	Jer. 30. 18–24	John 10. 22–30
25	W	Jer. 31. 1–9	Matt. 15. 21–31
26	Th	Jer. 31. 10–17	Matt. 16. 13–end
27	F	Jer. 31. 31–37	Heb. 10. 11–18
28	Sa	Isa. 51.17 – 52.2	Eph. 5. 1–20
29	S	**THE FIRST SUNDAY OF ADVENT**	
30	M	**ANDREW**	

December 2020

1	Tu	Zeph. 3. 14–end	1 Thess. 4. 13–end
2	W	Isa. 65.17 – 66.2	Matt. 24. 1–14
3	Th	Mic. 5. 2–5a	John 3. 16–21
4	F	Isa. 66. 18–end	Luke 13. 22–30
5	Sa	Mic. 7. 8–15	Rom. 15.30 – 16.7, 25–end
6	S	**THE SECOND SUNDAY OF ADVENT**	
7	M	Jer. 7. 1–11	Phil. 4. 4–9
8	Tu	Dan. 7. 9–14	Matt. 24. 15–28
9	W	Amos 9. 11–end	Rom. 13. 8–end
10	Th	Jer. 23. 5–8	Mark 11. 1–11
11	F	Jer. 33. 14–22	Luke 21. 25–36
12	Sa	Zech. 14. 4–11	Rev. 22. 1–7
13	S	**THE THIRD SUNDAY OF ADVENT**	
14	M	Isa. 40. 1–11	Matt. 3. 1–12
15	Tu	Lam. 3. 22–33	1 Cor. 1. 1–9
16	W	Joel 3. 9–16	Matt. 24. 29–35
17	Th	Ecclus. 24. 1–9 *or* Prov. 8. 22–31	1 Cor. 2. 1–13
18	F	Exod. 3. 1–6	Acts 7. 20–36
19	Sa	Isa. 11. 1–9	Rom. 15. 7–13
20	S	**THE FOURTH SUNDAY OF ADVENT**	
21	M	Num. 24. 15b–19	Rev. 22. 10–21
22	Tu	Jer. 30. 7–11a	Acts 4. 1–12
23	W	Isa. 7. 10–15	Matt. 1. 18–23
24	Th	*At Evening Prayer, the readings for Christmas Eve are used. At other services, the following readings are used:*	
		Isa. 29. 13–18	1 John 4. 7–16
25	F	**CHRISTMAS DAY**	
26	Sa	**STEPHEN**	
27	S	**JOHN THE EVANGELIST (THE FIRST SUNDAY OF CHRISTMAS)**	
28	M	**THE HOLY INNOCENTS**	
29	Tu	Mic. 1. 1–4; 2. 12–13	Luke 2. 1–7
30	W	Isa. 9. 2–7	John 8. 12–20
31	Th	Eccles. 3. 1–13	Rev. 21. 1–8

CALENDAR 2020

JANUARY						
Su	..	X^2	B	E^2	E^3	..
M	..	E	13	20	27	..
Tu	..	7	14	21	28	..
W	1	8	15	22	29	..
Th	2	9	16	23	30	..
F	3	10	17	24	31	..
Sa	4	11	18	25	..	..

FEBRUARY						
Su	..	Pr	L^{-3}	L^{-2}	L^{-1}	..
M	..	3	10	17	24	..
Tu	..	4	11	18	25	..
W	..	5	12	19	A	..
Th	..	6	13	20	27	..
F	..	7	14	21	28	..
Sa	1	8	15	22	29	..

MARCH						
Su	L^1	L^2	L^3	L^4	L^5	..
M	2	9	16	23	30	..
Tu	3	10	17	24	31	..
W	4	11	18	An	..	..
Th	5	12	19	26	..	..
F	6	13	20	27	..	..
Sa	7	14	21	28	..	..

APRIL						
Su	..	P	E	E^2	E^3	..
M	..	6	13	20	27	..
Tu	..	7	14	21	28	..
W	1	8	15	22	29	..
Th	2	M	16	23	30	..
F	3	G	17	24	..	..
Sa	4	11	18	25	..	..

MAY						
Su	..	E^4	E^5	E^6	E^7	W
M	..	4	11	18	25	..
Tu	..	5	12	19	26	..
W	..	6	13	20	27	..
Th	..	7	14	A	28	..
F	1	8	15	22	29	..
Sa	2	9	16	23	30	..

JUNE						
Su	..	T	T^1	T^2	T^3	..
M	1	8	15	22	29	..
Tu	2	9	16	23	30	..
W	3	10	17	24	..	..
Th	4	11	18	25	..	..
F	5	12	19	26	..	..
Sa	6	13	20	27	..	..

JULY						
Su	..	T^4	T^5	T^6	T^7	..
M	..	6	13	20	27	..
Tu	..	7	14	21	28	..
W	1	8	15	22	29	..
Th	2	9	16	23	30	..
F	3	10	17	24	31	..
Sa	4	11	18	25	..	..

AUGUST						
Su	..	T^8	T^9	T^{10}	T^{11}	T^{12}
M	..	3	10	17	24	31
Tu	..	4	11	18	25	..
W	..	5	12	19	26	..
Th	..	6	13	20	27	..
F	..	7	14	21	28	..
Sa	1	8	15	22	29	..

SEPTEMBER						
Su	..	T^{13}	T^{14}	T^{15}	T^{16}	..
M	..	7	14	21	28	..
Tu	1	8	15	22	29	..
W	2	9	16	23	30	..
Th	3	10	17	24	..	..
F	4	11	18	25	..	..
Sa	5	12	19	26	..	..

OCTOBER						
Su	..	T^{17}	T^{18}	T^{19}	T^L	..
M	..	5	12	19	26	..
Tu	..	6	13	20	27	..
W	..	7	14	21	28	..
Th	1	8	15	22	29	..
F	2	9	16	23	30	..
Sa	3	10	17	24	31	..

NOVEMBER						
Su	AS	A^{-3}	A^{-2}	A^{-1}	A	..
M	2	9	16	23	30	..
Tu	3	10	17	24	..	..
W	4	11	18	25	..	..
Th	5	12	19	26	..	..
F	6	13	20	27	..	..
Sa	7	14	21	28	..	..

DECEMBER						
Su	..	A^2	A^3	A^4	X^1	..
M	..	7	14	21	28	..
Tu	1	8	15	22	29	..
W	2	9	16	23	30	..
Th	3	10	17	24	31	..
F	4	11	18	X	..	..
Sa	5	12	19	26	..	..

CALENDAR 2021

JANUARY						
Su	..	X^2	B	E^2	E^3	E^4
M	..	4	11	18	25	..
Tu	..	5	12	19	26	..
W	..	E	13	20	27	..
Th	..	7	14	21	28	..
F	1	8	15	22	29	..
Sa	2	9	16	23	30	..

FEBRUARY						
Su	..	L^{-2}	L^{-1}	L^1	L^2	..
M	1	8	15	22	..	..
Tu	Pr	9	16	23	..	..
W	3	10	A	24	..	..
Th	4	11	18	25	..	..
F	5	12	19	26	..	..
Sa	6	13	20	27	..	..

MARCH						
Su	..	L^3	L^4	L^5	P	..
M	1	8	15	22	29	..
Tu	2	9	16	23	30	..
W	3	10	17	24	31	..
Th	4	11	18	An	..	..
F	5	12	19	26	..	..
Sa	6	13	20	27	..	..

APRIL						
Su	..	E	E^2	E^3	E^4	..
M	..	5	12	19	26	..
Tu	..	6	13	20	27	..
W	..	7	14	21	28	..
Th	M	8	15	22	29	..
F	G	9	16	23	30	..
Sa	3	10	17	24	..	..

MAY						
Su	..	E^5	E^6	E^7	W	T
M	..	3	10	17	24	31
Tu	..	4	11	18	25	..
W	..	5	12	19	26	..
Th	..	6	A	20	27	..
F	..	7	14	21	28	..
Sa	1	8	15	22	29	..

JUNE						
Su	..	T^1	T^2	T^3	T^4	..
M	..	7	14	21	28	..
Tu	1	8	15	22	29	..
W	2	9	16	23	30	..
Th	3	10	17	24	..	..
F	4	11	18	25	..	..
Sa	5	12	19	26	..	..

JULY						
Su	..	T^5	T^6	T^7	T^8	..
M	..	5	12	19	26	..
Tu	..	6	13	20	27	..
W	..	7	14	21	28	..
Th	1	8	15	22	29	..
F	2	9	16	23	30	..
Sa	3	10	17	24	31	..

AUGUST						
Su	T^9	T^{10}	T^{11}	T^{12}	T^{13}	..
M	2	9	16	23	30	..
Tu	3	10	17	24	31	..
W	4	11	18	25	..	..
Th	5	12	19	26	..	..
F	6	13	20	27	..	..
Sa	7	14	21	28	..	..

SEPTEMBER						
Su	..	T^{14}	T^{15}	T^{16}	T^{17}	..
M	..	6	13	20	27	..
Tu	..	7	14	21	28	..
W	1	8	15	22	29	..
Th	2	9	16	23	30	..
F	3	10	17	24	..	..
Sa	4	11	18	25	..	..

OCTOBER						
Su	..	T^{18}	T^{19}	T^{20}	T^L	A^{-4}
M	..	4	11	18	25	..
Tu	..	5	12	19	26	..
W	..	6	13	20	27	..
Th	..	7	14	21	28	..
F	1	8	15	22	29	..
Sa	2	9	16	23	30	..

NOVEMBER						
Su	..	A^{-3}	A^{-2}	A^{-1}	A	..
M	AS	8	15	22	29	..
Tu	2	9	16	23	30	..
W	3	10	17	24	..	..
Th	4	11	18	25	..	..
F	5	12	19	26	..	..
Sa	6	13	20	27	..	..

DECEMBER						
Su	..	A^2	A^3	A^4	X^1	..
M	..	6	13	20	27	..
Tu	..	7	14	21	28	..
W	1	8	15	22	29	..
Th	2	9	16	23	30	..
F	3	10	17	24	31	..
Sa	4	11	18	X	..	..

A = Ash Wednesday, Ascension, Advent
A^- = Before Advent
A^{-4} = also All Saints, 2021 (if trans.)
A^{-1} = Christ the King
An = Annunciation
AS = All Saints
B = Baptism
E = Epiphany, Easter
E^4 = also Presentation, 2021 (if trans)
G = Good Friday
L = Lent
L^- = Before Lent
M = Maundy Thursday
P = Palm Sunday
Pr = Presentation
T = Trinity
(T^8 = also James, 2021)
(T^{11} = also Blessed Virgin Mary, 2021)
(T^{19} = also Luke, 2020)
T^L = Last Sunday after Trinity
W = Pentecost (Whit Sunday)
X = Christmas
(X^1 = also John, 2020)